VIOLENCE
AGAINST WOMEN

Other Books in the Current Controversies Series:

VIOLENCE AGAINST WOMEN

David Bender, *Publisher*
Bruno Leone, *Executive Editor*

Bonnie Szumski, *Managing Editor*
Katie de Koster, *Senior Editor*

Karin L. Swisher, *Book Editor*
Carol Wekesser, *Book Editor*
William Barbour, *Assistant Editor*

CURRENT CONTROVERSIES

Cover photo: © Rick Reinhard/Impact Visuals

Library of Congress Cataloging-in-Publication Data

Violence against women / Karin L. Swisher, Carol Wekesser, book editors, William Barbour, assistant editor.
    p. cm. — (Current controversies)
    Includes bibliographical references and index.
    Summary: Articles present opposing opinions on the seriousness of violence against women, including issues of rape, domestic violence, sexual harassment, and pornography.
    ISBN 1-56510-070-0 (lib : alk. paper). — ISBN 1-56510-069-7 (pbk. : alk. paper)
    1. Women—United States—Crimes against. 2. Abused women—United States. [1. Women—Crimes against. 2. Abused women. 3. Violence. 4. Violent crimes.] I. Swisher, Karin, 1966-   . II. Wekesser, Carol, 1963-   . III. Barbour, William, 1963-   . IV. Series.
HV6250.4.W65V553   1994
362.82'92'0973—dc20   93-1807
                                                                CIP
                                                                 AC

Printed on
recycled paper

© 1994 by Greenhaven Press, Inc., PO Box 289009, San Diego, CA 92198-9009
Printed in the U.S.A.

Contents

suffer from a mental condition—"cognitive distortion"—that allows them to justify their actions.

Chapter 3: Can Reforms in the Criminal Justice System Decrease Violence Against Women?

Yes: Changes in the Criminal Justice System Can Decrease Violence Against Women

Chapter 4: Does Pornography Promote Violence Against Women?

Chapter 5: How Can Violence Against Women Be Reduced?

Chapter 6: How Widespread Is the Problem of Rape?

Rape Is a Widespread Problem

information-gathering methods for rape guarantee that it will
continue to be underreported. More accurate, private studies
indicate that the incidence of rape is greater than realized.

Rape Is Not a Widespread Problem

Chapter 7: Is the "Battered Woman's Syndrome" a Legitimate Defense?

Yes: The "Battered Woman's Syndrome" Is a Legitimate Defense

No: The "Battered Women's Syndrome" Is Not a Legitimate Defense

Foreword

By definition, controversies are "discussions of questions in which opposing opinions clash" (Webster's Twentieth Century Dictionary Unabridged). Few would deny that controversies are a pervasive part of the human condition and exist on virtually every level of human enterprise. Controversies transpire between individuals and among groups, within nations and between nations. Controversies supply the grist necessary for progress by providing challenges and challengers to the status quo. They also create atmospheres where strife and warfare can flourish. A world without controversies would be a peaceful world; but it also would be, by and large, static and prosaic.

The Series' Purpose

The purpose of the Current Controversies series is to explore many of the social, political, and economic controversies dominating the national and international scenes today. Titles selected for inclusion in the series are highly focused and specific. For example, from the larger category of criminal justice, Current Controversies deals with specific topics such as police brutality, gun control, white collar crime, and others. The debates in Current Controversies also are presented in a useful, timeless fashion. Articles and book excerpts included in each title are selected if they contribute valuable, long-range ideas to the overall debate. And wherever possible, current information is enhanced with historical documents and other relevant materials. Thus, while individual titles are current in focus, every effort is made to ensure that they will not become quickly outdated. Books in the Current Controversies series will remain important resources for librarians, teachers, and students for many years.

In addition to keeping the titles focused and specific, great care is taken in the editorial format of each book in the series. Book introductions and chapter prefaces are offered to provide background material for readers. Chapters are organized around several key questions that are answered with diverse opinions representing all points on the political spectrum. Materials in each chapter include opinions in which authors clearly disagree as well as alternative opinions in which authors may agree on a broader issue but disagree on the possible solutions. In this way, the content of each volume in Current Controversies mirrors the mosaic of opinions encountered in society. Readers will quickly realize that there are many viable answers to these complex issues. By questioning each author's conclusions, students and casual readers can begin to develop the critical thinking skills so important to evaluating opinionated material.

Current Controversies is also ideal for controlled research. Each anthology in the series is composed of primary sources taken from a wide gamut of informational categories including periodicals, newspapers, books, United States and foreign government documents, and the publications of private and public organizations. Readers will find factual support for reports, debates, and research papers covering all areas of important issues. In addition, an annotated table of contents, an index, a book and periodical bibliography, and a list of organizations to contact are included in each book to expedite further research.

Perhaps more than ever before in history, people are confronted with diverse and contradictory information. During the Persian Gulf War, for example, the public was not only treated to minute-to-minute coverage of the war, it was also inundated with critiques of the coverage and countless analyses of the factors motivating U.S. involvement. Being able to sort through the plethora of opinions accompanying today's major issues, and to draw one's own conclusions, can be a complicated and frustrating struggle. It is the editors' hope that Current Controversies will help readers with this struggle.

"The emotional, physical, and social consequences of . . . violence are profound for all women—indeed, for all of society."

Introduction

On October 18, 1978, while walking home from her job at a nursing home, sixteen-year-old Ruth Schmidt was raped. She was attacked by a serial rapist, a man who had already raped ten other women. Fifteen years later, Schmidt describes how the rape still affects her:

> There are so many things I will never do again. I will never walk on the same side of the road where a single man or a group of men is walking. I will never go past the house where I grew up without my first thought being that the rapist knew that I lived there. I will never meet a man without my first thought being, "Is he capable of rape?" . . . I see differently. I hear differently. I surely believe differently.

Women who have been raped, abused, or attacked carry both physical and emotional scars. Fear, shame, anxiety, and anger are some of the emotions experienced by these women. A large percentage of raped women consider suicide. Both raped and battered women often suffer lowered self-esteem and face feelings of self-blame. Many battered women are emotionally incapacitated by their abuse, making it difficult for them to leave the abuser. Fear that leaving will exacerbate the abuse—a justified fear, according to statistics—also paralyzes women. Many women who do choose to leave an abuser find themselves and their children homeless. According to a Ford Foundation report, 50 percent of all homeless women and children in the United States are fleeing domestic violence.

Even women who have not personally experienced violence may be hobbled by its pervasive threat. The fear of assault, like violence itself, causes emotional devastation and social dislocation for many women. As writer Susan Kushner Resnick declares, "Like most American urban women, I find that fear has become part of my life." In their book *The Female Fear*, Stephanie Riger and Margo Gordon found that one-third of the women they surveyed always worry about being raped. More than 25 percent of the women never walk in their neighborhood after dark (compared with less than 3 percent of the men); 52 percent of the women cross the street when they see someone who seems strange or dangerous (compared with 25 percent of the men).

This awareness of the constant potential for danger affects women emotionally, socially, and physically. Writer Kerry O'Neil describes how her fear of passing strange men on the street colors her view of all people, men in particular:

> I realize . . . I am reducing myself to prey and every male that passes by into a predator. . . . Without question, when I view my world as unfriendly—specifically, as a place that breeds male monsters—I am also cutting off the potential of a larger me and a larger concept of men. When I obey a code of conduct that instructs me to put up walls and keep my face taut, I am squelching deep impulses to engage with the mysteries of the outside world.

Gordon asserts that the guarded stance described by O'Neil also affects women physically. She contends that "fear of attack is draining on people's mental health, which leads to physical problems. It makes women more susceptible to flus and other diseases." Resnick agrees, stating that few people "realize that when a woman is constantly tensing, jumping, clenching her fists, tightening her shoulders, and filling her veins with adrenaline she's becoming vulnerable to heart attacks, high blood pressure, and all the diseases that stem from a compromised immune system."

More than 1 million women seek medical treatment for abuse every year, and more than 150,000 women are raped. The emotional, physical, and social consequences of this violence are profound for all women—indeed, for all of society. *Violence Against Women: Current Controversies* addresses the impact of violence on women, explores possible causes of violence, and offers some possible solutions. Ending violence is crucial for all women, for as columnist Ellen Goodman states, "Women cannot feel free unless they feel safe."

Chapter 1

What Causes Violence Against Women?

Chapter Preface

A 1990 Senate committee report indicates that three out of four women will be victims of violent crime during their lifetime. According to a national crime survey, since 1974 assaults against women have risen 50 percent, while assaults against young men have declined by 12 percent. The Bureau of Justice Statistics says that 95 percent of the victims of domestic violence are women. These statistics reveal that violence against women is a grave and frequent problem. What the statistics do not reveal is that the majority of these crimes are committed by men, usually someone the victim knows. They also conceal what causes these men to commit violent crimes against women.

Experts who study what causes some men to become violent cite a host of biological, personal, and social factors. Experts hypothesize that societal approval of violence, a family history of violence, sexism, and tradition, among many other factors, can all cause violence against women. Therapist and author Ron Thorne-Finch concurs: "While each individual is unique as to the exact configuration of crucial influences in his life, a multitude of powerful social forces foster, allow, and legitimize male violence."

Experts have concluded that no single cause exists to explain the violent acts committed against women. The viewpoints in the following chapter discuss some of these factors.

Traditional Male/Female Roles Promote Domestic Violence

by Bernadette Dunn Sewell

About the author: *Bernadette Dunn Sewell is an attorney with Morrison, Mahoney, and Miller in Boston.*

Domestic violence is one of the most underestimated and underreported crimes in the United States today. It represents the single greatest cause of injury to women, and affects more than two million women each year. Its origins, however, lie not in the violence of our contemporary society, but in the historical subjugation of women in patriarchal societies.

Traditionally, female family members existed only in terms of their relationships to men. As daughters, subject to the control and whim of fathers, women represented a means of economic or political gain through marital arrangements. As wives, they became their husbands' property, and symbols of power and status. Violence against women served to coerce their acquiescence in this scheme and perpetuate subservience to male relatives.

Spouse Abuse Is Now a Crime

Legally permitted abuse of women continued to exist in many Western cultures until the late nineteenth century. Currently, however, every American state legislatively recognizes spouse abuse as a criminal act and authorizes punishment of abusers. Women are no longer deemed men's property and now possess personal rights and a legal status separate from their husbands. Yet wife beating continues. It does so because the historical abuse of women is ingrained in contemporary social attitudes and reflected in institutional responses to battered women. . . .

The observation that spouse abuse dates from the time men and women

From Bernadette Dunn Sewell, "History of Abuse: Societal, Judicial, and Legislative Responses to the Problem of Wife Beating," *Suffolk University Law Review* 23 (1989): 983-1017. Reprinted with permission.

19

formed monogamous relationships reveals something of the depth and intensity of the problem. Understanding the subject, therefore, requires a discussion of the history of wife beating and its impact on present day attitudes. Such an examination reveals society's traditional view of a woman's "proper" role and the systematic subjugation of women in a patriarchal society. Moreover, it exposes the axiom that while twentieth century laws have changed to herald the condemnation of wife abuse, public attitudes indeed remain in the Middle Ages.

Early Western Civilization

The patriarchal nature of early Roman society deemed a wife the property of her husband and therefore subject to his control. According to early Roman law, a man could beat, divorce, or murder his wife for offenses committed by her which besmirched his honor or threatened his property rights. Roman society considered enforcement of such rights of control essentially a private matter, moreover, and thus failed to subject the husband to either public scrutiny or disapproval.

Men retained much of this authority despite women's entry into the political, intellectual, and religious circles of later Roman society. As legislators, for instance, men continued to frame the law in their favor in order to maintain control over their spouses and daughters. Only unjustifiable, excessive violence by a husband provided a wife with sufficient reason for divorce, but such a privilege remained limited to the upper social strata.

Religious Attitudes

Both the Old and New Testament attest to the belief in early religious teachings in the subservience of women. Indeed, Eve's creation from the rib of Adam provided justification for early preachings regarding women's submissive role within the family. According to the teachings, a woman's virtues included docility, chastity, and passivity. Failure to conform to those standards, moreover, subjected an unruly wife to death by mutilation or stoning.

By the twelfth century, the position of women within the church, and thus within society, remained largely unimproved. A medieval publication of canon law, relying on Roman law, argued that women should remain subject to men and be deprived of all authority. The Catholic church's endorsement of the *Rules of Marriage*, a fifteenth-century publication, further demon-

> *"Traditionally, female family members existed only in terms of their relationships to men."*

strated the continued degradation of women within society. The *Rules* exhorted a husband to stand as judge of his wife and to beat her with a stick upon commission of an offense. According to the *Rules*, wife battering showed the husband's concern for his wife's soul, which ultimately benefitted both husband and wife.

Historians indicate that the advent of the Modern Period brought changes in society's political, economic, and religious institutions. These changes, however, merely solidified male domination within the family unit and perpetuated the subjugation of women. Nevertheless, the era did see the development of certain restrictions limiting the type and extent of physical punishment that a husband could inflict upon his wife. Furthermore, when a husband overstepped the bounds of allowable punishment, he often became subject to ridicule from neighbors. Although rare, such an event remained relatively lighthearted in comparison with community condemnation of recalcitrant wives.

> *"The historical abuse of women is ingrained in contemporary social attitudes."*

The prevailing common law of England reflected the attitudes characterized by such community activities. For example, an English husband possessed a legal right to beat his wife in the interest of maintaining family discipline and order. Sir William Blackstone, the eminent British jurist, rationalized the necessity of such correctional power based on a common law rule imputing a wife's misbehavior to her husband.

American Responses to Spouse Abuse

Blackstone's commentaries, and English law as a whole, greatly influenced early American legal systems, both generally and in the area of wife abuse. In 1824, for instance, the Supreme Court of Mississippi affirmed ancient English common law noted by Blackstone, by granting a husband the right to chastise his wife. Although the court limited the punishment to moderate chastisement, it nevertheless showed general support for the principal. The court further indicated that a man should neither be subjected to "vexatious prosecutions" by his wife for exercising that right, nor should courts be eager to reveal such private conduct to the public eye.

Such inherent inequality, although prevalent, did not always exist in early American history. The Puritans openly professed their abhorrence of family violence, believing it a threat to the settlement's orderliness and stability. During the mid-1600s, Massachusetts Bay and Plymouth Bay colonies enacted the first laws in the Western world which prohibited wife abuse. The *Body of Liberties*, passed in Massachusetts Bay in 1641, prohibited a husband from beating his wife unless in self-defense. Similar laws enacted in Plymouth Bay in 1672 punished wife abuse with fines and whippings.

These seemingly humanitarian and revolutionary early laws, however, lacked strict enforcement. Colonial courts, for instance, preferred to reconcile couples regardless of complaints of abuse. Failing that, courts issued orders compelling runaway wives to return to the family home. Moreover, Puritans remained tolerant of physical abuse of family members so long as justification existed for the abuser's actions. Social changes within these early religious communities weakened the already tenuous commitment to the protection of abuse victims. After 1680, for instance, the colonial court system came under increasing pressure to align its jurisprudence with that of England. Immigrants from Western Europe settling in the communities further diluted the ties binding the family, church, and state. Prosecutions of private moral crimes, such as wife beating, incest, and child abuse declined, while public moral crimes such as drunkenness, prostitution, and vagrancy filled the courts. In essence, public support of state interference in domestic matters for the good of the community yielded to the concept of family privacy.

Nineteenth-Century America

Although societal changes in the latter part of the nineteenth century presented a challenge to white male supremacy, the early decades evidenced strong judicial approval of their rights and privileges. In 1836, for example, a New Hampshire court articulated well-established principles concerning a husband's control over his wife and the wife's proper role within the family. The court held that a wife who failed to submit to the legitimate authority of her husband and who manifested characteristics unbecoming a lady could not obtain a divorce. The court also indicated that a woman who provoked her husband's anger, or who refused to remain silent in the face of his temper, deserved any abuse inflicted upon her as a result of her disobedience and had no cause for complaint. The reasons, the court opined, lay in the husband's position as head of the household, and the woman's parallel station of subordinate. The court added that since the law deemed the husband answerable for his wife's debts, crimes, and torts, it also wisely granted him authority to control her actions. The court concluded that although society condemned the husband's unmanly conduct in beating his wife, it abhorred even more the wife's unseemly rebellion against the proper exercise of his authority.

With the rise of activist organizations in the late nineteenth century, domestic violence once again emerged as a reform issue. While movements with otherwise disparate goals found common ground in the fight against wife abuse, each retained their own view of the cause of the problem and its possible remedies. Temperance campaigners viewed domestic violence as inextricably connected with the evils of alcohol, and thus sought abolition as a means of protecting abuse victims. Social purist reformers and feminists argued that physical and sexual abuse of women stemmed from a husband's rights of ownership of his spouse's body and campaigned for emancipation to remove that privilege.

> *"Spouse abuse dates from the time men and women formed monogamous relationships."*

Courts were initially slow to heed the change in public opinion and continued to adhere to the rationale of English common law. They emphasized the importance of family autonomy and privacy by displaying a hesitancy to invade the domestic forum. They only did so with reluctance, for instance, when the husband exceeded the bounds of moderate chastisement. Both public and judicial opinion began to shift by the late 1800s, however, heralding a second era of reform against wife

> *"Eve's creation from the rib of Adam provided justification for early preachings regarding women's submissive role."*

abuse. In 1871, both Alabama and Massachusetts judicially abrogated a husband's right to physically abuse his wife. The Alabama court held husband and wife equal before the law, each endowed with civil and political rights, and public privileges. In Massachusetts, the court indicated that even a drunken or insolent wife deserved protection from her husband's abuse. . . .

Twentieth-Century America

Despite the favorable statutory and judicial reforms of the late nineteenth century, domestic violence largely subsided as a critical social issue in the following decades. The few changes implemented reiterated traditional doctrine concerning the family and proper gender roles within the family. For instance, the early twentieth-century family court system championed family preservation and curative, rather than punitive, solutions to the spouse abuse problem.

Courts uniformly discouraged separation and divorce of couples, and boasted of their record of reconciling couples. Often, however, such attempted reconciliations translated into judicial coercion of abuse victims by badgering wives into withdrawing complaints, denying petitions for financial support from husbands, or assigning cases to a social service organization. The courts also often failed to provide a battered woman with physical protection after filing a complaint, the absence of which increased the possibility of retaliatory assault from her abuser.

The battered woman's situation remained largely unchanged and unnoticed for the first six decades of the twentieth century. The work of psychoanalysts during that period, however, had a tremendous effect on public perception of domestic violence. Some psychiatrists attributed domestic violence to the victim's inherent sexual and biological problems. One Freudian disciple argued that masochism played a significant role in women's lives, causing them to provoke, and then remain in, battering situations. Her theory persuaded both practicing psychiatrists and the general public.

The feminist movement of the 1960s challenged existing mysogynist views and served as a catalyst for the emergence of the battered women's movement a decade later. Initially, however, the women's movement ignored the plight of battered wives, and not until the issue of rape emerged as a feminist concern did abused wives finally receive attention. The battered women's movement also grew from a recognition among legal aid lawyers and feminists that the law provided little or no relief to abused wives. In response, activists developed services to aid and shelter abuse victims. Advocates also pressured police, courts, social service agencies, and legislators to recognize the immensity of the spouse abuse problem and to provide assistance to its victims. Furthermore, they strove for public education about domestic violence through the media, public speaking engagements, and outreach programs.

Since the emergence of the battered women's movement in the 1970s, activists have continued to achieve success in obtaining state and federal legislation and funding for the protection of abused women, along with educating the public about the horrors of domestic violence. Their efforts, however, have faced periodic opposition. Moreover, despite the successes, spouse abuse remains a shameful major social problem. . . .

A History of Oppression

The existence of wife beating is reflected in the historical subjugation of women within the family and society. Secular and religious laws, for instance, attest to the continued powerless and inferior status of women throughout time. These laws systematically excluded women from positions of influence or importance within the church and society, and subjected them to the ignominy of male dominance. This served to encourage husbands to exercise and maintain control over their wives by means of physical force.

Women traditionally remained with an abusive husband because the law provided little means of escape. As a wife, the law subsumed her legal identity into her husband's, transferred title of her property to him, restricted her access to divorce, and denied her the right to sue the abuser for tortious actions. Currently, statutes provide a wife with protection from an abusive spouse. Pursuant to these statutes, a wife may seek a divorce, file criminal charges, or bring a civil action based on a husband's abusive behavior. Many abuse victims, however, are unable to take advantage of these statutory protections because of society's adherence to the traditional marital hierarchy and the corresponding belief that a woman's "proper" place is in the home. When persons assigned to aid victims retain such beliefs, it reinforces these social attitudes and contributes to the victim's sense of helplessness and lack of self-worth, thereby reducing the chances that she will seek future legal protection from abuse.

> *"An English husband possessed a legal right to beat his wife."*

As in the past, society seeks to justify its silent condonation of wife abuse by relying on the shield of family privacy. Societal emphasis on the benefits of preserving family unity, however, fails to consider the devastating effects domestic violence wreaks on family members. Society also often chooses to ignore domestic violence, despite evidence that the home is something other than a safe, secure place. . . .

Wife beating emerged from a religious, ideological, and moral framework of male-dominated marriages, and societal legitimization and reinforcement of a husband's power. It perpetuated through adherence to the sacrosanct values of family privacy and unity and society's willingness to subjugate women to benefit the family ideal. While such values remain largely unchanged, widespread condonation of wife abuse is eroding. The battered women's movement's success in obtaining nationwide abuse prevention laws, federal funding to finance shelters and programs to aid abuse victims, and its campaign to sensitize the public to the horrors of domestic violence suggests a weakening of society's tolerance of wife abuse. Mere understanding of the battered woman's plight, however, is insufficient. Society must act upon its repugnance and enforce abuse prevention laws to ensure maximum protection of abuse victims.

Society's Belief in Family Privacy Contributes to Domestic Violence

by Elizabeth M. Schneider

About the author: *Elizabeth M. Schneider, a law professor at Brooklyn Law School, was a visiting professor of law at Harvard University in Cambridge, Massachusetts, in 1991.*

Protection of a sphere of family privacy from state interference has been viewed as "good." Yet, understood through a lens of gender, and more particularly shaped by the experiences of battered women, the concept of privacy is more complex and ambiguous. . . .

For women in the United States, intimacy with men, in and out of marriage, too often results in violence. The concept of freedom from state intrusion into the marital bedroom takes on a different meaning when it is violence that goes on in the marital bedroom. . . .

Privacy and Battering

This viewpoint explores the ways in which concepts of privacy permit, encourage, and reinforce violence against women, focusing on the complex interrelationship between notions of "public" and "private" in our social understandings of woman-abuse. Historically, male battering of women was untouched by law, protected as part of the private sphere of family life. Over the last twenty years, however, as the battered women's movement in this country has made issues of battering visible, battering is no longer perceived as a purely "private" problem and has taken on dimensions of a "public" issue. There has been an explosion of legal reform and social service efforts: the development of battered women's shelters and hotlines, many state and federal governmental reports and

From Elizabeth M. Schneider, "The Violence of Privacy," *The Connecticut Law Review* 23 (1991): 973-99. Reprinted with permission.

much state legislation. New legal remedies for battered women have been developed which have been premised on the idea of battering as a "public" harm. However, at the same time, there is widespread resistance to acknowledgment of battering as a "public" issue. . . .

The concept of privacy poses a dilemma and challenge to theoretical and practical work on woman-abuse. The notion of marital privacy has been a source of oppression to bat-

> *"There is widespread resistance to acknowledgement of battering as a 'public' issue."*

tered women and has helped to maintain women's subordination within the family. However, a more affirmative concept of privacy, one that encompasses liberty, equality, freedom of bodily integrity, autonomy, and self-determination, is important to women who have been battered. The challenge is not simply to reject privacy for battered women and opt for state intervention, but to develop both a more nuanced theory of where to draw the boundaries between public and private and a theory of privacy that is empowering. . . .

Privacy: The Meanings of Public and Private

Historically, the dichotomy of "public" and "private" has been viewed as an important construct for understanding gender. The traditional notion of "separate spheres" is premised on a dichotomy between the "private" world of family and domestic life (the "women's" sphere), and the "public" world of marketplace (the "men's" sphere). . . . In the public sphere, sex-based exclusionary laws join with other institutional and ideological constraints to directly limit women's participation. In the private sphere, the legal system operates more subtly. The law claims to be absent in the private sphere and has historically refused to intervene in ongoing family relations. [As Taub and Schneider state]:

> Tort law, which is generally concerned with injuries inflicted on individuals, has traditionally been held inapplicable to injuries inflicted by one family member on another. Under the doctrines of interspousal and parent-child immunity, courts have consistently refused to allow recoveries for injuries that would be compensable but for the fact that they occurred in the private realm. In the same way, criminal law fails to punish intentional injuries to family members. Common law and statutory definitions of rape in most states continue to carve out a special exception for a husband's forced intercourse with his wife. Wife beating was initially omitted from the definition of criminal assault on the ground that a husband had the right to chastise his wife. Even today, after courts have explicitly rejected the definitional exception and its rationale, judges, prosecutors, and police officers decline to enforce assault laws in the family context.

Although a dichotomous view of the public sphere and the private sphere has some heuristic value, and considerable rhetorical power, the dichotomy is overdrawn. The notion of a sharp demarcation between public and private has been widely rejected by feminist and Critical Legal Studies scholars. There is no realm of personal and family life that exists totally separate from the reach of the state. The state defines both the family, the so-called private sphere, and the market, the so-called public sphere. "Private" and "public" exist on a continuum.

> *"The battered women's movement revealed to the public hidden and private violence."*

Thus, in the so-called private sphere of domestic and family life, which is purportedly immune from law, there is always the selective application of law. Significantly, this selective application of law invokes "privacy" as a rationale for immunity in order to protect male domination. For example, when the police do not respond to a battered woman's call for assistance, or when a civil court refuses to evict her assailant, the woman is relegated to self-help, while the man who beats her receives the law's tacit encouragement and support. Indeed, we can see this pattern in recent legislative and prosecutorial efforts to control women's conduct during pregnancy in the form of "fetal" protection laws. These laws are premised on the notion that women's childbearing capacity, and pregnancy itself, subjects women to public regulation and control. Thus, pregnant battered women may find themselves facing criminal prosecution for drinking liquor, but the man who battered them is not prosecuted.

The Message: Women Do Not Merit Protection

The rhetoric of privacy that has insulated the female world from the legal order sends an important ideological message to the rest of society. It devalues women and their functions and says that women are not important enough to merit legal regulation. [As Taub and Schneider state]:

> This message is clearly communicated when particular relief is withheld. By declining to punish a man for inflicting injuries on his wife, for example, the law implies she is his property and he is free to control her as he sees fit. Women's work is discredited when the law refuses to enforce the man's obligation to support his wife, since it implies she makes no contribution worthy of support. Similarly, when courts decline to enforce contracts that seek to limit or specify the extent of the wife's services, the law implies that household work is not real work in the way that the type of work subject to contract in the public sphere is real work. These are important messages, for denying woman's humanity and the value of her traditional work are key ideological components in maintaining woman's subordinate status. The message of women's inferiority is compounded by the totality of the law's absence from the private realm. In our society, law is for business and other important things. The fact that the law in general claims to have so little bearing on women's day-to-day concerns reflects and underscores their insignificance. Thus, the le-

gal order's overall contribution to the devaluation of women is greater than the sum of the negative messages conveyed by individual legal doctrines.

Definitions of "private" and "public" in any particular legal context can and do constantly shift. Meanings of "private" and "public" are based on social and cultural assumptions of what is valued and important, and these assumptions are deeply gender-based. Thus, the interrelationship between what is understood and experienced as "private" and "public" is particularly complex in the area of gender, where the rhetoric of privacy has masked inequality and subordination. The decision about what we protect as "private" is a political decision that always has important "public" ramifications.

In general, privacy has been viewed as problematic by feminist theorists. Privacy has seemed to rest on a division of public and private that has been oppressive to women and has supported male dominance in the family. Privacy reinforces the idea that the personal is separate from the political; privacy also implies something that should be kept secret. Privacy inures to the benefit of the individual, not the community. The right of privacy has been viewed as a passive right, one which says that the state cannot intervene.

However, some feminist theorists have also explored the affirmative role that privacy can play for women. Privacy is important to women in

> *"One woman in the United States is beaten every 18 seconds."*

many ways. It provides an opportunity for individual self-development, for individual decision making and for protection against endless caretaking. In addition, there are other related aspects of privacy, such as the notion of autonomy, equality, liberty, and freedom of bodily integrity, that are central to women's independence and well-being. For women who have been battered, these aspects of privacy are particularly important. . . .

Dimensions of Privacy

The battered women's movement grew out of the rebirth of the women's movement in the 1960s, and it is one of the areas in which the women's movement has made an enduring contribution to law. Like sexual harassment, the "problem" of battering and the social and legal construct of a "battered woman" did not exist in this country until the women's movement named it. The battered women's movement revealed to the public hidden and private violence. Over the last 20 years the battered women's movement has been involved in efforts to provide services for battered women, to create legal remedies to end abuse, and to develop public education efforts to change consciousness about battering. The battered women's movement saw battering as an aspect of fundamental gender relations, as a reflection of male power and female subordination.

As a result of the battered women's movement during the last two decades, the general problem of domestic violence and the more specific problems of battered women have entered public consciousness in the United States. The severe problems that battered women face have been documented by government reports, legal and social science literature, and media reports, including front-page headlines, coverage of trials, and television programs. State and federal legislative reforms have focused on improving the legal remedies available to battered women, and many battered women's shelters, hotlines, advocacy programs, and support services for battered women have been developed.

> *"Woman-abuse is an aspect of the basic gender inequality built into the very fabric of American family law."*

Domestic violence is the leading cause of injury to women in the United States. According to FBI statistics, one woman in the United States is beaten every 18 seconds. Between 2000 and 4000 women die every year from abuse. Thirty percent of all women killed every year are slain by their partners. Battering of women by their husbands or men with whom they are in an intimate relationship cuts across racial, class, ethnic, and economic lines. Police involvement, nationally, in cases of domestic violence exceeds involvement in murder, rape, and all forms of aggravated assault.

Woman-abuse is an aspect of the basic gender inequality built into the very fabric of American family law. Myths concerning battered women, for example, that they provoke and like the violence, are widespread. The police and the courts have historically failed to intervene to protect battered women because battering is perceived as a "private" problem, neither serious nor criminal. When the battered women's movement began, battered women had, effectively, no legal remedies.

Over the last twenty years, there has been considerable change. There are now a wide range of groups and organizations that have emerged around the country to assist battered women. These groups have developed a range of approaches. They have focused their efforts on providing services to battered women, by founding shelters for battered women, setting up telephone hotlines, challenging police practices that fail to intervene effectively to protect battered women, and working to advance legislation that offers legal remedies for battered women. Some groups also have developed programs to work with battering men.

Acknowledgment of the Problem

Today there is greater public familiarity with these problems. Federal and state task forces have recommended reforms of legal, social welfare, and health care systems. Lawsuits have resulted in improved police and court practices. Lawsuits against the police have compelled police departments to arrest batterers vigorously. Almost all states now have domestic violence legislation providing for orders of protection for women, and legal sanctions for their violation and/or criminal remedies for battering. In short, there has been an explosion of law reform efforts to assist battered women.

Work on issues of battered women is now at a turning point. Some reforms have been institutionalized, and problems of battered women have achieved credibility and visibility. To some degree, a public dimension to the problem is now recognized. However, federal, state, and private funding resources put into these reform efforts have been small. There has been little change in the culture of female subordination that supports and maintains abuse. At the same time, there is a serious backlash to these reform efforts and many of the reforms that have been accomplished are in serious jeopardy. For the last several years, while writing a report on national legal reform efforts for battered women for The Ford Foundation, I have been amazed at the enormous accomplishments of the battered women's movement over the last 20 years. Indeed, I can think of few recent social movements that have accomplished so much in such a short time.

However, I have also been stunned by the depth of social resistance to change. Although battering has evolved from a "private" to a more "public" issue, it has not become a serious political issue, precisely because it has profound implications for all of our lives. Battering is deeply threatening. It goes to our most fundamental assumptions about the nature of intimate relations and the safeness of family life. The concept of male battering of women as a "private" issue exerts a powerful ideological pull on our consciousness because, in some sense, it is something that we would like to believe. By seeing woman-abuse as "private," we affirm it as a problem that is individual, that only involves a particular male-female relationship, and for which there is no social responsibility to remedy. Each of us needs to deny the seriousness and pervasiveness of battering, but more significantly, the interconnectedness of battering with so many other aspects of family life and gender relations. Instead of focusing on the batterer, we focus on the battered woman, scrutinize her conduct, examine her pathology, and blame her for not leaving the relationship, in order to maintain that denial and refuse to confront the issues of power. Focusing on the woman, not the man, perpetuates the power of patriarchy. Denial supports and legitimates this power; the concept of privacy is a key aspect of this denial.

> *"Battering . . . goes to our most fundamental assumptions about the . . . safeness of family life."*

The Extent of Denial

Denial takes many forms and operates on many levels. Men deny battering in order to protect their own privilege. Women need to deny the pervasiveness of the problem so as not to link it to their own life situations. Individual women who are battered tend to minimize the violence in order to distance themselves from some internalized negative concept of "battered woman." I see denial in the attitudes of jurors, who try to remove themselves and say that it could never happen to me; if it did, I would handle it differently. I see denial in the public engagement in the Hedda Nussbaum/Joel Steinberg case which focused on Hedda Nussbaum's complicity, and involved feminists in active controversy over the boundaries of victimization. The findings of the many state task force reports on gender bias in the courts have painstakingly recorded judicial attitudes of denial. Clearly, there is serious denial on the part of state legislators, members of Congress and the Executive Branch who never mention battering as an important public issue. In battering, we see both the power of denial and the denial of power. The concept of privacy is an ideological rationale for this denial and serves to maintain it.

The concept of privacy encourages, reinforces, and supports violence against women. Privacy says that violence against women is immune from sanction, that it is permitted, acceptable, and part of the basic fabric of American family life. Privacy says that what goes on in the violent relationship should not be the subject of state or community intervention. Privacy says that it is an individual, and not a systemic, problem. Privacy operates as a mask for inequality, protecting male violence against women. . . .

The challenge is to develop a right to privacy which is not synonymous with the right to state noninterference with actions within the family, but which recognizes the affirmative role that privacy can play for battered women. Feminist reconstruction of privacy should seek to break down the dichotomy of public and private that has disabled legal discourse and public policy in this area. Male battering of women is a serious public problem for which we need to accept collective responsibility; it requires a dramatic program of mass public reeducation similar to the drunk driving campaigns over the last several years. At the same time, while claiming woman-abuse as a public problem, we do not want to suggest that state intervention is always the answer. . . .

However, we also do not want to reject the genuine values and benefits of privacy for battered women. Thinking about privacy as something that women who have been battered might want makes us think about it differently. Battered women seek the material and social conditions of equality and self-determination that make privacy possible. Privacy that is grounded on equality, and is viewed as an aspect of autonomy, that protects bodily integrity and makes abuse impermissible, is based on a genuine recognition of the importance of personhood. . . . Such a notion of privacy could challenge the vision of individual solution, rather than social responsibility, for abuse. Conceived differently, privacy could help keep women safe, not battered.

Sexism Promotes Violence Against Women

by Nancy Hutchings

About the author: *Nancy Hutchings is a professor of social work at Southern Connecticut State University in New Haven and the author of* The Violent Family.

Why do we think of violence when studying family life in the United States in the 1990s? Probably because there are so many newspaper and television stories about women and children being beaten, being abused, and murdered. There has been a real increase in family violence in this country in the last decade. Many people ask: is there more violence or is it finally being discussed in public? Both answers seem correct; there is more violence but it is also being talked about by the police, by the courts, and by the media.

Dangerous Households

In the world today, bombings, hijackings and terrorism are *normal*, yet in the United States the locus of most of our violence is in the home. Other countries have civil wars or have problems with terrorism and our country is considered peaceful. Yet the households of the United States are very dangerous. There is violence between spouses, between siblings, between parents and children, and most recently towards the elderly relatives who are often living in the home. Violence is self-perpetuating so that once it is accepted in a family as a means of communication or as punishment, it is hard to change this behavior.

The recent statistics on domestic violence often seem overwhelming yet, according to most experts, wife battering, rape, child abuse and abuse of the elderly are crimes that often go unreported to the authorities, so that the statistics are still not reliable.

It was not until 1968 that all states mandated the reporting of child abuse.

Nancy Hutchings, "Family Violence," *Peace Review*, Fall 1992. Reprinted with permission.

Even today, with this mandate, private doctors may still not be reporting cases of abuse. Many people believe that abuse only occurs among the poorer classes and the minorities, but this belief stems from the mandated reports that come from hospital clinics and public health agencies. The husband who beats his wife or the parents who abuse their children may often go unreported by their private physician.

> *"The households of the United States are very dangerous."*

The belief that severe physical discipline is essential to child rearing has been prevalent for centuries; children have been punished with canes, rods, and whips by parents, guardians and teachers. In a well known text of the Bible it says, "Thou shall beat him with rods and thou shall save his soul from hell." The doctrine of original sin says that children were born corrupt so that parents believed they were beating the devil from them. Literature abounds with examples of child abuse. Perhaps the writings of Charles Dickens are the best known example.

These same theories permeate religious tradition regarding violence towards women. For many centuries, a husband was legally allowed to beat his wife. The phrase *rule of thumb* referred to the English common law that sanctioned a husband beating his wife providing the switch was no thicker than the thumb. Most religions support the theory that the male is the head of the family and the wife must obey and be submissive. Her role is to take care of the household and the children. Violence between spouses seems to be on the increase and it has become more severe. Murders of ex-wives and ex-lovers are prominent in the newspapers. Recently the *Boston Globe* reported sixteen such murders in a period of six weeks. Historically, a man's home was his castle and he was given the right to privacy for his behavior. Since his wife and children were considered his property, what went on behind closed doors was permitted by society.

An Overwhelming Problem

The research by Murray A. Straus, S.K. Steinmetz, and Richard J. Gelles on family violence revealed startling statistics about the acceptance of violence by marriage partners, parents and children. One out of six wives are beaten each year and here again this figure is probably higher. Three out of five parents use physical punishment with their children and one out of two families is a scene of some sort of domestic violence each year. The increase in sexual abuse of children, or at least in the increase in knowledge about it, is staggering. One of six teenage girls will be abused by the time she is eighteen years of age. Foster homes, group homes and mental institutions are crowded with boys and girls that have been abused either physically or sexually by their relatives. Some psychologists and social workers estimate that 80 percent of the residents of the mental institutions have been abused.

Since violence is so acceptable in this country, it is not surprising that violent crimes are increasing. Children who have been exposed to violence will become violent adults.

What are the causes of family violence? I have alluded to some of them already. There's the belief that the husbands and fathers [have] that women and children are like property to be controlled. Another cause of violence is the dependence of wives and children on men to give them economic support—to provide the basic necessities of food and shelter. Women who are unable to support themselves and children who are weak and helpless are in vulnerable situations and are unable to leave them or change other people's behavior.

Sex-role stereotyping has been prevalent in psychology for years. Sigmund Freud has been blamed because of his themes of psychosexual development, but other theorists also emphasized the differences in the developmental patterns between the two sexes. Men were physically stronger and more dominant, women were more passive and given to nurturing their mates and children. One of Freud's theories was that anatomy was destiny so that men should be in control. Yet there are different cultures where men are more nurturing and the women are warriors. Today, in the United States, we are seeing families where the wife is the economic support for the family and the husband is staying home with the children. This should be acceptable, but many people ridicule these *new families*. It is true, however, that boys and girls are trained differently at home, in school, and in the community. It is acceptable for boys to have fights and to be more aggressive and competitive, but girls are not allowed these same behaviors.

> *"Most religions support the theory that . . . the wife must obey and be submissive."*

Today's women are expected to be the primary caregivers in the home, and their jobs are more passive, nurturing ones. The media, particularly advertising, encourages stereotyping. Women are depicted as housekeepers, as mothers, or as sexual partners. How many commercials or advertisements show women as prominent executives, doctors, or lawyers? The result of sex-role stereotyping is that women feel they are in a secondary position in society and they learn as they are growing up to value themselves in relation to their male partners, or to the men with whom they work.

The Economic Factor

Control over economic resources is a key source of power in all industrialized nations. There are public and private institutions within our society where this power is exercised. Laws, social policies and physical strength tend to give male members in our society more power than females. Even women who make it up the corporate ladder say that subtle sexism often deprives them of real power. In the early days of the Industrial Revolution, there was a division of labor and men were the wage earners and women were the housekeepers and mothers of the children. The role of women was defined by the family structure. The husband's role as wage earner gave him more power; this power has then been strengthened by social, religious, and political institutions. The wife's sphere of control in the home is very limited, although many different cultures will admit that their mothers dominated their families. If a man feels, however, that he does not have enough power of control at his employment, or status in the community, he then may abuse his power with his wife and children. His control over the flow of money into the household allows him to perpetuate abuse at home.

A Labor of Love

In the 1990s at least 60 percent of married women are working, yet they are also housewives and mothers. Combining a job plus the role of homemaker often means that women are working 100 hours each week. Housework for their husband and children is considered a *labor of love*, for which they receive no wages or Social Security. Because women produce and nurture the young, it was considered that they had limited abilities to produce in a productive economy. It was also believed that they did not have the physical strength to do hard manual labor. Women working in factories during World Wars I and II proved the fallacy of this theory. When women were forced to work in an earlier day, in the textile factories in New England, they were given half the pay of their male co-workers. Even today, in corporations, women executives do not receive the same pay as men.

So many career opportunities have grown from an extension of their domestic roles. Nursing came from caring for soldiers during war times, teaching came with the extension of public education, and the nurturing roles of social work came with the increase of awareness of the mentally ill, which was emphasized by draft boards in World War II, who denied many draftees for service because of mental illness.

Some careers from women came from the volunteer movement. The Industrial Revolution brought problems of poverty and illness, and women were the first volunteers as nurses, teachers and social workers.

"Sex-role stereotyping has been prevalent in psychology for years."

Since these careers often grew out of the unpaid status of volunteers, it was natural for women to receive low wages. Today, the political climate is again encouraging volunteerism as a substitute for government allocations in health, education, and welfare. There may be a *compassion trap* that has kept women in the lower paying nurturing and teaching positions. Most often the staff members are women but the administrators in health, education, and welfare are usually men. Volunteers at an agency or school also have no power in decisions that affect their services.

Unions have been very resistant to allowing women to come into construction or other industries. Even though women proved that they had strength to handle factory employment during World War II, they were paid less than men. Minority women were even more discriminated against with salaries. Union opposition to female participation has been well documented. This opposition has been caused by women's willingness to work for lower salaries, but also possibly out of a deeper fear that women will threaten their jobs because they could be equally qualified. By 1980, very few women belonged to labor unions and until issues like equal pay, equal opportunity, and sexual harassment are addressed women will probably remain outside unions.

The largest percentage of women in the labor force are in clerical occupations. This is a career where the worker helps to maintain and nurture her boss, usually a male. This can be degrading work and often entails situations of sexual harassment, sometimes subtle, other times more overt. The problem for women employees is that sexual harassment can be a threat to her economic livelihood; she sometimes is the sole support of her family. Attempting to fight sexual harassment may mean loss of a job and difficulty working elsewhere. Economic institutions, even those controlled by men, have to give more organized support to women in these situations.

> *"Battered wives often stay in their marriages because they are too afraid to change."*

Women are entering the bottom level of support services in many organizations, yet they often are being denied the management positions. Women may not know how to play office politics or how to talk in locker room vocabularies. There are rites of passage in achieving promotions and white males know the game plan better than females. Possibly, the competitive aggression that was allowed to male children helps them succeed where women's nurturing of her coworkers may cause her failure. It still seems that women are being denied in terms of their nurturing, supportive natures and that they will receive lower salaries and have fewer opportunities. Changing this will mean a loss of power for men and change in the traditional economic structure.

Victims Need Help

The victims of family violence often have to turn to public institutions to achieve independence. Women usually do not have salaries or personal savings to support them in a personal crisis. They have been dependent on their families and husbands for financial security. Battered wives often stay in their marriages because they are too afraid to change. The public assistance program, Aid to

Families with Dependent Children, gives a mother below-poverty-level financial assistance when she is eligible. Twenty-five percent of our children are being brought up in below-poverty homes in the United States. The mother who wants to work and not receive public assistance has to depend on day care for her younger children. Shelters for battered women only provide emergency care for sixty days, so that a battered wife is dependent on public institutions such as welfare and day care to help become independent. The bureaucracy of both of these institutions often deprive her of a chance to leave her violent home. The lack of affordable decent housing is another problem for victims of domestic violence. The United States does not provide proper public assistance, quality day care, or affordable public or private housing; thus victims of violence have difficulty accessing the present system.

> *"We need a real shift in social, political and economic structures to outlaw domestic violence."*

Media Violence

Another cause of violence, although a controversial one, is the violence on television, in the movies, in the videos we watch, and the songs we listen to. Pornography is a big business in this country. Magazines and videos are earning billions of dollars depicting women and children in sadistic and violent episodes. Anyone can get a movie or a magazine that degrades women and encourages violence for sexual pleasure. There certainly has been an increase in violence and an emphasis on women and children as objects for sexual gratification in the 1980s. Many psychologists believe that this encourages children and adults to be more violent; there is a belief that society is condoning violence, rape and murder. If we can purchase media, then society must be supportive of the themes. Censorship is controversial, but it is possible that media violence is among the main causes of the increase in family violence.

To summarize, women and children are still dependent on men to provide support and care for them. Sexism, stereotyping and the lack of equal economic opportunity have kept women in a dependent status. If she and her children are being abused, public institutions are not sufficient to grant her independence and freedom. The media and advertising seem to emphasize a woman's role as secondary, and also seem to be encouraging violence. We need a real shift in social, political and economic structures to outlaw domestic violence and to enable its victims to become free and independent.

Men's Participation in Sports Causes Violence Against Women

by Ron Thorne-Finch

About the author: *Ron Thorne-Finch is a therapist at Klinic, Inc., a community health center in Winnipeg, Manitoba. He is the author of* Ending the Silence: The Origins and Treatment of Male Violence Against Women, *from which this viewpoint is excerpted.*

Sport has many positive aspects. It can be a forum for learning about co-operation and healthy solidarity, setting and pursuing goals, building team spirit, seeking excellence, recognizing the value of losing as well as winning, and establishing a context for the healthy expression of aggression. It can also be a vehicle enabling an individual to take better care of his or her mind and body; when one reviews the statistically average North American's high caloric intake, generally poor cardiovascular health, and propensity to watch rather than to participate in sports, it is clear that more physical activity is needed. The positive effects of sport are commonly acknowledged. What is not as widely recognized, however, is that sport also contributes to the creation of violent men. . . .

All Classes Are Equally Violent

Sport has many critics. Some have a strong class bias. The presumption is that it is not so much the team sports per se which cause the violence, as the greater representation of unemployed and working-class individuals within those sports. This notion derives from a physiological myth that the lower classes are more violent than the more refined and wealthy—who are more likely to be involved in individual, rather than team, sports. If there are differences in the class composition of individual and team sports, this is more likely a function of working-class individuals simply not having the resources to engage in the typically more expensive individual sports than of a preference for team sports. Shooting a few baskets into a hoop on a vacant lot is feasible for most inner-city poor; escaping to the mountains for downhill skiing is not. There do not exist any studies indicating that when the wealthy are involved, the levels of violence are significantly less.

> *"Sport both mirrors and perpetuates the class divisions within our society."*

Sport both mirrors and perpetuates the class divisions within our society. At one level, there are many noble ideals about sport as a great leveller between the classes. On the playing field all are to be equal. It is the skill of the players that is being tested and nothing else. The reality, however, is different. Children of the wealthy can afford better equipment and coaches. Even when the poor kids win a game at the expense of the wealthy, the victory does not immediately alter the relations between the classes. Mike Messner has said that it is not uncommon for a losing team of rich kids to assuage their sorrow with a team cheer: 'That's all right, that's OK, you'll be working for us someday!'

Other critics of sport, arguing that it is not the class origins of individual players that is of concern, have focused on large team sports as the real culprit in the creation of violent men. They emphasize sport's perpetuation and glorification of male violence through large, organized team competitions such as hockey, football, soccer, baseball, and basketball. Many parents also fear that their community and high-school leagues may contribute to this process. They recognize that, whether at the local or the professional level, sport frequently becomes more valued as a vehicle for earning money, prestige, and power for those involved; winning becomes more important than playing the game.

While these criticisms of team sports are valid, numerous individual sports such as boxing, weight-lifting, fencing, javelin, and shotput also can contribute traits which encourage male violence. It is not simply the type of sport that is the problem, but rather the social context in which it is undertaken. This involves all that is associated with organizing, teaching, practising, evaluating, or advertising the game. Engaging in physical activity—team or individual—can expose an individual to powerful pressure to conform to the currently hegemonic notions of masculinity and femininity. It is in this sense that sport has contributed to some very dangerous traditions.

Sport Encourages a Deference to Authority

The large and necessarily hierarchical structure of team sports can encourage in the individual a greater deference to authority. John Mitzel, in *Sports and the Macho Male*, has provided one of the best critiques of sport's role in creating a

40

hierarchy which encourages deference among individuals. He points to all that is involved in selection of those who get to play the specific sport, in the training needed to regiment them, in the submission to a greater authority as a requirement of a team effort, and in the broader context, in the exploitation of men, women, and children to manipulate them into fans. He recognizes the importance of the team hierarchy to which all adhere: rookies, seasoned players, captains, assistant coaches, head coaches, managers, and owners. The existence of this system, with its rules and regulations, can be very restrictive for the individual player.

Winning Becomes Paramount

Too often the primary overt or covert goal is to create a winning team, and the degree of regimentation needed to achieve this can be very harmful to the development of the individual. Coming late for practice, not working one's hardest (in the estimation of the coach), or merely questioning the content and duration of the exercises can get one thrown out of the organization. If a person does persist, he or she may be subjected to gruelling practices under some less-than-desirable conditions—for instance, very early in the morning or late at night. Children are often tired and tears are not uncommon as the kids agonize over not achieving the perfection desired by their coaches, parents, or team-mates. Already rampant numbers of sports injuries are escalated by the pressure on children to do physical things that are not natural for any human, or that should only be undertaken when the body is more mature. One example is the pressure on boys not to throw a baseball 'like a girl'—which is to say, in more of a shotput style, with the hand and ball starting behind the ear and the elbow leading the way. Drilled into young boys is the fear of derision if they do not throw 'like a man'—pulling the arm straight back as far as it will go and snapping the ball overhand past the ear. This is done despite the evidence that 'throwing like a girl' is actually more anatomically correct for the human arm, and the fact that many Little League Pitchers seriously damage their shoulders. It is clear that the intent here is not simply to teach a sport, but rather to identify a specific type of activity as masculine and thus afford it significantly more value. Those who achieve this skill can win the rights of privilege; those who fail suffer the scorn of the crowd.

> *"For men sport is an important training ground for the military life."*

The parallels to military basic training are unmistakable. As in the army, young recruits are moulded through physical and emotional endurance tests to obtain the skills and embrace the values of hegemonic masculinity. Mitzel emphasizes that for men sport is an important training ground for the military life. Physical fitness and a willingness to defer to authority are two attributes needed to advance within the ranks of the

41

army. Mitzel argues that the sport and military hierarchies are very similar, as evidenced particularly by the support afforded each by our society. Robert Kennedy, at one time the U.S. attorney general, recognized the links between sport and the military: 'Except for war, there is nothing in American life—nothing—which trains a boy better for life than football.'

Whether in the military, in sport, or elsewhere, becoming part of a larger whole can be a very positive and rewarding experience. One can feel supported by other individuals while the group cooperates to pursue similar goals. Yet problems can arise in group settings when individuals relinquish some, or all, responsibility for their thoughts, principles, and actions. This may help lead the team to victory. But reducing one's ability to question or dissent from a perceived group consensus can be very dangerous; it can, in some contexts, facilitate male violence.

Individuals may lose their capacity to disagree with the group's goal. At a larger level, this is part of what occurs every time citizens put their unquestioned faith in their leaders. The phenomenon of Nazi Germany is an extreme example of what can occur when we abandon individual reasoning to defer to a larger authority. Another example—this one more related to the experiences of many women—is the deference to authority that occurs among a group of men when they gang rape a woman. Studies repeatedly indicate that many of the males involved in a gang rape do so more to fit in with a group of males, or out of fear of disagreeing with the perceived group consensus that it is acceptable for men to abuse women, than out of a desire to rape. Yet another example—this one being more common and socially acceptable—is when men in a group chuckle as their peers joke or talk about being violent to the women in their lives. Once again, while their thoughts may differ, they defer to the group, and their responses support the violence. In both examples, whether the men are too afraid to stand on their own, or recognize the potential rewards for being part of the group, or are being goaded by an individual male within the group who is testing the loyalty of the other group members, the violence toward women is condoned. As is too often the case, a woman's body is the testing ground for male rivalry.

> *"A woman's body is the testing ground for male rivalry."*

Sport Reinforces Masculinity's Links with Violence

One of the key components of most sporting activities is competition. It is not an inherently evil quality. Competition can be an incentive to improve one's skill and performance levels. It is something different, though, when winning the game becomes the overriding reason for playing. This reinforces the goal-focused component of hegemonic masculinity. In order to win the game men may refuse to cooperate, be willing to disregard the needs of others, and ultimately use physical force to achieve a goal—and they are generally rewarded by society for having done so.

The social context in which sport occurs too frequently gives positive reinforcement only to hegemonic masculine behaviour—win at all costs, might is right, and cooperate only if it helps you reach your goal. It is from engaging in sports that many adolescent males first learn they are

> *"Like enemy territory during war, [women] are to be conquered."*

'not man enough' to compete and endure the derision of their peers and family. A male not interested in being overly competitive or aggressive quickly learns that if he does not want to be excluded from a team or a highly valued peer group, he needs to play the game like the 'big boys.' If he has not already done so, he may bury his sensitivity. He hides his interest in things such as plants, insects, flowers, or the creation of beauty. Instead, he crushes, stomps on, and obliterates anything in his path that may betray his tenderness or vulnerability. One thinks of a twelve-year-old boy playing hockey. He tries his best with a shot on goal, but misses. Instead of commending his effort, the loudest roars from the crowd deride him for his incompetence, or question his sexual preference—as if this were something all twelve-year-olds have even sorted out, or as if being gay precludes the capacity to score a goal. To win the approval of that crowd and of others, weight and barbell sets are purchased, by the parent, the son, or both, so he can bulk up his muscles to look like the stereotypical (super)man.

The Charles Atlas scenario typifies the dreadful alternative if one does not measure up to the physical standards of hegemonic masculinity. If one is a 'ninety-eight-pound weakling,' like the protagonist, not only will one get sand kicked in one's face; there is also the probability of losing one's girlfriend. Aside from not giving the girlfriend any cognitive capacity to decide with whom she wishes to spend her time, the ad epitomizes the way in which sport is sold as an important vehicle for conformity to hegemonic masculinity.

Masculinity, Sport, and the State

This form of masculinity also has been important to the nation-state. The connections between masculinity, sport, and the state, in fact, were central to the revival of the Olympic Games, the pinnacle of sporting events, by Baron Pierre de Coubertin in the late nineteenth century. Born in Paris in 1863 to a wealthy French family, de Coubertin witnessed first the humiliating defeat of his country in the Franco-Prussian War of 1870 and then the continued ascension of German and British power over France during the next several decades. He developed a belief that Frenchmen must be toughened up by sport in order to return their nation to its rightful place among world powers. . . . This tradition of using the Olympics as a way of proving superiority—either the individual's or the nation's—continues unabated.

For a long time in sport, there have been certain myths cultivated regarding the superiority or inferiority of specific groups of people. While it is not as easily done in the contemporary period, in the past, sport was an important means of segregating sexes, races, and classes. People of colour or those of the lower classes (which were often one and the same) at one time were not allowed to partake. This began to change, however, after several important challenges to the colour bar—Satchel Paige struck out top white players in an exhibition game, Jesse Owens captured the gold at the 1936 Olympics in Berlin, and Jackie Robinson broke into the all-white baseball leagues.

While the colour and class barriers have either become more subtle or have disappeared altogether, the division between the sexes continues—not until 1984, for example, were women officially permitted to run in the Olympic marathon. There is evidence that within the next few decades, male and female athletes may compete on an equal basis, thanks to the steadily declining gap in various performance records. Yet many people in our society continue to firmly believe that girls and boys should or should not play various gender-coded sports.

The continuing popularity of such myths has prompted Lois Bryson to critically analyse connections between sport and hegemonic masculinity. Bryson argues that sport 'serves to ritually support an aura of male competence and superiority in publicly acclaimed skills, and a male monopoly of aggression and violence. A corollary of this is an inferiorization of women and their skills, and their isolation from the ultimate basis of social power—physical force.'

Hegemonic men have largely appropriated sport and used it to perpetuate various class and gender inequities. One of the results is the pervasive manner in which sporting metaphors are used to describe actions valued within hegemonic masculinity and certain nation-states. In the discussion of sexual exploits, for example, certain phrases are common: 'Did you get to first base?' 'Did you steal a base?' 'Did you make it all the way to home?' 'Did you score?' (And if so, 'how many times?') When describing military activities, individuals may talk about a nation's 'first-strike' nuclear capacity, or accuse another country of 'not playing by the rules.' Organized sport reinforces a notion central to traditional male culture that all male interaction—whether at the individual or national level—is adversarial and requires competitive skill and cunning to be practised successfully. Whatever the metaphor, the notion regarding women is the same. Like enemy territory during war, they are to be conquered and this is best done by able-bodied athletic hulks. Limp-wristed faggots need not apply.

While many of the negative hegemonic traits reinforced by sport may be learned elsewhere, when one considers the large amount of time many men spend throughout their lives either participating in or watching sport, this important agent of male socialization needs to be held accountable for its contribution.

Chapter 2

What Causes Rape?

CURRENT CONTROVERSIES

The Rapist: An Overview

by David Gelman et al.

About the author: *David Gelman is a reporter for* Newsweek, *a national weekly newsmagazine.*

They say a lot of things lead up to rape, but I never thought about it. I don't know what the hell I was looking for. The opportunity occurred and I just took advantage of it.

—Convicted rapist Roger Smith, 26, interviewed in
Atlanta's Metro Correctional Institution

Why do they do it? What impels men to commit, sometimes casually, sometimes with practiced cunning, one of the most primitively brutal of crimes—the pre-empting of another person's body for the gratification of their own needs? Data to help solve that frightening riddle is in short supply. Most of it comes from rapists who are caught and convicted, representing only a slice of the real total. Meanwhile, disturbing statistics are emerging on the sheer incidence of sex crimes. The 1990 Senate Judiciary Committee hearings on violent crime against women concluded that rape increased four times as fast as the overall crime rate over the previous decade. A woman is raped every six minutes, the committee said, but only half the rapes are ever reported. The statistics . . . are giving new urgency to the quest to understand the phenomenon of sexual violence.

No Single Profile

No single profile provides an answer to why men rape. Opportunity, emotional illness, lust—it happens for all of those reasons, yet often for none of them. There is Roger Smith, a married mechanic oppressed by mortgage payments on his trailer home, stopping to do a good deed for a woman whose car had broken down and tarrying, unexpectedly, to assault her. But there is also "Bill," a serial rapist who methodically sought out his victims in their own apartments, attacking seven women at knifepoint before he was caught. Some are like "Vince," a sexually troubled youngster who began by peeping through bedroom windows in his teens, committed a rape murder in his early 20s, and then went to prison for molesting his own stepdaughter. Others are like "James," a 42-year-old Miami business manager with four children, aware only of a vague "frustration" in

> *"No single profile provides an answer to why men rape."*

his life, who liked to pick up females in pairs and rape one of them in front of the other. "Inside is a rage," said James, who completed a sexual-offender program in June 1989, after serving 10 years for rape.

Anger, deep and dark, is a common thread among rapists. Something has invariably gone wrong with their lives, often from almost the very beginning. A 1982 study of rapists in Oregon found that as many as 80 percent were abused children, and their own victimization results in a kind of emotional death. They grow up feeling martyred, self-justifying—unwilling or unable to extend compassion to the people they in turn abuse. Many depersonalize their victims. "The offender views rape the same as kicking a tire," says William Pithers, director of the Vermont Center for the Prevention and Treatment of Sexual Abuse. Yet others are so shamed by their acts they grow suicidal. William Samek, a Miami-based clinical psychologist, remembers one extreme instance in which the rapist handed his gun to his woman victim, exclaiming: "I can't stand it anymore, please blow me away."

How Should Rapists Be Treated?

The inability to make useful generalizations about rapists has fostered a somewhat schizoid attitude about how to treat them. "They're not all mad dogs," says Pithers. "Rape is a sick act committed by sane people." That poses a conundrum to police and mental-health authorities, who sometimes split between favoring imprisonment without treatment and treatment without imprisonment. Typically, Washington state has one of the country's more innovative programs for sex offenders—and also the toughest pack of laws to keep released offenders under police and public surveillance.

Inevitably, the quarrel evokes shades of the ancient nature versus nurture argument. Some treatment experts, for example, support the use of Depo-Provera, a drug that brings about impotence, and is thus sometimes labeled "medical castration." They feel rapists suffer from a biological defect, and can't be cured, only controlled. (Some still advocate literal castration.) Others argue that potency is not the problem, since many rapists are unable to penetrate their victims or achieve orgasm when they rape. "We believe that what's wrong with a sex offender is what's between his ears, not his legs," says Richard Seely, director of Minnesota's Intensive Treatment Program for Sexual Aggressiveness, who refuses to use the suppressant drug. "It's his thinking that's dysfunctional, not his sexuality," he says. "Rapists are who they learn to be—it's not a product of their hormones."

Experts have hotly debated for years whether rape is an act of violence or an act of sex. Current thinking seems to be that it is both, but there are still differences of emphasis. "We look at rape as the sexual expression of aggression, rather than as the aggressive expression of sexuality," says psychologist Nicholas Groth, director of Forensic Mental Health Associates, who has seen more than 3,000 sex offenders in 25 years of practice. Most of his patients, Groth points out, were not sexually deprived at the time they committed rape.

Anger and Power

In about 1980, Groth established a typology of rapists that is still a standard, although some psychologists feel parts of it are outdated. Broadly speaking, rapists fall into three motivational types, said Groth: anger, power and sadism. In anger assaults, the rapist is getting even for "some wrong he feels has been done to him, by life, by his victim at the time. He's in a frame of rage and attacks someone sexually." The anger rape is usually unpremeditated and impulsive, but the impulse drives the rapist into excessive force: the victim is punched, choked, kicked into submission. Most such offenders derive little pleasure from the act, says Groth, but "they want to degrade their victims, and sex is something bad, dirty, the worst thing you could do to someone. That reflects a lot of our values in society."

> *"A 1982 study of rapists in Oregon found that as many as 80 percent were abused children."*

Anger rapists can be the most ruthless. "Forrest," 33, went to see a friend once, and found he had moved. When the woman living in the house invited him in to use the phone, he grabbed her and her then 86-year-old mother-in-law, pushed them into the bedroom, tore their clothes off and penetrated the older woman with his finger. Then he panicked and fled. "Rape was always a big issue for me," says Forrest, who was caught soon after the attack. . . . The father of three children, addicted to drugs and drink, he had been thrown out by his wife after beating her repeatedly. Often, he says, he had rape fantasies about his mother, who had beaten him "nonstop since the age of 8." Forrest joined the sex-offender treatment program at Washington's Twin Rivers prison and is off drugs.

Power rape, Groth says, is a form of compensation, committed usually by men who feel unsure of their competence. Rape gives them a sense of mastery and control. Power rapists usually hunt for a victim, or seize an opportunity: finding a young girl in the house after a break-in, for example. "Tom," 37, an abuser of alcohol and drugs, was forced as a child to perform oral sex on his grandfather and had a history of window peeping, flashing, compulsive mastur-bation and making obscene phone calls by the time he committed his first rape, at 20. He admits to about a dozen sexual assaults since then, although he was caught only twice. He recalls feeling nothing for his victims. "There were only thoughts of me. I'd say, 'I have a knife, and I'll cut your eye out.'" Once he smashed a woman's face into a car because she kicked him in the groin. But often "there was just pleasure in the humiliation."

Just after serving his first prison term for rape, "Tom" kidnapped a woman at a parking ramp, and forced her to perform oral sex on him three times. He has gained enough insight from counselors to say, "A lot of what I did had to do with my own feelings of inadequacy." But he is also perceptive enough to add: "I can't say I'll never rape again."

Sadistic and Gang Rape

Groth defines his third type, sadistic rape, as eroticized aggression. The very act of forcible sex excites rapists in ways that consensual sex can't. "If the anger components of aggression are eroticized," he explains, "then you see sadistic acts, such as deliberate sexual torture, using an instrument to rape the victim." Something like that may have incited a group of Glen Ridge, N.J., high-school football teammates in March 1989, when they allegedly sexually assaulted a mentally impaired woman with a miniature baseball bat, a broom handle and a stick [three were found guilty of first-degree aggravated sexual assault in April 1993]. A sadistic impulse may be the only explanation for such a horror. But gang rapes have a dynamic of their own. Alone, the participants may be inca-pable of sexual assault; together, they may bait each other into monstrous acts, as police contend the Glen Ridge footballers and the Central Park jogger's at-tackers did. They tend to be more opportunistic than ordinary marauders. "A lot of times you may have one or more individuals in the group who have the same arousal patterns as a rapist," says psychologist Gerald Kaplan, executive director of Alpha Human Services in Minneapolis, a community-based sex-offender pro-gram. "But the typical gang rape is not like having a whole pack of rapists. In fact, most rapists are isolated people who travel by themselves. It's a very hidden part of their lives."

Gang rapers are usually quite young, and vulnerable to peer pres-sure: they play follow the leader. The rape is a rite of passage, and the un-willing rapist may be even more un-willing to oppose the group. The gang, moreover, often builds to extreme vio-lence, as members are challenged to outdo each other. Some studies suggest that offenders slow down as they age. Older men simply don't travel in packs. "You're not going to find a group of 40-year-old rapists out there as a group,"

"What's wrong with a sex offender is what's between his ears, not his legs."

49

says Kaplan.

One of the most consistent elements in rape of all kinds is the absence of empathy; attackers are able to persuade themselves that the victim wanted or deserved to be raped. Dr. Gene Abel, a professor of psychiatry at Emory University who has studied hundreds of rapists over the past 20 years, believes that rapists suffer from a form of cognitive distortion that allows them to justify their actions in the face of stark evidence to the contrary. Abel saw a patient who claimed he had never raped a woman, despite an arrest record showing repeated rape charges. When he asked the patient how he would know a woman wanted to have sex with him, he replied that she was obviously willing if she spoke to him or invited him up to her apartment. How would he know if she *weren't* willing, Abel asked. The patient responded, seeing nothing askew in his answer: "If she fought me the whole time we were having sex."

> *"Power rape . . . is a form of compensation, committed usually by men who feel unsure of their competence."*

Probably these distortions set in early, as a child protects himself from unbearable reality. Only 10 percent of rapists appear to have a history of psychiatric illness. But by the time they are ordered into treatment, their careers may be well advanced; some list hundreds of victims as they pour out their stories. Few rapists ever seek treatment on their own, says Theoharis Seghorn, a clinical psychologist at New England Forensic Associates: "Rapists don't reach out because they don't trust."

Responsibility and Empathy

Treatment may not be able to cure rapists, but the majority can be helped. Most programs aim to get patients to stop rationalizing and accept responsibility. The rapists may not be able to feel actual empathy, but counselors urge them to behave as if they do, if only to keep them out of prison. "For many of them, it has to be on the level of their own self-interest," says Stephen Huot, an associate director at the Minnesota Correctional Facility in Oak Park Heights.

Oak Park teaches inmates to acknowledge blame by sharing written autobiographies in group therapy. After identifying their patterns of assault, they work on conscience-building by putting themselves in the victims' shoes. Occasionally they even write letters to their victims. They also learn to change their fantasies and distorted thinking. At the Vermont center, newcomers invariably say they were drunk when they raped. Long-termers tell them: "We'll respect you a lot more around here if you cut out that bullshit." To help such people discover empathy is a complicated job, says director Pithers. "They need to experience their own feelings before they can identify with others." The offenders start by writing down every emotion they can remember feeling. One 15-year-old, in after committing his fifth rape, could name only four: depression, rage, anger and frustration.

Pithers shows them films like "To Kill a Mockingbird" or "A Christmas Story," a simple '40s tale about a boy who wants a rifle for Christmas, and has the offenders try to identify the emotions of all the characters, noting those that weren't acceptable in their own families. He has them read victims' recollections or watch videotapes of their victims' testimony, and jot down when they recognize how one of the victims might have felt. For most people who can feel for others almost as naturally as they breathe, it may be hard to imagine *not* feeling. But many young offenders are "numbed out," says Lynn Reynolds, clinical director of the Institute Against Social Violence, in Briarcliff Manor, N.Y. "I had one boy who saw his father pull his mother down the steps by her hair and stab her," says Reynolds. "That's not an excuse, but it does explain his desensitization to violence." Adds Eugene Porter, an Oakland, Calif., psychologist: "I haven't seen a rapist who didn't have a childhood horror story."

Some programs still employ behavior modification techniques, such as administering mild shocks while inmates view pornographic material, or "masturbatory reconditioning"—getting them to masturbate to "healthy" images. Some men never do develop the connection to others that allows them to care. With many, impulsiveness and sexual arousal are the main issues, and thus they need both punishment and treatment, says Porter. "Punishment drives home the point, it serves to correct the 'responsibility imbalance.'" In recent years the burden of treatment has shifted from mental-health departments to corrections departments, an issue bitterly debated in some states.

> *"The very act of forcible sex excites rapists in ways that consensual sex can't."*

The public, for its part, generally opposes money for treating rapists. Funding tends to increase only after widely publicized assaults. After a series of rape-murders in Minnesota a few years ago, the legislature increased both sentences and treatment dollars for rapists, notes Huot. Now, sexual offenders may wait a year to get into treatment, and then spend 18 months in therapy programs—often after a year of chemical-dependency treatment.

Ominous Trends

Meanwhile, mental-health and corrections officials across the country are seeing an ever more youthful population of sex offenders, some—both abused and abusing—as young as 8. According to the National Center for Juvenile Justice, the arrest rate for 13- and 14-year-olds accused of rape doubled between 1976 and 1986. Although experts agree that younger offenders respond better to treatment, they often fall between the cracks of the social-welfare system. "Every state is trying to figure out what to do with these kids," says June Binney, of the Department of Mental Health in Massachusetts.

Teenagers are not the only group contributing to the rise in sex offenses. Part of the jump is due to a staggering increase in reported "date" or acquaintance rape. An estimated 75 percent of rapes occur between people who know each other. "Men may well mistake [sexual] liberation for license," says Eleanor Holmes Norton, a lawyer and activist on women's issues.

More than that, many people blame the escalating violence in popular culture for fueling the growth in rape statistics across the board. After two decades of the newly "sensitive," nurturing male, the macho stud seems to have come back in magnum force. In sexually explicit movies and books, as well as increasingly suggestive music videos and television shows, men flex pectorals and women acrobatically surrender to them. "Our insensitivity to the violence of rape is un-doubtedly fostered by our massive diet of entertainment," says Dr. Thomas Radecki, research director for the National Coalition on Television Violence, based in Champaign, Ill.

Radecki cites statistics showing one out of eight Hollywood movies depicts a rape theme; and by age 18, the average American will have seen 250,000 acts of violence and 40,000 attempted murders on television. Radecki's position with a special-interest group may make such figures a little suspect, and in light of the wave of reaction against funding sexually explicit art, critics should be wary of encouraging censorship. But neither a Radecki nor a National Endowment is needed to convince most people that something has run amok in the culture.

H. Rap Brown once raised middle-class hackles by declaring that violence "is as American as cherry pie." Examining our national rape statistics, the Senate Judiciary Committee noted that when ranked against other nations, the United States leads the way, with a rape rate four times that of Germany, 13 times as much as England, 20 times as much as Japan. Sadly, sexual violence, too, may now be an emblem of the American way.

Society Encourages Rape

by Alice Vachss

About the author: *Alice Vachss was an assistant district attorney in Queens County, New York, from 1982 to 1991. She is the author of* Sex Crimes, *from which this viewpoint is excerpted.*

The first sexual offender I tried—Johnny Washington—was also the first felony trial for the judge who presided. At the initial conference between the judge, the defense attorney and me, the judge offered to let the defendant plead to the charges in exchange for a minimum sentence. I objected, but the judge ignored me. It was the defense attorney who turned down the offer. But in light of the judge's generosity, the defense attorney waived a jury—preferring to let this judge issue the verdict on the guilt of the defendant. Right then, I should have known.

The First Case

Carmen was petite, dignified—and terrified when she took the witness stand. She testified that she had returned home from her job as a bank teller at around 6:30 in the evening. A stranger, later identified as Washington, had followed her onto the elevator in her apartment building. When Carmen tried to get off at her floor, the stranger grabbed her from behind. He told her he had a knife and that he would kill her if she didn't cooperate. At the roof, he dragged her over to an electrical shack, where he made her undress and lie down on the gravel. He covered her face with his jacket while he raped her and sodomized her. Then he made her give him her watch and money.

After he left her on the roof, she crawled down the outside of the building to her apartment. Her sister, a social worker who counseled rape victims, testified about seeing Carmen appear at her door, her clothes in disarray and scrape marks all over her back and legs. They called Carmen's boyfriend, who was a police officer, to take them to the precinct to make the complaint.

From *Sex Crimes* by Alice Vachss. Reprinted by permission of Random House, Inc.

Four days later, Carmen saw Washington on the street and called the police. This is the man, she said, who raped her.

Unbelievably, the judge decided that because Carmen hadn't seen the rape, she couldn't be sure of the penetration. He wanted nauseatingly graphic details.

I told the judge he was saying that a blind woman couldn't prosecute a rape case in Queens County. That quote was picked up by the media— with two results: Although the judge

> *"There seems to be a residuum of empathy for sexual predators that crosses all gender, class, and professional barriers."*

did not find Washington guilty of rape, he felt compelled to impose the maximum sentence on him for the lesser offenses, including first-degree sexual abuse; it added up to the same sentence as a rape conviction. And the judge hated me for life.

Collaborators

My first lesson about sex-crimes prosecution was that perpetrators were not the only enemy. There is a large, more or less hidden population of what I later came to call collaborators within the criminal justice system. Whether it comes from a police officer or a defense attorney, a judge or a prosecutor, there seems to be a residuum of empathy for sexual predators that crosses all gender, class and professional barriers. It gets expressed in different ways—from victim-bashing to jokes in poor taste, and too often it results in giving the sexual offender a break.

It didn't take me long to get the reputation of someone willing to take on any rape prosecution. Other trial attorneys "gave" me their sex cases. Mostly what I got were the ones nobody else wanted: cases in which the proof was weak or the victim unlikable—or simply cases that involved a lot of work.

The victim was a big, homely, unlikable teenager. She had a crush on one of the popular boys—a handsome athlete who was everything she wasn't. One night, she ran into him in the neighborhood. Probably she would have been willing to do anything he asked of her. Instead he forced her to have sex with him and his friend. If the term had been fashionable then, it would have been called date rape. He did it to be doing it, because he could, and who, he thought, would care?

He was almost right. Her family didn't care. Her brothers yelled at her for getting raped. Her mother wouldn't interrupt her bowling night to take the girl to the police precinct.

The victim, nevertheless, on sheer courage alone, went to the police. One of the rapists, the friend, was arrested. He went to trial. Sure enough, the jury didn't like the victim. She was sullen where she could have been sympathetic, unresponsive in cross-examination. She didn't expect a jury to believe her. She knew she needed to do this for herself. It made me angry. I tried the whole case angry.

And the jury convicted.

It was more than a year later before the co-defendant was found and arrested. I contacted the victim. She had built a new life for herself, met a man and had a son. She still was willing to prosecute. I put together enough of a case so that Mr. Popularity pleaded guilty. When I told the victim *both* rapists were in prison, she was happier than I thought she could be. She said when her son got older, she would tell him.

I'd like him to know that his mother taught me something about bravery.

Courage Is Common

Being a sex-crimes prosecutor meant, for me, eyewitnessing courage. It was the one common denominator among the victims I had the privilege of accompanying into a courtroom to testify that they had been raped.

Other prosecutors in the office insisted on more common denominators than that. They wanted their rape victims to fit an image. How the jury responds to a victim is an enormous percentage of the verdict in any sex-crimes trial—which is why prosecutors want "good victims."

> *"Rapists tend to go to trial more often than any other kind of criminal, believing in their souls that all men . . . would rape if they only had what it takes."*

In New York City, good victims have jobs (like stockbroker or accountant) or impeccable status (like a police officer's wife); are well-educated and articulate; and are, above all, presentable to a jury: attractive but not too attractive, demure but not pushovers. They should be upset, but in good taste—not so upset that they become hysterical.

Such attitudes not only are distasteful, they are also frightening. They say it's OK to rape some people—just not *us*.

Rapists tend to go to trial more often than any other kind of criminal, believing in their souls that all men, including those on the jury, would rape if they only had what it takes. They are supported too often in this belief by the fact that what the defense puts on trial is the victim.

People do say that anybody can be raped, that rapists don't discriminate. It is true that rape victims include among their ranks heiresses and nuns and great-grandmothers. But they also include crackheads and dope dealers, junkies, whores, thieves and liars.

Rapists Discriminate

Rapists do discriminate—they look for whatever vulnerability might insulate them from capture and punishment. Sometimes that means raping a child, because we seem as a country to doubt the word of children who say they've been raped. And sometimes that means trying to sell the rest of us on the concept that it isn't really rape if the victim is someone we don't like.

The one truth that is more important to me than all the rest is that what the public is entitled to from prosecutors is not any particular verdict but the willingness to step into the ring again and again.

I remember, for example, Terry Pittman. He didn't have in him what quality it is that makes the rest of us human. He'd lucked into a teenager who asked if he knew where to buy marijuana. He took her to his apartment and raped her. She struggled so hard she kicked out a window. He twisted her neck so violently that he paralyzed her. She begged: "Help me, help me I can't move!" It aroused him, and he raped her again. When he was done with her, he dumped her, naked, on the driveway. Neighbors called the police.

The victim's parents didn't think she had the strength to prosecute. I did. I believed her when she told me, "If I have to testify, I'll testify—whatever it is— just so long as he gets punished." Pittman pleaded guilty. The day she could walk on her own again, with crutches, she came to the courthouse to find me. She brought me a rose.

From the beginning, I never had a caseload made up solely of sex crimes. I found out that not every rapist got charged with sexual assault. Rapists always knew what I had to learn: There is more than one way to penetrate a victim. People who think rape is about sex confuse the weapon with the motivation.

Domestic Violence

Robert Roudabush was charged with attempted murder. It was Christmastime. He was supposed to take his wife, Maureen, shopping for gifts. Instead he got drunk and stayed late at his office Christmas party. When she complained, they argued. He decided he knew how to settle it, once and for all. He went into the bedroom and assembled a minor arsenal—two rifles, a shotgun.

Maureen took her 1-year-old into the kitchen to prepare a bottle for him. She was standing at the refrigerator with the baby in her arms when Roudabush spoke from behind her: "Don't move, I'm going to kill you." As she turned instinctively toward the sound, he shot her. The first bullet lodged in her neck, near the spinal column. She and the baby both went down. That was

"I'm so scared of him. . . . I'm so scared the jury is going to let him go, and he'll kill me."

why the other shots missed them. Roudabush kept firing until the rifle jammed.

She screamed for the neighbors to call 911. They took her in an ambulance. They took him in a police car.

Maureen later told me she had to keep phoning the DA's office from the hospital, insisting that her husband be prosecuted. They told her her husband would never be convicted. Besides, sooner or later she would drop the charges.

Maureen was terrified that her husband would get out of jail and kill her. At a preliminary hearing, the judge believed her and kept her husband in jail. They gave the case to me.

Living in Fear

Even after I starting pushing, Roudabush's case stayed pending for almost a year. Maureen got divorced, moved in with her mother, waited. Maureen and I talked before and after each court appearance. I started each conversation telling her that her ex-husband's bail status hadn't changed. She needed to hear it. She still lived in fear.

Roudabush wrote to Maureen while he was in jail. He tried all the angles. One letter would declare his love and repentance and beg her forgiveness. The next would be full of threats. Some letters would tell her he'd found God. None of these worked. Finally, we went to trial.

There was more proof against Roudabush than I was used to having. Maureen was young, pretty and distraught, with her Irish-rose face radiating credibility. At one point in her testimony, she broke down in tears. I talked to her on the break, and she said, "I'm so scared of him. He's sitting looking at me, and I'm so scared the jury is going to let him go, and he'll kill me." The jury seemed to understand her feelings. In addition, there were recovered weapons, ammunition, a confession and injuries serious enough for a jury not to discount the crimes as "only" domestic violence. The People's case was persuasive, powerful—it felt like a conviction.

> *"We have allowed sex crimes to be the one area of criminality where we judge the offense not by the perpetrator but by the victim."*

Then the defense called a neurologist as a witness. The defendant had a history, from birth complications through childhood epilepsy, the neurologist said, that together with a lifelong propensity toward sudden violence, led to a diagnosis of "episodic dyscontrol." According to the doctor, Roudabush did not "intend" his crimes. His episodic dyscontrol meant he had irresistible urges to commit violence—episodes of rage beyond his control.

Because the testimony came as a surprise to me, the judge gave me the weekend to prepare my cross-examination. I needed every minute of it. What the doctor said sounded logical, but its consequences were devastating. It he convinced the jury, Roudabush simply went free.

That Friday night was one of the lowest times for me that I can remember during a trial. What if the neurologist was right? But while I was worrying the problem to death, I had a moment of simple perception that felt like it applied to a lot more than one trial.

Chapter 2

Monday morning, I cross-examined the neurologist for several hours. Then I delivered the payload question. If Roudabush suffered episodic dyscontrol, how come the only victim of his violence was his wife? How come he never had these fits at work or driving his car? The jury convicted. Roudabush did 10 years of a 6- to 18-year sentence before being paroled out of state. He hasn't had any incidents of "episodic dyscontrol" since the trial.

When I decided to become a sex-crimes prosecutor, I had no idea what it would feel like to convict a rapist—to create a little piece of justice on this planet. All along, from the first sex crime I prosecuted to the last day, there were people "in the know" saying that what I wanted couldn't be done.

We have allowed sex crimes to be the one area of criminality where we judge the offense not by the perpetrator but by the victim. There is an essential difference between sex crimes and other crimes, but it has nothing to do with the victims. Most other crime is in response to a need that the offense itself seeks to meet: Some people kill because they are angry; some people steal because they want money. But as each rape is committed, it creates a greater need. Rape is dose-related—it is chronic, repetitive and always escalating.

Rapists cross a line—a clear, bright line. Absent significant, predictable consequences, they are never going to cross back. Too often, instead of consequences, what we give them is permission.

Collaboration is a hate crime. When a jury in Florida acquits because the victim was not wearing underpants, when a grand jury in Texas refuses to indict because an AIDS-fearing victim begged the rapist to use a condom, when a judge in Manhattan imposes a lenient sentence because the rape of a retarded, previously victimized teenager wasn't "violent," when an appellate defense attorney vilifies a young woman on national TV for the "crime" of having successfully prosecuted a rape complaint, when a judge in Wisconsin calls a 5-year-old "seductive"—all that is collaboration, and it is antipathy toward victims so virulent that it subjects us all to risk.

Judging the Rapist

There are always going to be rapists among us. We need to stop permitting it to be socially and politically acceptable to give them aid and comfort. We need to recognize rape for the antihuman crime that it is. Rape is neither sexual nor sexy—it is an ugly act of dominance and control. We need to start judging sex crimes by the rape and by the rapist—not by the victim.

A rapist is a single-minded, totally self-absorbed, sociopathic beast—a beast that cannot be tamed with "understanding." We need to stop shifting the responsibilities, to stop demanding that victims show "earnest resistance," to stop whining and start winning. And one of our strongest weapons must be fervent intolerance for collaboration in any form.

We need to go to war.

Society Encourages Rape by Athletes

by Julie Cart

About the author: *Julie Cart is a staff writer for the* Los Angeles Times, *a daily newspaper in Los Angeles, California.*

Seven high school athletes [were implicated] in Glen Ridge, N.J., [in the] raping [of] a retarded girl with a baseball bat and other wooden objects.

The 17-year-old girl is described by police as being a sports fan and the boys are well-known sports stars. According to police reports, the girl—who has the mental capacity of an 8-year-old—was brought to the basement of a house where the boys and six others the victim could not identify sexually assaulted her.

The boys were members of the Glen Ridge High football and baseball teams.

Athletes and Rape

Athletes and rape—awful anomaly or growing problem? Social critics believe the latter is the case. . . .

A woman is raped every six minutes in this country. As members of society, athletes are going to be statistically represented in that crime, and they are. In fact, some would say athletes are overrepresented in the area of sexual assault.

A 1990 study found that 2% of athletes surveyed admitted they had committed date rape, more than four times the frequency reported by non-athletes.

What society has fostered is a segment of the population—elite athletes—that has learned from an early age that they are special. Often they form the idea that rules don't apply to them.

Institutions that thrive from the athlete's labor are tolerant of their sometimes abhorrent behavior. Too often, the institutions assist the athlete to cover up or avoid punishment for his crime.

It often is not difficult. Rape is one of law enforcement's most under-reported crimes and its most difficult to prosecute. The nationwide conviction rate for rape is 10%.

Athletes are frequently heard to complain that they are held to different standards than the general public.

But what the statistics regarding rape among athletes reveal is that the standards might not be high enough.

Terminal Adolescence

It is not enough to say that there seems to be a high incidence of sexual assault among athletes. Police blotters confirm that. An attempt must be made to explain the *why*.

Tom House, pitching coach for the Texas Rangers, sees athletes as part of a system that treats them as objects, thus athletes tend to treat others as objects.

House is uniquely qualified to comment. He holds a doctorate in psychology and has written a book, *The Jock's Itch*, in which he describes athletes as being in a state of terminal adolescence.

House believes this country's huge athletic system is turning out dysfunctional people. Athletes have difficulty identifying society's boundaries because of their programmed insensitivities, House said.

"The easiest way to say it is that they [athletes] don't have a thermostat for empathy," House said. "They don't have a thermostat for the reality of human interaction. They have a real problem with this thing called empathy, putting themselves in another person's shoes and feeling what that other person feels. That is a computer chip they don't have.

"Athletes are expected to understand two things: anger and aggression. Those are the only emotions they are really capable of dealing with. The more violent the sport, the less they are able to empathize for the 'other' they are dealing with."

Sexual assault cases among athletes appear to occur most often in team sports. "We never see golfers or swimmers," said one researcher. But it's not always the athletes in showcase sports.

At St. John's University in New York, five members of the lacrosse team and one member of the school's rifle club were accused of raping a student on March 1, 1990.

"A woman is raped every six minutes in this country."

The woman was brought to an off-campus house where, prosecutors said, she was pressured to drink a powerful vodka and juice mix, and she passed out. Roommates who shared the house testified the woman was lying limply on a couch with her eyes closed and was repeatedly sodomized by the men, who then bragged about it. Other witnesses testified that the woman was heard screaming and that during the attack the men were cheering each other on.

Police said other women came forward and told of similar assaults at the house. Informants told police that the practice of luring a woman to the house and then gang raping her was referred to by the men as "hooking up." Police said the men's practice was to take a "souvenir" from the woman, such as an identification card, and tack the item to a house bulletin board, which was known as a "score sheet.". . .

House won't defend what he calls "repulsive" behavior, but he asks that it be understood in its social context.

"These are not bad kids," he said. "They have been programmed to be dysfunctional when it comes to the real world of human interaction."

At the University of Oklahoma, five members of the football team imprisoned a college student in an athletic dorm room and took turns raping her. Many others watched or heard the attack.

Two players received prison sentences.

Teresa Bingman is the Cleveland County assistant district attorney who helped prosecute the case. She says the case still haunts her. One reason was the attitude of the football players during the trial. They appeared to believe they were above the law.

The other thing she remembers was how, even after their convictions, the players were revered by many people in the community, simply because they were star athletes.

> *"Institutions that thrive from the athlete's labor are tolerant of their sometimes abhorrent behavior."*

"I think the system fosters these types of attitudes," Bingman said. "These individuals are young, and when they attend college they are automatically placed on a pedestal."

Society confers a privileged status to athletes, whether they ask for it or not, and whether they deserve it or not. But an icon's burden is heavy. As writer Simone de Beauvoir observed, a pedestal, like a prison, can be a tiny place.

Superiority, Sexism, and Fame

Some studies suggest that rapists are likely to have been fostered in male-only clubs and organizations such as fraternities and athletic teams.

In . . . *Nice Boys, Dirty Deeds: Gang Rape on Campus*, psychologist Chris O'Sullivan details 40 cases of collegiate gang rape. Of the cases, 30% involve athletes; 90% involve fraternities.

In one gang rape case at the University of Kentucky involving football players, it was said that there was a line of players outside the door where the victim was being held. Witnesses testified that the players were chanting, "Me next, me next."

Not surprisingly, experts say that gender segregation reinforces ignorance, stereotypes and disregard for the feelings of the "other" group. These elements can be heightened among male athletes.

"There are a number of factors," O'Sullivan said. "One is that they do something that women can't do. They tend to feel superior to people who don't have the [physical] talents they have. By definition, women are outsiders, they can't cut it, they can't compete.

> *"This country's huge athletic system is turning out dysfunctional people."*

"There is also the sexism. These athletes do get an awful lot of attention from women, which of course exacerbates this feeling of superiority. And the feeling that they can take what they want."

Successful athletes are often famous persons. They grow accustomed to the attention of women, some of whom are eager to sleep with them because they are well known. Some athletes have trouble differentiating between the groupie who wants sex and the fan who wants an autograph.

All-Pro wide receiver James Lofton was accused of sexual assault on two occasions when he played for the Green Bay Packers. The first incident took place at an exotic dance club and the second in a stairwell of a popular nightspot. Lofton was fined for trespassing in the first case and acquitted of rape in the second.

In a story about Lofton's trade to the Los Angeles Raiders in 1987, *Los Angeles Times* reporter Mark Heisler asked Lofton, who was married at the time of the incidents, what he was doing in a nightclub and bar in the first place.

Lofton said: "Oh, c'mon. Anybody could be in that bar. And anybody could sit around and let women flirt with them. And how many men turn down sex? I think that really is the question. At some point the brain just cuts off and [says], 'Well, I'm having a good time, what the heck.'"

Other than Enlightened Attitudes

O'Sullivan and others say that the emotional climate in which many elite athletes work is something other than enlightened.

"Look at the coaches," she said. "They certainly foster in the players that a real man is an abusive man. Look at football players— these guys have to take a lot of pain. They have to be tuned out to their own pain, so that other's pain becomes unreal to them. Hurting somebody is something they do all the time."

Extensive research links the male hormone testosterone to aggression. . . .

Some women say men display an insensitivity to rape. In the Oklahoma gang rape case, one of the defendants, Bernard Hall, testified that he did not rape the women because "she was not my type."

Remember Indiana basketball Coach Bob Knight telling television interviewer Connie Chung, "I think that if rape is inevitable, relax and enjoy it."

There is also the question of believability. It has been noted that if a robbery victim resists, such action is considered stupid, but a rape victim is expected to display visible wounds in order to be believed.

A female student at Cal [the University of California at Berkeley] in 1986 reported a harrowing case of gang rape to police, charging several members of the Cal football team. On the surface, the woman appeared to have a strong case.

But, in explaining his decision not to prosecute, Martin Brown, assistant district attorney, told the Sacramento *Daily Californian:* "I believed what the [victim] told us, but she was acquainted with the boys and there were no bruises."

O'Sullivan said that because of their sense of entitlement and commonplace use of power, some male athletes might have misconceptions about what constitutes rape.

"I talked to a former pro basketball player who told me he had raped women for years but didn't know it at the time," she said. "He's horrified now. At the time he always thought it was much better that way. That he scored more points with the other men. I think the point was, if he didn't have to use a little force to get sex, then it was a disappointment to him."

If athletes learn from an early age that they are above the rules, who is teaching them this?

> *"Society confers a privileged status to athletes . . . whether they deserve it or not."*

"It starts when they are 8 years old, with their peer group, their teachers—the people who have impact in their social environment and allow them to be a *what* and not a *who*," House said. "Their status as jocks precludes their development as a responsible human being. They have had responsibility all their lives, but they have never been held accountable. When they do something that escalates beyond what their immediate close system can protect, all of a sudden they are saying, 'Why is this happening?'"

Sports—Protector and Exploiter

Too often in the case of athletes who break the law, the protector is also the exploiter—intercollegiate and professional sports.

In college, athletic teams represent millions of dollars to the university. At the professional level, athletes are chess pieces to be moved and traded at the whims of management. If the pawn makes a mistake that might embarrass the school or franchise, it seems prudent to apply full-scale damage control.

What do athletes learn from coaches bailing them out of trouble? Bingman said the attitude she observed at the University of Oklahoma was troubling.

"I had the impression they thought they would not be convicted," she said. "They thought they were untouchable. That's very disturbing to me, it really is. We all know there are certain people who feel they are above the law. And some of them manage to get by with committing crimes."

On the college level, school administrators are often co-conspirators in either covering up reports of sexual assaults or in pressuring the complainant into dropping charges to avoid negative publicity.

Failed Cover-Ups

The strategy backfired at the University of Maryland. Lefty Driesell, then the school's basketball coach, repeatedly called a woman to persuade her to drop sexual misconduct charges against basketball player Herman Veal.

The woman didn't drop the charges and pressed charges against Driesell for harassment. He was reprimanded and made to apologize publicly. Veal was suspended for four games.

The case of the Arkansas basketball players is another where university officials were found to have acted improperly to resolve a charge of rape.

Four Arkansas players, including All-American Todd Day, were accused of raping a woman in a campus athletic dormitory in February of 1991. The woman identified the players to police, but never pressed charges. The players conceded they had sex with the woman, but said that she consented.

However, according to a report issued by the president of the University of Arkansas system, school officials "up and down the line"—including the university chancellor, Athletic Director Frank Broyles and Coach Nolan Richardson—erred in not taking immediate action.

"It looked like we were not in control of the situation," said B. Alan Sugg, Arkansas system president. "It looked like we were not concerned about it. It looked like we were not concerned about the conduct of athletes. It sent a terrible message to the state of Arkansas and, actually, the nation.

"I do believe [the players] broke a university student conduct regulation by participating in a degrading act by engaging in serial consensual sexual intercourse. I consider this conduct simply wrong."

Having said that, Sugg then reduced the athletes' suspensions from one year to six months. The reduction allowed the players to miss only one tournament and a few nonconference games. Sugg's ruling also allowed the players to practice with the team during the suspension.

> *"The emotional climate in which many elite athletes work is something other than enlightened."*

Sugg was criticized for his seemingly contradictory position and for showing less concern about the welfare of the players than their eligibility. However, the public relations lesson was apparently learned. Two months later, when an Arkansas football player was charged with rape, the athlete's scholarship was revoked and he was dismissed from the football team.

Perhaps the most blatant example of complicity came to light in January 1992. A Florida State Board of Regents committee report sharply criticized administrators at the University of South Florida for their handling of multiple sexual assault complaints against a basketball player.

The report reveals that school officials took no action against Marvin Taylor—the basketball team's starting point guard—for more than 1½ years, despite complaints filed by six women.

The 60-page report charges that the school's vice president of student affairs gave special handling to Taylor's case. Even though she reported the alleged incident immediately, the alleged rape victim was never interviewed by anyone at the school. The first official to ask for her version of the events was the investigator appointed by the board of regents, nearly two years later.

> *"If [an athlete] didn't have to use a little force to get sex, then it was a disappointment to him."*

Taylor was accused of raping an acquaintance in 1989. By the next year, four more women lodged complaints of sexual assault or harassment against Taylor. In another case that wasn't handled by campus authorities, Taylor was prosecuted in Tampa criminal court for battery after he knocked a woman down and kicked her in the stomach.

During this period, the South Florida vice president responsible for both intercollegiate athletics and student discipline took personal control of Taylor's case. The school official, who is a member of the Green Jackets athletic booster club, repeatedly ignored the school's written discipline procedures, according to the board of regents' report.

An Unbelievable Case

After Taylor's conviction in the battery case, another school official overturned a school hearing officer's recommendation that the basketball player be suspended from school for one year. Taylor was placed in a program for first offenders, even though court records showed he was on probation for a burglary conviction in another state.

Finally, the report said, the alleged rape victim was treated unfairly by the school and offered none of the help and support that was afforded Taylor. The school vice president told the media that the alleged victim had recanted her story, which he later acknowledged that she never did. The same official also removed all records of the women's complaints from Taylor's file.

The board of regents' investigation also showed that the woman and others had been continually harassed into withdrawing their complaints against Taylor. At least one of the women reported the harassment to school authorities, who took no action. The parents of another woman took their daughter out of school rather than face continued harassment.

In February 1991, with his eligibility nearly over, Taylor was finally kicked off the team for a curfew violation.

Dan Walbolt, the South Florida vice president criticized in the report, resigned January 31, 1992.

Florida's top school official called the case unbelievable.

What is the solution? Will the sports system continue to turn out seeming sociopaths unequipped to deal with a complex world? Will the "indiscretions" of athletes be tolerated by a society that looks the other way? Or will parents and others responsible for the welfare of young athletes do what Tom House suggests and "make them take out the garbage"?

Not all athletes are the spoiled products of coddling and special privileges. House cites Ranger pitcher Nolan Ryan, who—even when he showed amazing athletic aptitude at a young age—was never treated differently by his parents. And he always had to take out the garbage.

Women's Naivete Contributes to Rape

by Camille Paglia

About the author: *Camille Paglia is the well-known author of several contro-versial books, including* Sexual Personae *and* Sex, Art, and American Culture, *from which this viewpoint was excerpted.*

Rape is an outrage that cannot be tolerated in civilized society. Yet feminism, which has waged a crusade for rape to be taken more seriously, has put young women in danger by hiding the truth about sex from them.

Dramatizing Rape

In dramatizing the pervasiveness of rape, feminists have told young women that before they have sex with a man, they must give consent as explicit as a le-gal contract's. In this way, young women have been convinced that they have been the victims of rape. On elite campuses in the Northeast and on the West Coast, they have held consciousness-raising sessions, petitioned administrations demanded inquests. At Brown University, outraged, panicky "victims" have scrawled the names of alleged attackers on the walls of women's rest rooms. What marital rape was to the '70s, "date rape" is to the '90s.

The incidence and seriousness of rape do not require this kind of exaggera-tion. Real acquaintance rape is nothing new. It has been a horrible problem for women for all of recorded history. Once fathers and brothers protected women from rape. Once the penalty for rape was death. I come from a fierce Italian tra-dition where, not so long ago in the motherland, a rapist would end up knifed, castrated, and hung out to dry.

But the old clans and small rural communities have broken down. In our cities, on our campuses far from home, young women are vulnerable and de-fenseless. Feminism has not prepared them for this. Feminism keeps saying the sexes are the same. It keeps telling women they can do anything, go anywhere, say anything, wear anything. No, they can't. Women will always be in sexual danger.

One of my male students recently slept overnight with a friend in a passageway of the Great Pyramid in Egypt. He described the moon and sand, the ancient silence and eerie echoes. I will never experience that. I am a woman. I am not stupid enough to believe I could ever be safe there. There is a world of solitary adventure I will never have. Women have always known these somber truths. But feminism, with its pie-in-the-sky fantasies about the perfect world, keeps young women from seeing life as it is.

> *"Women will always be in sexual danger."*

We must remedy social injustice whenever we can. But there are some things we cannot change. There are sexual differences that are based in biology. Academic feminism is lost in a fog of social constructionism. It believes we are totally the product of our environment. This idea was invented by Rousseau. He was wrong. Emboldened by dumb French language theory, academic feminists repeat the same hollow slogans over and over to each other. Their view of sex is naive and prudish. Leaving sex to the feminists is like letting your dog vacation at the taxidermist's.

Gender Wars

The sexes are at war. Men must struggle for identity against the overwhelming power of their mothers. Women have menstruation to tell them they are women. Men must do or risk something to be men. Men become masculine only when other men say they are. Having sex with a woman is one way a boy becomes a man.

College men are at their hormonal peak. They have just left their mothers and are questing for their male identity. In groups, they are dangerous. A woman going to a fraternity party is walking into Testosterone Flats, full of prickly cacti and blazing guns. If she goes, she should be armed with resolute alertness. She should arrive with girlfriends and leave with them. A girl who lets herself get dead drunk at a fraternity party is a fool. A girl who goes upstairs alone with a brother at a fraternity party is an idiot. Feminists call this "blaming the victim." I call it common sense.

For a decade, feminists have drilled their disciples to say, "Rape is a crime of violence but not of sex." This sugar-coated Shirley Temple nonsense has exposed young women to disaster. Misled by feminism, they do not expect rape from the nice boys from good homes who sit next to them in class.

Aggression and eroticism are deeply intertwined. Hunt, pursuit, and capture are biologically programmed into male sexuality. Generation after generation, men must be educated, refined, and ethically persuaded away from their tendency toward anarchy and brutishness. Society is not the enemy, as feminism ignorantly claims. Society is woman's protection against rape. Feminism, with its solemn Carry Nation repressiveness, does not see what is for men the eroticism or fun element in rape, especially the wild, infectious delirium of gang rape. Women who do not understand rape cannot defend themselves against it.

The date-rape controversy shows feminism hitting the wall of its own broken promises. The women of my '60s generation were the first respectable girls in history to swear like sailors, get drunk, stay out all night—in short, to act like men. We sought total sexual freedom and equality. But as time passed, we woke up to cold reality. The old double standard protected women. When anything goes, it's women who lose.

Cold Reality

Today's young women don't know what they want. They see that feminism has not brought sexual happiness. The theatrics of public rage over date rape are their way of restoring the old sexual rules that were shattered by my generation. Because nothing about the sexes has really changed. The comic film *Where the Boys Are* (1960), the ultimate expression of '50s man-chasing, still speaks directly to our time. It shows smart, lively women skillfully anticipating and fending off the dozens of strategies with which horny men try to get

> *"Women who do not understand rape cannot defend themselves against it."*

them into bed. The agonizing date-rape subplot and climax are brilliantly done. The victim, Yvette Mimieux, makes mistake after mistake, obvious to the other girls. She allows herself to be lured away from her girlfriends and into isolation with boys whose character and intentions she misreads. *Where the Boys Are* tells the truth. It shows courtship as a dangerous game in which the signals are not verbal but subliminal.

Neither militant feminism, which is obsessed with politically correct language, nor academic feminism, which believes that knowledge and experience are "constituted by" language, can understand pre-verbal or non-verbal communication. Feminism, focusing on sexual politics, cannot see that sex exists in and through the body. Sexual desire and arousal cannot be fully translated into verbal terms. This is why men and women misunderstand each other.

Trying to remake the future, feminism cut itself off from sexual history. It discarded and suppressed the sexual myths of literature, art, and religion. Those myths show us the turbulence, the mysteries and passions of sex. In mythology we see men's sexual anxiety, their fear of womens' dominance. Much sexual violence is rooted in men's sense of psychological weakness toward women. It takes many men to deal with one woman. Woman's voracity is a persistent motif. Clara Bow, it was rumored, took on the USC football team on weekends. Marilyn Monroe, singing "Diamonds Are a Girl's Best Friend," rules a conga line of men in tuxes. Half-clad Cher, in the video for "If I Could Turn Back Time," deranges a battleship of screaming sailors and straddles a pink-lit cannon. Feminism, coveting social power, is blind to woman's cosmic sexual power.

To understand rape, you must study the past. There never was and never will be sexual harmony. Every woman must take personal responsibility for her sexuality, which is nature's red flame. She must be prudent and cautious about where she goes and with whom. When she makes a mistake, she must accept the consequences and, through self-criticism, resolve never to make that mistake again. Running to Mommy and Daddy on the campus grievance committee is unworthy of strong women. Posting lists of guilty men in the toilet is cowardly, infantile stuff.

The Italian philosophy of life espouses high-energy confrontation. A male student makes a vulgar remark about your breasts? Don't slink off to whimper and simper with the campus shrinking violets. Deal with it. On the spot. Say, "Shut up, you jerk! And crawl back to the barnyard where you belong!" In general, women who project this take-charge attitude toward life get harassed less often. I see too many dopey, immature, self-pitying women walking around like melting sticks of butter. It's the Yvette Mimieux syndrome: Make me happy. And listen to me weep when I'm not.

The date-rape debate is already smothering in propaganda churned out by the expensive Northeastern colleges and universities, with their overconcentration of boring, uptight academic feminists and spoiled, affluent students. Beware of the deep manipulativeness of rich students who were neglected by their parents. They love to turn the campus into hysterical psychodramas of sexual transgression, followed by assertions of parental authority and concern. And don't look for sexual enlightenment from academe, which spews out mountains of books but never looks at life directly.

As a fan of football and rock music, I see in the simple, swaggering masculinity of the jock and in the noisy posturing of the heavy-metal guitarist certain fundamental, unchanging truths about sex. Masculinity is aggressive, unstable, combustible. It is also the most creative cultural force in history. Women must reorient themselves toward the elemental powers of sex, which can strengthen or destroy.

The only solution to date rape is female self-awareness and self-control. A woman's number one line of defense is herself. When a real rape occurs, she should report it to the police. Complaining to college committees because the courts "take too long" is ridiculous. College administrations are not a branch of the judiciary. They are not equipped or trained for legal inquiry. Colleges must alert incoming students to the problems and dangers of adulthood. Then colleges must stand back and get out of the sex game.

Declining Moral Standards Cause Rape

by Dwight D. Murphey

About the author: *Dwight D. Murphey teaches business law at The Wichita State University in Wichita, Kansas.*

Many Americans are favorable to "feminism" in a broadly practical sense that supports, say, a right of women to equal pay for equal work or to have access to jobs and the professions. A much smaller number, however, subscribe fully to modern feminist theory as it has been proclaimed since the early 1960s, and which constitutes "feminism" as an ideological movement. As I discuss this ideological feminism, it will be worthwhile to keep it mentally separate from the attitudes of American women in general. Feminism as an ideology is part of today's intellectual culture, which seeks both to influence and to stand in opposition to mainstream America.

It is commonplace in America's fashionable—or, today, "politically correct" —thinking to accept the notion that women and ethnic minorities are the continuing "victims" of a domineering, exploitive and insensitive mainstream culture. "Victimology" has become the latest variation of the Left's 170-year-old refrain about "exploitation.". . .

Collective Villainy

Linda Bourque tells us in a recent book that "publication of Betty Friedan's *The Feminine Mystique* in 1963 and the formation of the National Organization for Women in 1966 marked the beginning of the contemporary women's movement." Within a short time thereafter, the new ideology began to focus on rape as a symbol of men's collective villainy. Bourque says that "it was with the publication in 1975 of Susan Brownmiller's book, *Against Our Will: Men, Women and Rape*, that feminist psychosocial-cultural theories of rape were first

From Dwight D. Murphey, "Feminism and Rape," *Journal of Social, Political, and Economic Studies* 17 (Spring 1992): 13-17. Reprinted with permission.

set forth."

The rape theme proclaimed by Brownmiller has become a foundation-stone for a grand theory of victimization, according to which all women are the victims of all men. It is repeated as revealed truth today both in academic journals and the popular media. Here are its main components:

Brownmiller's book chronicled many thousands of the occasions upon which men have, over history, forced themselves upon women. From this history she then took a giant inductive leap, concluding that "from prehistoric times to the pre-

> *"Feminism . . . postulates . . . ideas, each of them consistent with its theory of 'victimization,' that deserve to be called myths in their own right."*

sent, I believe, rape has played a critical function. It is nothing more or less than a conscious process of intimidation by which *all men* keep *all women* in a state of fear" (her emphasis). She explained that "a world without rapists would be a world in which women moved freely without fear of men. That *some* men rape provides a sufficient threat to keep all women in a constant state of intimidation. . . . Men who commit rape have served in effect as front-line masculine shock troops, terrorist guerrillas in the longest sustained battle the world has ever known." And again: "Rape is to women as lynching was to blacks: the ultimate physical threat by which all men keep all women in a state of psychological intimidation."

Her inductive leap had its origins in the radical Left, reformulating its alienation with a new cast of heroes (or, in this case, heroines) and villains. She said that "when the women's liberation movement was birthed by the radical left, the first serious struggle we faced was to free ourselves from the structures, thought processes and priorities of what we came to call the *male* left."

She related this to her own development, telling how "as a rebellious young woman during the height of McCarthyism, . . . I took myself down to the old Jefferson School and enrolled in a night course taught by Dr. Herbert Aptheker, the American Communist historian. . . . I owe a debt to Aptheker, who was the first to tell me that rape was a political crime, who taught me the tools of dialectic logic, and who shouldn't be surprised that I have carried his argument further than he intended."

Are All Men Really Rapists?

During the years since 1975, Brownmiller's revelation that the rapist is an extension of all men has become an accepted truism to many feminist authors. (A side observation: So far as I have discerned, no one among the feminists seems bothered by the fact that it is put forth as a Truth, not merely as an hypothesis, and that even as an hypothesis it is of a nature that is not susceptible to refutation by counter-evidence, since obviously its proponents won't accept any amount of kindness by men to women as a rebuttal. Thus, it stands as one of the best examples of the intellectual vacuity of so much feminist ideology going back over the past century and a half. My impression is that, overall, the intellectual quality of feminist thought has been very poor.)

In academic writing, we see the Brownmiller thesis echoed in Diana Scully's *Understanding Violence: A Study of Convicted Rapists* (1990). Scully says "P. Bart refers to rape as a paradigm of sexism. . . . Feminist theorists have pointed out that, because it preserves male dominance, sexual violence benefits all men, not just those who actually rape. . . . J. Herman concludes that the United States is a rape culture. . . ." (We will see later that the charge against the United States is based on egregious abuse of statistics; and we may wonder why the United States is singled out, since the thesis asserts a universal phenomenon. The answer almost certainly lies in the Left's special hatred for the United States.)

In popular literature, Brownmiller's point often shows up as a reductionist argument that "rape doesn't have anything to do with sex; it is exclusively an assertion of power over and hatred toward women." Thus, in the May 1990 *McCall's* it is said that "rape has been characterized as 'an all-American crime.' Its roots are planted in the culture. . . . Feminists have long argued that it is a crime of violence and not an act of passion . . . and one that reflects the sexist stratification of society."

> *"Feminists have in effect promoted a cultural environment in which rape is more likely to occur."*

The October 1988 *Ebony* points out in authoritative tones that "rape is not about sex per se. Instead, rape is the sexual expression of anger or aggression. 'It's a power trip'. . . ." And Joan Beck, a nationally published columnist based with the *Chicago Tribune*, was able to say in April 1991 that "if there is still any lingering misconception that rape is a crime of sexual passion, it's important to drive a stake through the heart of that idea as quickly as possible. . . . What it really is—a hate crime against women."

Fearing Men

A corollary expressed by Brownmiller as central to her thesis is that women live their lives subject to a brooding fear of rape and that this fear is itself a mechanism of overall male control. This is the focus of Margaret T. Gordon and Stephanie Riger's book *The Female Fear*.

"How widespread is this fear?" Gordon and Riger ask. "Every woman has it to a degree, and all women are affected by it. It 'keeps women off the streets at night. Keeps them home. Keeps women passive and modest. . . .'" The echo in popular literature appears in Rochelle Distelheim's article in the September

73

1989 *McCall's:* "Learning to fear rape is a process that begins in childhood and continues throughout a woman's life.". . .

One of the myths embraced by feminist thought is precisely the notion that the American public clings to a variety of "myths." Feminism also postulates a number of other ideas, each of them consistent with its theory of "victimization," that deserve to be called myths in their own right.

• One of these notions is that until it was enlightened by feminism American society considered women to have less value than men. Thus, a certain Lucille Pfleeger writing a recent letter-to-the-editor about rape was able to say that "the feminist movement has attempted to teach young girls and women that they are of as much value as males." And although it is not quite the same point, Susan Brownmiller wrote that men harbor "a contempt for women."

Wives and Mothers

Critique: The ideas that "women were given less value" and "were objects of contempt" are derivatives of the idea that women are victims. As with the axiom itself, they are not propositions about which the ideologues will allow any refutation. I remember from my childhood the many women in my family—going back to a whitehaired great-grandmother who served cookies whenever we visited—who were wives and mothers, and I know that it never entered our minds to think of them as less than loved ones and as vitally important people in our lives. The thought of measuring their comparative "value" would have seemed alien, even contemptible; and it was love, not disdain, that the members of the family of both sexes felt toward them. But would feminist theorists accept any of this as disproof of their theses? Certainly not.

• With reference to today's culture, many of the feminist attitudes scoff at conventional morality and justify the moral permissiveness that the intellectual culture so strongly favors as part of its long-standing "anti-bourgeois" orientation. By promoting permissive behavior, liberals, including feminists, have actually contributed to the destruction of traditional morals. This morality caused males to abhor rape. It reflected a family-oriented and woman-respecting culture which saw rape as a deeply rooted offense against the ideal of the family, and of the dignity of women. Some conservative males regarded rape as an even more debasing and heinous crime than murder. By opposing this morality, feminists have in

> *"Contemporary permissive culture . . . has created a situation in which former muggers and woman-harassers like Mike Tyson find it easy to rape women."*

effect promoted a cultural environment in which rape is more likely to occur.

Thus, it was possible for Dianne Klein, in her Sept. 16, 1991 column emanating from the *Los Angeles Times* that discussed the charge that heavyweight boxing champion Mike Tyson had raped a beauty contestant, to write in words literally dripping with sarcasm: "Why would a woman agree to a date if sex were not part of her plan? And meeting someone in his hotel room? Ha! Why not just wear a sign? I mean, what did she expect? Respect?" Contemporary permissive culture, to which the feminist ideology has contributed, has created a situation in which former muggers and woman-harassers like Mike Tyson find it easy to rape women who behave in a permissive way. The older pre-feminist morality would have warned that such behavior is dangerous.

Destroying Traditional Ethics

Indeed, feminists now have to argue that, as Katie Sherrod put it, writing for the *Fort Worth Star-Telegram*, "No woman's behavior gives a man the right to rape." That is entirely true, but why did feminists destroy the traditional ethic of male respect for females, as honored wives and mothers, only to create a culture in which many women behave in a way that invites rape?

Sometimes, however, there is simply an unabashed declaration that reminds me of the old saw "we're all socialists now"—except that today it amounts to an acknowledgment that, in effect, "we're all whores now." (At least it would if the word "whore" had not quietly dropped out of our vocabulary as too much a throwback to the age of morals.) Naomi Wolf, writing for the *Washington Post*, spreads it out for all to see that "my other best friend . . . wears dangling earrings, began her sex life at 16, tried drugs, went to parties and has also had a few lovers.

"Why did feminists destroy the traditional ethic of male respect for females . . . only to create a culture in which many women behave in a way that invites rape?"

. . . And me, of course. . . . Sexually active in my teens, I went to late-night parties, had several non-marital relationships. . . ." Her generalization: "If it is Bad to have a sexual history by your mid-20s in 1991 . . . then let's face it: There are no good girls." (She reneged a bit by speaking of the mid-20s; we had reason to think she was talking about a girl's mid-*teens*.)

Critique: These are propositions that weave such plausibility as they have out of partial truths. It is certainly true as a purely categorical matter that no man has a right to rape a woman under any circumstances; and it is also true that a woman should be able to come and go without her activities being taken as a standing invitation. But is it also true that modern women should be encouraged to place themselves in dangerous situations? Feminists allege that men rape freely, while they attack traditional morality which placed women in a protected category. They defend female behavior such as that described by Naomi Wolf, who sings the siren song of a permissiveness unlike any we've seen before in our history.

Much of this destruction of what the Left denigrates as "bourgeois" standards has to do with manners and lifestyles that are more general than we might envision if we think simply of rape-conducive situations. We live in a time when the T-shirts worn on our campuses include slogans (which I've seen recently) that would have been unthinkable before the Berkeley Free Speech Movement: "Shit happens" and "Fuck Me, Fuck You, Fuck Everybody." One that is now being sold in large numbers by a clothing company says "Button Your Fly." The sports section of the *Wichita Eagle* on November 14, 1991, featured a large photo of a sweet-looking couple sitting with a baby on the young woman's lap. The caption: WSU's Mornay Annandale says his girlfriend, Tammy West, and son, Nathan, help keep his mind focused. Thus, the cohabitation of unmarried couples receives respectful acceptance in the popular press. If Jonathan Swift were to return today, he would no doubt be prompted to write a sequel to his story about the Yahoos. But he would have to up the ante, since to be satire today something far more bizarre is required.

Traditional Morality

It is in this context, strangely, that feminism presents us with the demand that men at all times adhere to traditional concepts of morality regarding their behavior toward women, remain professional, never say anything suggestive unless they are certain in advance that it is "not unwelcome" to the woman with whom they are speaking, and never take advantage of any situation sexually. At the very same time, we have the reality of women who attend class at a university wearing jeans that are purposely made (and purchased) to press up into their crotches, leaving nothing to the imagination. Any amount of tease is welcome, and any amount of actual promiscuity. The press reports of women sexually abused after putting themselves in compromising situations are endless. In one, a 32-year-old Wichita woman is said to have been "raped" by her boyfriend—with whom she lived—after they went out drinking. In another, "a 17-year-old reported that she was raped . . . at a man's home . . . (after they) had been drinking. . . . When she said no, he raped her.". . .

In the midst of all this militancy against both men and the United States, what is conspicuous by its absence is any mature understanding of either aggression or sexuality. The well-springs of the human psyche are mysterious and complex far beyond anything feminist philosophy, derived from Herbert Aptheker's dialectical Marxian logic, has the imagination to conceive. I see in that philosophy no attempt to understand the electricity that snaps and pops between the sexes, or the subtleties of the infinity of situations that bring the sexes together.

Hatred of Women Causes Rape

by Anne Roiphe

About the author: *Anne Roiphe is the author of the novel* If You Knew Me.

Me, waiting for the elevator in my lobby, gray-haired, carrying a bag from the deli with vegetarian dip. Him, a toy rifle slung over his shoulder, mittens attached to his jacket by clips. His mother, holding a blue sheet of construction paper covered with bright paint slashes, trying not to crush or wrinkle it. He points the rifle at me, level with his own eye: "Boom, ack, ack," he says. "I blasted your vagina." His mother turns bright red, white, stares at her boots.

Hatred of Vaginas

I think of the football heroes of Glen Ridge, New Jersey, who allegedly put a broomstick into the vagina of a mentally disabled girl so eager to please she couldn't refuse, so innocent of power she confused it with friendship. They allegedly used a baseball bat for further exploration, these handsome young men whose hormones were stirring while their superegos slept. But it wasn't just hormones run amok. If it were, we might have forgiven them their opportunism, their pragmatic approach to age-appropriate itches. We might have forgiven their ignorance of each woman's potential for giving and receiving pleasure through all the hidden crannies, down all the hidden nerve paths. We might have seen this encounter as a vicious child's game of exploitation, a bullying that was nasty but not criminal. The issue of consent would have been blurred; the matter would have never come to trial.

No, it isn't because this merry band's hormones were exuberant and inappropriate that so many of us want to see them tossed into a dungeon, the keys fed to alligators in the surrounding swamp. This isn't why they should be derailed from their destiny as fraternity brothers, attendees at bachelor parties where girls with sparklers on their nipples jump out of cakes, as middle-aged users of escort services when business finds them in strange cities. Our anger stems from the real activity in that suburban basement.

They were attacking a vagina. They were hurting and humiliating the young woman, but their motive was simpler, more childish than sexual. They were ack-acking her vagina. This has nothing to do with sexual urges or reproductive passions. It has nothing to do with courtship and mating. It has to do with hatred of vaginas. This particular one belonged to a vulnerable girl with an eight-year-old's mind.

Yes, the mysteries of female biology can be unnerving, and of course men can be confused, thinking that there may be teeth in the vaginal bite and blood-letting in the act of sex. In many societies, males are protected by law from the impurity of menstruating women. Disguised behind these laws, behind custom and tradition, are primitive and childish habits of hatred. Hatred is the theme behind this New Jersey story too, and that's what makes our hearts pound and the blood run cold.

Standard Suburban-Issue Males

These boys are not Jeffrey Dahmers or Draculas, not Serbian militia or Nazi SS. They are what they look like, standard suburban-issue American males. They are many years older than my elevator companion but very like him: alarmed at the vagina, wanting to harm it to prove some superiority, some safety, some point about their own sexual organs. That scares me. Misogyny lurks there, and with misogyny comes clitorectomies, unnecessary hysterectomies; maybe the whole rotten system of patriarchal religion and boys' clubs and unequal pay for equal work is all based on the fear of the vagina.

> *"This has nothing to do with sexual urges. . . . It has to do with hatred of vaginas."*

Women have their own basic instinct and historical angers, and who knows what we'd do if we had absolute political and social power: wrap men up in scarves so only their eyes showed, make them walk on one leg like herons, improve the size of their organs with silicone? Any woman who believes that women are the gentle sex hasn't looked far enough into her own heart, where puppy dogs' tails wag amid the sugar and spice.

How to Make Peace?

If men and women are unable to like, admire and accept each other's biological givens, then how are we to lie together, trusting, in each other's arms? If I am always female, with the strange vagina and milky breasts, if he is always male, frightened of the way I bleed, awed by my power to give birth, disgusted by how my body's tissues grow soft, then what will we do with each other?

How to make peace, how to love, how to grow up, really grow up? Drenched as we most often are in wanted and unwanted desire, how are we to muddle through, preserving some shards of human harmony, if sex is always tainted by aggression and Eros always carries a whip?

A person could go crazy thinking of men as four-year-olds with guns pointed at the vaginas of passing women. "Did you have a toy gun when you were a child?" I asked my husband. "I made one out of sticks," he says. It's his birthday. The candles on the cake light his face. I try to look at him as if we hadn't met before. I look as carefully as I can. I don't see a child with a gun. I see a man with his fork in the air, ready to taste his cake.

I think of the painting in the arms of the mother in my lobby. Lovely blue, bright red, a smudge and some drips: He had done that, too, my four-year-old neighbor. He may become an architect, a surgeon, a maker of deals. Soon he'll learn to shoot only bad guys and then just to enjoy the vicarious violence of TV car chases and football games. One day, he'll wait with his heart in his throat for a girl to pick up the phone, to go for a walk with him, to hold his hand, to let him touch her, to touch him where he wants to be touched. The years will bury his ack-acking, and he will be ready, if he doesn't turn out like the Glen Ridge boys, to be loved for his true self, which, while it will carry along inside it this four-year-old blasting away at my personal parts, will include everything else that is human and dear, gentle and tender, sexy and kind. Maybe.

Chapter 3

Can Reforms in the Criminal Justice System Decrease Violence Against Women?

Chapter Preface

According to the U.S. Department of Justice, only about half of all violent crimes committed against women are reported. Independent surveys say that the percentage may be even lower, especially when the crime is rape. For example, researchers Mary Kay Biaggio, Arlene Brownell, and Deborah L. Watts surveyed staff, faculty, and students at a midwestern university and found that of those women who had been sexually assaulted, only 4.4 percent reported the crime to the police. Statistics from the Department of Justice also indicate that of those women who reported being raped, only 17 percent expected the offender to be punished. Clearly, many women feel the criminal justice system in the United States is ineffective in addressing violence against women.

Women's reluctance to report crimes against them stems from a wide variety of social factors, but many simply distrust the criminal justice system. That distrust is well-founded, researchers say. Often when women report a violent crime, police, prosecutors, and even judges somehow—overtly or subtly—blame the victim for the crime. Biaggio and her colleagues discovered that "there seems to be quite a bit of fearfulness associated with formal reporting. . . . The tendency of victims to encounter difficulties from the human service and criminal justice systems has been characterized as the 'second wound.'" This "second wound" discourages victims of both domestic violence and sexual assault from seeking help from the justice system.

Despite this distrust, the criminal justice system can sometimes prevent repeat episodes of violence by rapists and batterers. Lawyer Jessica Goldman contends that "arrest and punishment send a valuable message: battering is against the law and perpetrators will be punished." Police and Justice Department studies support Goldman's contention that a strong criminal justice response can deter violence. A National Institute of Justice report quotes a former battered woman who says, "The judge told him, in no uncertain terms, that the law doesn't allow him to assault me just because I'm his wife. He said that he'll send him to jail if he's brought back for another offense. . . . You should have seen the look on his face. I think he knew the judge wasn't kidding, and that's when he decided to do something about it." In this case the criminal justice system was effective.

While the criminal justice system can and should be an effective route to decreasing violence against women, experts concur that the system as a whole must become more sensitive and receptive to cases involving abused women. Perhaps then the often-accurate perception that the female victim rather than the male perpetrator gets punished can be erased. The viewpoints in the following chapter debate whether various reforms will help the criminal justice system more effectively address violence against women.

Reforming the Criminal Justice System Can Decrease Violence Against Women

by Matthew Litsky

About the author: *Matthew Litsky is a 1991 graduate of New York Law School in New York City.*

The battering of women has reached epidemic proportions in the United States. Surveys indicate that between one-third and one-half of the 4,611 women murdered in the United States in 1988 were killed by a husband, boyfriend or ex-mate.

Unfortunately, information about the severity of such violence is sparse, because little data has been collected on actual injuries sustained in any particular incident. Nevertheless, Finesmith has reported that "the average severity of the injuries sustained by victims of spousal assaults is significantly greater than those sustained by victims of assaults by strangers." More women are admitted to emergency rooms after being battered by their partners than are treated for muggings, car accidents, and rapes combined.

Violence between partners is often serious and even fatal. Fatalities from abuse are all too common: the batterer may kill his victim, she may kill him or one of them may commit suicide in order to escape an unbearable situation. Moreover, statistics indicate that domestic disturbances account for a substantial portion of all crime-related injuries and deaths of intervening police officers.

The Failure of the Courts

These chilling statistics, which document the plight of battered women, reflect a traditional problem: women have been battered for centuries without any protection from the courts. Although public perceptions of the battered woman and

From Matthew Litsky, "Explaining the Legal System's Inadequate Response to the Abuse of Women: A Lack of Coordination," *New York Law School Journal of Human Rights* 8 (1990): 149-55, 160-81. Reprinted with permission.

her abusive male partner have improved, misconceptions about the reality of the battering relationship still permeate the legal system. The law's dedication to the elimination of the problem is half-hearted and its reaction remains misguided.

Powerful social forces permit and even encourage abuse. These forces continue to influence legal institutions and personnel, and undermine the legal system's desire and ability to combat the problem. Even if these forces were purged from the legal system, they would probably continue to operate in society at large. As long as social forces and attitudes condone battering, the legal system alone can never provide a complete solution to battering. Nevertheless, the law and those responsible for enforcing it can play a critical role in reducing domestic violence. Someone must move against abuse, and no other societal institution has the legal system's clout to protect victims and to force batterers to face the consequences of their transgressions.

The legal system must respond in unison. There must be coordinated intervention among legislators, police, prosecutors and judges. . . .

The Legislative Response

Historically, the law has not afforded battered women much protection from their male abusers. Until the early twentieth century, the law explicitly permitted men to beat their wives. American common law in the early nineteenth century allowed a man to chastise his wife "[w]ithout subjecting himself to vexatious prosecutions for assault and battery, resulting in the shame and discredit of all parties concerned" [as was cited by an 1824 Mississippi court decision, *Bradley v. State*].

The legislative response to judicial reluctance to support the rights of battered women was painstakingly slow. Eventually, intensified public concern with family violence brought about legislative attempts to act. By the latter half of the 1970's, many legislative initiatives had been undertaken to pass legislation in aid of battered women. For example, Pennsylvania enacted a law enlarging the number and scope of alternative dispositions available to a court confronted with an abused spouse case. A Massachusetts statute spelled out the duties of investigating law enforcement officials in protecting abused spouses and expanded the number of circumstances under which arrests could be made for offenses committed outside a law officer's presence. The two most common types of statutory enactments were (1) laws allowing victims to obtain protective orders against abusers and (2) laws providing aid to supportive services, such as emergency shelters for battered victims.

"Powerful social forces permit and even encourage abuse."

As the 1970's progressed, the trend of legislative initiative moved away from helping the abuse victim and towards imposing criminal sanctions on the abuser. The change in legislative direction was reflected in legislation creating new "family violence" offenses by using existing assault laws to punish violent acts within the family.

Although the 1970's witnessed an emergence of new legislative initiatives in the area of wife-battery, important proposals were rejected in many states and on the federal level. Much of the legislation designed to protect battered wives did not provide adequate funding or resources to accomplish the objectives of the draftsmen. Police and state officials undermined the effectiveness of legislation by failing to vigorously implement the statutes. As recently as 1978, only nine states had legislation which dealt seriously with domestic violence, although several other states had begun to make provision for shelter homes for battered women.

In response to this legislative rejection, advocates for battered women worked to create a legal system responsive to the needs of the abused. Indeed, most of the domestic abuse laws have been enacted largely as a result of the work of legal services attorneys and the staffs of battered women's shelters. As a result, many states have passed extensive legislation to provide early intervention in domestic abuse cases and to reform existing domestic violence laws. . . .

> *"The law and those . . . enforcing it can play a critical role in reducing domestic violence."*

Civil orders of protection are the most widely used remedy for wife beating. Battered women prefer obtaining an order of protection to initiating a criminal prosecution. Numerous studies indicate, however, that these orders are not effective in stopping the battering of women. The fact remains that "Orders of Protection are only worth the paper they are written on," [as E. Yaroshefsky states]. Existing civil protection order legislation must be improved by increasing access and improving procedures. Finally, the legislature must take heed of the plight of the battered woman. The question remains, however, whether the legislature's efforts have been supported by the other arms of the legal system.

The Police Response

As society's peacekeepers, law enforcement personnel are in a position to help battered women. Police involvement in domestic disturbances exceeds their combined involvement in murder, rape, and all other forms of aggravated assault. Police policy toward battered women assumes many forms, varying from outright refusal to arrest batterers and recognize domestic violence as a criminal matter, to a practice of giving domestic violence calls lower priority than non-domestic disputes. This is logical considering that official police policy has often stressed avoidance of arrest whenever possible. Sometimes police policy is explained in written manuals and other times it is demonstrated by a pattern of police behavior that treats assaults by men against their wives less seriously than assaults by strangers.

Despite the belief and preference of some people that police respond to the crime of wife battering by enforcing the law against the wife batterer, the policy of many jurisdictions is to encourage nonarrest or mediation by police officers.

> *"The legislature must take heed of the plight of the battered woman."*

In one survey it was found that less than twenty-five percent of the jurisdictions examined required the full enforcement of the law and the arrest of the wife batterer. The results of this survey show that police policy was a clear reflection of either strong or weak state laws in the jurisdictions examined.

Recent history sheds an unfavorable light on the police response to domestic violence. During the 1950's and 1960's the police response could best be classified as one of passive reluctance to help the victim. For example, the police in Detroit, Michigan, during the 1950's often refused to take action when confronted with domestic disputes and when they did arrest it was usually followed by a referral to a misdemeanor complaint bureau which did no more than to release the abuser on an informal, unenforceable bond. Similarly, in Chicago in the early 1960's, the primary police responses were ad hoc informal attempts at conflict resolution by police responding to calls for help.

Rationalizations for Police Inaction

The justifications for police non-enforcement policies in wife abuse cases are numerous. The many rationalizations include preserving the traditional principle that "a man's home is his castle," [as Finesmith states,] avoiding arrest in situations in which the physical abuse of a woman by her husband is purported to be acceptable within the couple's culture, and maintaining the efficient and economic administration of the state's law enforcement agencies by regarding wife battering as a minor crime and the arrest of wife batterers as a low priority. Other rationalizations have been: avoiding arrest in situations in which the family could ill afford the economic impact of the husband's arrest (*e.g.*, time lost from work) and respecting a couple's privacy by not interfering in private marital matters. Regardless of the specific rationalization, none of these policies can accomplish the broad reach of arresting the batterer. Arrest is the linchpin of an effective police response because it communicates to the battered woman that the legal system does not blame her for the abuse inflicted and that she will not have to tolerate it. Arrest conveys a similar message to the batterer. It signifies that society condemns his conduct and will hold him accountable for it. Moreover, even if an arrest does not lead to a conviction, it is the most effective way for police to protect women from further abuse. . . .

The legal system, however, cannot rely completely on the police to use their discretion wisely in battering cases. Support from the other arms of the legal system is unquestionably needed to insure an effective police response.

The Prosecutorial Response

The police can only activate the legal process. In order to interrupt the cycle of violence permanently, prosecutors must intervene in the battering relationship and use their power to stop abuse. Like the police, prosecutors have erred in their historical reactions to abuse. Prosecutors have often viewed women's abuse complaints as extralegal family matters which have no place in the judicial system. They have argued that the heavy penalty and high bail for such crimes, in light of the domestic relationship, increases the chance that either the man will contest the charges, or the woman will drop the charges, with the result often being no conviction. Prosecutors have developed various diversion techniques to avoid prosecuting women abuse cases. District attorneys are known to have flatly refused cases of battered women without any consideration of the particular facts, and frequently, after taking the case for evaluation, they refuse to prosecute for spurious reasons or to simply avoid aggravating the situation.

The prosecutorial response has been ineffective for the same reasons that the judicial response has failed: both legal arms have neglected to treat women abuse seriously enough. Prosecutors, like police officers, are reluctant to pursue a criminal charge against a man who has abused his wife or woman friend, even when there has been an arrest. A lack of perseverance has been common. For example, Denise Markham, lawyer and supervisor for the Domestic Violence Advocacy Project in Chicago, estimates that about 90% of the domestic violence cases in Cook County, Illinois, are charged as misdemeanors, no matter how severe the injuries.

A troubling issue for prosecutors which may deserve some of the blame for the reluctant prosecutorial attitude towards wife abuse is the manner in which to proceed when a battered woman is either reluctant to press charges or wants to drop charges in a pending matter. Estimates of domestic violence victims who drop charges or refuse to cooperate with prosecutors can be staggering. In New York City these estimates range from 50% to 80%. The reasons for the abundance of dropped complaints vary. Frequently, the charges are dropped by the battered woman be-

> *"Arrest is the linchpin of an effective police response."*

cause she is "sweet-talked" into dropping her complaint or because of threats made to herself or her children.

Prosecutorial response to the "dropped complaint" problem is evidence that prosecutors have allowed the victim to be the leader of prosecutorial efforts, instead of a mere witness whose participation the state must support and encourage. It should be made clear that the prosecutor, not the victim, is responsible for enforcing the law. When prosecutors deal seriously with abuse and convince the batterer that the former "mean business" the batterer will often plead guilty.

One solution that has been presented by prosecutors' offices is adoption of "no-drop" policies in abuse cases. Where such policies exist, the prosecutors will decline to drop charges merely on the victim's request. The basic theory behind no-drop policies is sound, since it constitutes a strong statement of societal responsibility for deterring batterers. Additionally, such policies rob the abuser of much of his coercive power against the victim. However, except in cases of severe violence or recidivism, battered women should not be further victimized by being held in contempt if they remain staunch in their unwillingness to testify.

The State Must Intercede

Another suggestion has focused on the prosecutor's understanding of the victim's concerns and his setting goals for prosecution which correspond to these concerns. For example, the prospect of a stiff fine or incarceration may dissuade a battered woman from continuing with prosecution if she has young children and no means of support. This theory reasons that when prosecutors tailor their strategies to the relief battered women desire from the criminal justice system, both victims and prosecutors will benefit.

> *"Prosecutors must intervene in the battering relationship and use their power to stop abuse."*

The creation of any special relationship cannot excuse a lack of prosecutorial initiative. When a victim is able to reach her decisions freely, this "concern-tailored" approach can be useful. However, when the accused has great emotional and physical influence over the victim, the state must intercede forcefully on behalf of the victim. There must be a commitment by prosecutors to assume responsibility for the prosecution of woman abuse. This commitment must be translated into concrete policies that are carried out. Prosecutors' offices must make pursuit of battery cases a priority, and must have trained staff who are experts in dealing with the problem.

Whatever the solution, it will only materialize when prosecutors accept the serious criminal nature of woman abuse and conclude that the state has a duty to prosecute wife beating cases, not to dismiss them.

The Judicial Response

Until quite recently the role of judges in domestic violence cases has received scant public attention. Despite marked progress over the last decade in changing police department policies to protect battered women, judicial attitudes and courtroom practices have for the most part lagged behind. This discrepancy may result in part from the impact of public attention on police policies while judges are relatively removed from public scrutiny. The paucity of the judicial response to the plight of battered women is derived mostly from judicial misconceptions about the nature of woman abuse. Judges are subject to the same myths about domestic violence as are members of the general public. The results are disappointing. For example, many judges believe

> *"Many judges believe that battered women are masochists."*

that battered women are masochists or that they exaggerate the seriousness of the violence they suffer to punish "philandering husbands or boyfriends," [according to a study by the U.S. Commission on Civil Rights]. Other judges adhere to "family privacy" myths, one going so far as to chide a battery victim for washing her "dirty linen in public."

It is not uncommon for a woman who has overcome the complex procedures of family court to face a judge who may be predisposed against the use of the courts in family disputes. Many judges feel that woman-abuse court processes are an unfair weapon in a family quarrel. Judges often inquire into victim provocation and abuser excuses and may consider both as mitigating factors. Even if the batterer is convicted, the penalty may be nothing more than a stern lecture from the judge, perhaps ending with the extraction of a promise that the abuser will not hurt his wife again. Judges routinely allow first offenders and even repeaters to be freed on low or no bail. [According to Blodgett in *Violence in the Home*,] "Judges don't usually do anything the first time a man violates an order of protection." The reluctance of judges to sentence batterers to jail can often have tragic consequences.

The Duty of Protection

The judicial response, however, has not always been negative. [One] New York case depicts a judiciary that was willing to contribute once the battering relationship reached the courtroom. In *Baker v. City of New York*, a husband shot his estranged wife while in the waiting room of the domestic relations court. She had held a protective order issued in her favor against her husband. About a month prior to the incident, the police responded to a call from the woman, but when presented with the protective order, they had refused to take further action, saying it was "only a piece of paper" and "no good." Upon seeing her husband several weeks later at a scheduled meeting in the domestic relations court, the woman expressed her fear of being exposed to him and requested permission to remain in the office where she was located. The court personnel denied her request and sent her to the waiting room where some twenty minutes later her husband shot her. The court held that the existence of the protective order was sufficient to create a special relationship and therefore the police owed a special duty of protection to its carrier. . . .

Baker . . . symbolizes an effective judicial response at different points in the battering relationship. In *Baker*, the court reached the only applicable holding possible once the wife had been shot, namely, holding the police liable for their failure to protect the wife. . . . The judicial response, although no guarantee of safety for the seriously-injured wife, . . . shows that judges can be far from ambivalent towards the abuse of women.

The importance of judges' attitudes and their behavior cannot be taken lightly. Within their own courtrooms, judges can communicate a powerful message about the justice system's view of domestic violence. Although decisions such as *Baker* are a hopeful indication that judicial abstention from the domestic violence realm has ended, judicial misconceptions about the problem of battered women and the legal system's appropriate response can still be improved.

Coordination Between Police, Courts, and Legislatures

The legal system as an entity has not produced a uniform and coordinated response to the problem of battered women. This final section is divided into two parts: (1) a discussion of how the individual arms of the legal system can coordinate their actions in order to achieve a more effective response; and (2) why societal beliefs, reflected in the legal system's response, may be the ultimate barrier against the battering relationship.

Although the least visible, the legislature has enough resources to initiate a more effective response through the prompting of the other legal arms. The legislature can guide the police by enacting mandatory arrest legislation. A police policy of mandatory arrest is the product of strong domestic violence legislation. In support of mandatory arrest legislation is a Police Foundation study finding that arrest is the most effective police response to the battering of women. The study compared three forms of police response to domestic violence: arrest, counseling, and sending the assailant away for a few hours; the conclusion was that arrest was the most effective response in reducing domestic violence. There are other compelling benefits of mandatory arrest laws. Arrest advances the goal of short-term victim safety and abuser deterrence. Family violence occurs in an emotionally charged atmosphere with the threat of physical injury too often becoming the reality. If the spouses are not separated and the husband's rage is not given time to dissipate, the beating may continue after the police leave. This possibility is increased when an arrest is made or a misdemeanor citation is issued and the abuser is released from custody immediately. Arrest also conveys

> *"Judges can communicate a powerful message about the justice system's view of domestic violence."*

a message to the batterer that his conduct is wrong and that society and the legal system will hold him accountable for it. When succeeded by similarly strict measures from other legal personnel, arrest begins a process that tells the batterer that he can either be rewarded for stopping his actions or punished for continuing them. Incarceration tells the batterer that he cannot deny responsibility.

Counter-arguments to mandatory arrest laws have pointed to judicial lecturing of the batterer as a possible solution. A National Institute of Justice study of the criminal court response to non-stranger violence found that judges can deter future violence by issuing warnings or lectures to defendants concerning the inappropriateness and seriousness of their violent behavior. Other studies have shown that a stern admonition can help to persuade a defendant from future violence. Some experts have asserted that since neither party should be blamed for family disputes, battering can be treated with mediation techniques practiced by the police, rather than with criminal sanctions. In response to these arguments, both judicial admonition and police mediation have been attacked as ineffective. [As stated by Parnas in *Judicial Response to Intra-Family Violence:*] "No matter what role the judge assumes, even if he is the most knowledgeable, perceptive, compassionate and communicative judge imaginable, probably only temporary relief from violence can be accomplished by such a lecture before the next case in the day's long docket." Furthermore, the goals of mediation—communication, reasonable discourse and joint

> *"Societal acceptance of family violence has pervaded the legal system."*

resolution of adverse interests—work against the most immediate relief the battered woman desires. The goals she seeks are protection from violence, compensation, possession of her home without the batterer, and security for her children. The empirical data show that the therapeutic (mediation) model for handling battering is ineffective and that firm law enforcement including imprisonment is required to deter wife abuse. Because arrest is the legal system's most effective deterrent to battering, legislative enactment in that direction is a sensible long-term policy.

The Ignorance of Judges

Legislatures can also educate judges as to the criminal nature of woman abuse and the statutory tools available to confront the problem. As demonstrated by the Pamela Nigro Dunn case [in Somerville, Massachusetts], judges often fail to take domestic violence seriously, believing that victims' fears of future harm are unjustified. Additionally, many judges are unfamiliar with their respective state Domestic Violence Acts and may fail to provide adequate remedies because they are unknowledgeable about pertinent statutes. Legislatively-enacted training programs can educate judges about the courtroom attitude which will most effectively convey the legal system's condemnation of battering as a criminal act. A training program can also educate judges as to new laws on domestic violence which would encourage greater public compliance. The goals of all training programs should be to encourage judges to counter batterers' notions that the justice system quietly allows unpunished violence against women and to stress the importance of judges' behavior in ending domestic violence.

> *"No other social institution has the legal system's clout to protect victims."*

Legislatures can also act on a more comprehensive scale, affecting the entire legal system through the enactment of a single legislative act. . . .

While the legislature can mandate that the police take a tougher stance towards batterers, it is unlikely that police officers will begin or continue to arrest without prosecutorial support. It is not feasible to encourage police to arrest if a batterer will eventually be released to assault his wife within a few hours. It is well within a prosecutor's power to ask that a high bail be set for someone who is likely to pose a danger to the community. By bringing charges themselves, prosecutors not only remove from the battered woman some of the responsibility of instigating action against the batterer; they can also decrease the number of repeat offenders the police will have to arrest. The police, in return, can make the prosecutor's job easier by providing the latter access to reports of prior calls for assistance and arrest with reference to a specific batterer. This will enable repeat offenders to be identified more easily to prosecutors who in turn will be able to bring more severe charges against the batterer. Prosecutors can help the police by communicating their commitment to vigorous enforcement of anti-domestic violence laws. Such a commitment encourages both the arrest of batterers and sets a standard for the rest of the legal system.

Prosecutors can also help transform judicial perceptions. They can educate judges about the nature of the abusive relationship, including the uselessness of the lecture as a deterrent, and steer judges away from such false issues as provocation. Because judges look to prosecutors for information on a variety of issues, including bail and sentencing, judges might defer to the prosecutor's judgment if the latter seeks appropriate punishment for the abusers.

Societal Beliefs Are Reflected in the Legal System

At the core of the legal system's inability to bond and tackle the problem of woman-battery is the ingrained attitude of society that approves of the abuse of women. Societal acceptance of family violence has pervaded the legal system and caused it to offer the same justifications for condoning the battery of women which society has. When asked to defend this justification, legal personnel proffer a variety of superficially plausible reasons to explain their inaction. These reasons, because they are so widely accepted among legislators, police officers, prosecutors and judges, have developed into major obstacles blocking legal remedies for abused women.

Just as society has been reluctant to invade the sanctity of the family, the legal system has deferred to family privacy as a basis for nonintervention. Studies clearly indicate that police have traditionally been reluctant to interfere in family disputes and the rate of prosecution and conviction in criminal complaints drops strongly when there is a prior or present relationship between the alleged assailant and the victim.

Battered Women's Welfare Seen as Unimportant

Another societal belief that has been incorporated into the legal system is the idea that the cost required for stopping the abuse of women is better spent elsewhere. This argument assumes that the welfare of battered women and their children is unimportant compared to the time and safety of legal officials. The fear is that if the law started to take battering seriously, it would be overwhelmed by abuse cases. This response also extends past financial cost to other factors; for example, the police often view domestic quarrels as high danger, no-win situations in which the victim is uncooperative and the policeman's efforts are better spent apprehending "real" criminals.

All of these justifications can be exposed for precisely what they are: unjustifiable neglect. Legal doctrines that limit governmental interference with the family are grounded on reasons that have no application to the problem of woman battery. The law respects decisions on intra-family arrangements because society assumes that family members can reach responsible decisions free of governmental intrusion. This rationale must fail because the battering relationship is so blatantly harmful that no decision can be considered acceptable for the woman. Another justification offered is that policies favoring family autonomy may reflect a lack of confidence in governmental wisdom. This reasoning would allow families to make bad decisions for themselves for fear that governmental decisions may be worse. This reasoning is dangerous when battering is chosen as family behavior and the results are tragic. The legal system's rationalization that the cost of stopping wife abuse is a bad priority and outweighs its benefits is economically and morally wrong. Ignoring the problem will only compound it for future generations. Moreover, we

> *"The legal system as a whole can curtail the abuse of women."*

cannot accept the sacrifice of victims' lives as a fair price for the legal system's convenience.

If there is one excuse that has permeated the legal system through societal belief and has contributed to an uncoordinated response from the legal system, it is the belief that someone else is better able to deal with the problem. This argument offers the rationalization that legal institutions are ill-equipped to deal with complex social and psychological problems like battering and should thus avoid them. This argument fails to rebut the reality that when the stakes are high enough, and when the alternatives to legal intervention are inadequate, the legal system does not hesitate to intercede and resolve the problem. Although battery involves difficult and sensitive issues, it is clear that someone must move against abuse, and that no other social institution has the legal system's clout to protect victims and to force batterers to face the consequences of their transgressions.

The non-enforcement practice of the legal system with respect to the abuse of women is a reflection of prevailing societal values and attitudes regarding public intervention in domestic assault cases. Historically, women have been defined in our society as subordinate to men. As a result, men have been given a disciplinary role in the family, which has ostensibly legitimized the use of violence against women. Examining the history of the legal system's response to battery may lead many to believe that the legal system is the institution in our society which enforces those moral standards we establish for ourselves. If society condones battering, by action or inaction, the legal system absorbs this view and perpetuates the violence it is supposed to alleviate.

Sincere Efforts

The individual arms of the legal system have attempted to confront the problem of battered women. Legislatures have provided tools for the fight. The police response, once wholly unsatisfactory, has markedly improved. Prosecutorial inaction has been met with progressive solutions. Judges have attempted to eliminate their conformity to domestic violence myths by enforcing the law on those who refuse to protect abused women. The battering of women, however, remains a deadly reality. Powerful social forces which permit and encourage abuse have found reflection in the legal system's response to the problem. Moreover, for every person, whether legislator, police officer, prosecutor, judge, or citizen who has been enlightened about the abuse of women, there are countless who remain ignorant. By taking unequivocal action against battering, the legal system can eventually make inroads against the social forces that condone abuse. The individual arms of the legal system need to respond in unison and coordinate their response. The legal system as a whole can curtail the abuse of women.

Arresting Abusers Would Reduce Domestic Violence

by Jessica L. Goldman

About the author: *Jessica L. Goldman was a law clerk in the Washington, D.C. Federal Court of Appeals. She is now an attorney with the firm of Davis, Wright, Tremain in Seattle.*

The violent crime of domestic abuse persists in American society. Wife batter-ing has existed throughout history, at times accepted, often ignored, and, until re-cently, typically excused. Studies carried out by social workers can provide use-ful insights into the dynamics that cause battering and the "learned helplessness" that results. However, the traditional response of police, prosecutors, and judges often traps women in abusive relationships in which they are defenseless.

Over the last decade, ten states have instituted mandatory arrest policies. Such laws, specifically addressing domestic violence crimes, require police officers to make an arrest if probable cause exists that an individual either has committed a misdemeanor or has violated a restraining order. Most states, however, retain laws calling for arrest when probable cause exists that a felony has been com-mitted. Since most domestic violence assaults are classified as misdemeanors, traditional law leaves the decision of whether to arrest solely to the investigating officer. This often leaves the woman with little protection. Studies indicate, how-ever, that arresting the batterer and immediately removing him from the home can significantly reduce the chance of his again becoming abusive.

Abuse Often Not Viewed as a Crime

Left to their own discretion, many police, prosecutors, and judges do not view domestic assault as a substantial problem. Historically, many have not consid-

From Jessica L. Goldman, "Arresting Wife Batterers: A Good Beginning to Stopping a Pervasive Problem," *Washington University Law Quarterly* 69 (1991): 843-56, 865-73. Reprinted with permission.

ered it a crime. Hampered by stereotypes about the rights of men in marriage and the privacy of the marital relationship, the judicial system often responds ineffectively to protect battered women. The entire judicial system can become more accessible to victims of domestic violence if states and municipalities provide careful guidelines for police response.

This viewpoint argues that solely through mandatory arrest laws does the judicial system classify wife battering for what it is: a crime. . . .

The Battering Relationship

Estimates vary as to the extent of domestic abuse in the United States, but there is little doubt that it is widespread. Evidence suggests that one in every six American women is battered at some point in her life; at least two million women are subjected to physical abuse every year. Battering occurs at all socio-economic levels. One study indicates that white, educated, upper-middle class women and poor and minority women are equally likely to be victims.

Strong social and psychological forces tie battered women to the men who abuse them. The battered woman commonly holds traditional notions of marriage and the role of women within the family. She views the man as head of the household and thinks it her responsibility to provide for her husband's happiness. She further believes he has the right to punish her

"The traditional response of police . . . often traps women in abusive relationships."

violently for her perceived failures. Her success as a wife depends on her ability to control his violence. A woman finding herself unable to control this violence experiences self-blame and a deepened sense of failure.

Battered women often are unable to escape from abusive relationships without outside help. A battered woman also may deny that the abuse occurs. The woman, ashamed of the abuse, denies the reality to herself, thereby avoiding acknowledgment of the reality to others. This denial also allows the woman to keep her family together, a goal of overriding importance to her.

Practical considerations can also serve to bind the woman to her husband. In battering relationships the man characteristically dominates the woman in all aspects of the relationship, particularly in the area of family finances. The battered woman often has little or no independent or accessible resources sufficient to enable her to leave the common dwelling and provide for her children. Her lack of control over family assets may also lead to an inability to obtain legal advice. Even if a woman overcomes these obstacles and attempts to leave, she nevertheless may face more physical abuse from her husband.

Many battered women develop a condition termed "learned helplessness." Symptomatic of this is the battered woman's feeling that her life is out of her control. The longer the relationship, the more this perception may become real.

Repeated batterings erode her sense of strength and she ultimately becomes passive. The abused woman holds herself responsible for the battering and becomes unable to escape even though that may be the only option she can control in the relationship. Finally, many battered women love their husbands and endure the abuse in the hope that the abuser will change.

The batterer often possesses characteristics very similar to those of the woman he abuses. He has low self-esteem. He also usually subscribes to traditional notions of family in which the man is "king in his castle." Like his victim, the batterer denies his violence, to himself and to others.

The batterer tends to be overly jealous and protective of his wife. He sees her time spent with children, relatives, and friends, and at work as a threat; his desire to control her life then grows. Batterers commonly grew up in abusive families and may have learned such behavior from watching their fathers beat their mothers or from being beaten themselves. Despite the devastation batterers create in their homes, those outside the family often see them as likeable individuals. Because batterers often feel remorse for their behavior, they try all the harder to deny the destruction they cause.

Commonly, the battered woman is unaware prior to marriage that her partner is abusive. A woman struck for the first time reacts in disbelief and anger. The

> *"Arresting the batterer . . . can significantly reduce the chance of his again becoming abusive."*

batterer may be repentant, asking for forgiveness and promising that the violence will not happen again. The woman loves him and, therefore, believes his apologies and considers the incident an aberration. But, the battering continues and a cycle begins.

Psychologist Lenore Walker identifies a battering cycle with three distinct phases: 1) the tension-building period; 2) the severe battering incident; and 3) the quiet, loving reprieve. During the first phase, relatively minor battering incidents occur, while the woman struggles to halt the escalation of tension. The battering increases in frequency, with the relationship between the couple growing more strained. Finally the phase two severe battering incident occurs. After the severe battering the batterer commonly becomes loving and contrite and the couple may experience a period of closeness before the cycle begins again.

The Traditional Legal Response

Battered women often do not call the police when battering is imminent or occurring because they perceive that the police are ineffective in stopping the abuse. Often a police officer will only quiet the batterer, ascertain whether the woman requires medical care, and try to persuade the man and the woman to end the fighting. Frequently the battering temporarily stops after the police leave, but in some cases the battering resumes, sometimes with even greater intensity.

When the police answer domestic violence calls they often are unable to make arrests under existing state law. Beyond this, however, the opinions of individual officers, as well as general police department policies, also may explain police inaction.

Another possible source of police reluctance to deal with these cases is the traditional belief that wife battering simply is not a crime, or at best, not a relatively important crime. Some officers hold the traditional notion that the relationship between husband and wife lies within a realm of family privacy in which police should not intrude. Others believe in the antiquated right of men to "discipline" their wives. Additionally, many police officers, trained in the use of physical force, can relate to the batterer's use of force to control his wife.

> *"At least two million women are subjected to physical abuse every year."*

Beyond personal prejudices and socialization, police view involvement in domestic disputes as inherently more dangerous than other calls. A recent FBI Uniform Crime Report suggests, however, that police fears are exaggerated. The study showed that domestic calls are among the least likely calls to lead to an officer's death or injury. Furthermore police injuries have decreased in states where mandatory arrest policies exist.

Proof Difficult to Gather

Police are also reluctant to answer domestic violence calls because of problems they face in attempting to gather the requisite proof of abuse, compounded by the usual paucity of witnesses in cases of domestic violence. Furthermore, most jurisdictions classify battering as a misdemeanor and bar the police from effecting an arrest unless they witness the battering or have a court-issued arrest warrant. Those few witnesses to the battering often are children.

Police department policies, or the lack thereof, compound the aforementioned problems. One survey that covered the years 1984 and 1985 showed that almost fifty percent of the police departments surveyed failed to provide policy guidelines or training concerning domestic violence. Although this situation shows signs of improving, where it still exists it creates a system of complete discretion by default. States with little or no legislation leave the police even more discretion. Where policies exist, they commonly do not give domestic violence priority equal with other crimes.

The general non-interventionist policy pervading most police departments gained academic acceptance in the early 1970s when social work theories offering alternatives to punishment became the preferred method of dealing with certain crimes. Academics viewed mediation and on-the-scene counseling as more effective than arrest. Today, most observers discount this in situations involving violence. They view the justice system, criminal and civil, as the principal means of holding batterers responsible for their crimes and of ensuring justice and protection for the victims of abuse.

Even if the police arrest the batterer, prosecution may not ensue. Because prosecutors have wide discretion, the standards for when to prosecute are at least as vague as police arrest criteria. It may be that since the system does not value highly the successful prosecution of batterers, prosecutors have little incentive to pursue such charges vigorously. Charges that prosecutors do press usually are misdemeanors rather than felonies, no matter how serious the assault. If charges are brought the likelihood of the case continuing is diminished by the legal responsibilities imposed on the battered woman.

Battered women drop charges for several reasons. Many women are coerced by the fear of further violence at the hands of their batterers. Often the cumbersome nature of the legal system is overwhelming during a time of great personal and economic turmoil for the woman. Some battered women, simply not understanding how the judicial system works, have no one to explain the process to them. Battered women frequently love their batterers and do not want to see them jailed. Also, the couple may reconcile before the case

> *"Battered women . . . perceive that the police are ineffective in stopping the abuse."*

is brought to trial. Other women are unable for economic reasons to take the time necessary to see the prosecution through to completion. In many cases, the woman's decision to drop charges flows from the advice of prosecutors who may discourage her from pursuing the case. . . .

Legislative Mandates

Modern domestic abuse legislation was introduced in the early 1970s. At that time, every state authorized police officers to make felony arrests on probable cause without a warrant, while only fourteen states called for such arrests when probable cause indicated the commission of a misdemeanor. State laws authorized officers to make warrantless misdemeanor arrests only when they actually witnessed the commission of the crime, a rarity in domestic violence. Simple assault and battery, the crimes most commonly committed in domestic violence cases, are classified as misdemeanors in most states. Thus the arrest laws in the vast majority of states offered little protection to women, unless they took the time to file for an arrest warrant.

In the last decade, the requirement that the police officer witness the misdemeanor in order to make an arrest has become less universal. Nonetheless, most police departments today continue to discourage arrest as the preferred action in domestic violence cases. A survey of large city police departments in 1984 found that fifty percent had no policy concerning domestic violence, forty percent encouraged mediation, while only ten percent encouraged arrest.

Today, most jurisdictions fall under one of three statutory classifications: 1) those authorizing arrest only when probable cause of a felony exists; 2) those permitting arrest when the officer has probable cause to believe a misdemeanor was committed or a restraining order violated; and 3) those mandating arrest.

Mandatory Arrest Policies Are the Proper Response

Both permissive and mandatory arrest policies make arrest in domestic violence more likely than is the case under traditional law, which requires police to witness the commission of a misdemeanor to arrest. However, permissive arrest laws, which provide that police "may" arrest when probable cause exists that a domestic assault has been committed, still leave officers with potent discretion to forgo arrest. Mandatory arrest policies, on the other hand, require that police officers "shall" arrest if such probable cause exists. Therefore, the policy decision removed from the hands of individual police officers, properly rests with legislators or police chiefs.

Recently, there has been a growing consensus that mandatory misdemeanor arrest laws deter domestic abuse more effectively than either permissive misdemeanor arrest laws or probable cause felony arrest laws. The most prominent survey of the effects of various approaches was the Minneapolis Domestic Violence Experiment. The Minneapolis Experiment studied the effect of different modes of police intervention in domestic abuse calls over a six-month period.

> *"Mandatory misdemeanor arrest laws deter domestic abuse."*

Thirty-five police officers took part in the experiment. The police department randomly assigned one of three approaches with which to handle domestic violence calls: 1) arrest; 2) mediation; or 3) requesting that the batterer leave the home for eight hours. The study showed that when officers attempted to mediate there was a thirty-seven percent chance of further violence within the following six months; a thirty-three percent chance of subsequent violence existed among those temporarily sent away from the home. By contrast, there was only a nineteen percent chance of recurring violence when an arrest was made.

Other studies support the conclusions of the Minneapolis Domestic Violence Experiment. In 1984, the Attorney General's Task Force on Family Violence issued a report on police arrest policies; it recommended arrest as the preferred police policy. An experiment in California, modeled after the Minneapolis study, also showed that arrest deters spouse abuse more effectively than do other police responses. Studies in Canada and New Zealand demonstrate similar results. Thus, the implementation of mandatory arrest policies seems to decrease spousal abuse in the jurisdiction.

Wife abuse is a violent crime. American law has evolved from a system in which wife battering was not only acceptable, but legal. Deeply rooted historical prejudices made a criminal justice system that does not adequately serve the needs of victims of domestic violence. Police officers, prosecutors and judges must become more informed about the nature of the battering relationship and the needs of its victims in order to avoid using their discretion in ways that continue to reinforce outdated notions about the roles of men and women.

"Many batterers and their victims continue to adhere to notions that men have the right to beat their wives."

Police officers, prosecutors and judges influence each other's reactions and policies toward domestic violence. Because the police traditionally do not arrest, prosecutors do not take abuse cases to trial. As a result of hearing few domestic violence cases in their courtrooms, judges often underestimate the severity of the problem. When judges do hear cases, some fall into the old trap of blaming the victim and impose lenient sentences. Prosecutors then get the message that domestic violence is not a high judicial priority, and hence avoid prosecuting cases. Police officers, in turn, see it as a waste of time to take the domestic violence call seriously since nothing will come of it.

Educating judicial officers about the criminality and prevalence of battering can only occur if batterers are arrested. Studies indicate that, left to their own discretion, many police officers choose not to arrest. Mandatory arrest laws and policies must be implemented in order to institute a systemic change from the bottom, up.

Many batterers and their victims continue to adhere to notions that men have the right to beat their wives. Arrest and punishment send a valuable message: battering is against the law and perpetrators will be punished. This knowledge may strengthen the resolve of battered women to stand up to their batterers and impress upon police the criminal nature of these assaults.

Clarifying the Role of Police

Mandatory arrest laws clarify the police officers' role in domestic abuse cases. Wife battering incidents present the police with complicated situations, the dynamics of which they often may not fully comprehend. This has led, in the past, to a police preference for mediation or inaction, both of which are inappropriate in cases of violent crime. When all parties are aware that domestic abuse will result in arrest, any confusion surrounding the role of police is eliminated.

Mandatory arrest laws also enhance a battered woman's chance of success in suits against the police for inaction. The future of due process challenges was severely limited by the recent Supreme Court holding in *DeShaney*. Furthermore, equal protection actions commonly require a showing of discriminatory intent, difficult to establish in most cases. With mandatory arrest policies, women will no longer face the difficulty of establishing a causal link between police inaction and wife abuse in tort claims, since such statutes will establish that link for them.

Mandatory arrest laws preserve the integrity of the criminal justice system and publicly reject illegal behavior. Justice requires the similar treatment of like cases. Assaults upon spouses are as illegal and deplorable as those against strangers. Laws mandating arrest send a message to society that battering is considered unacceptable. A change in society's general acquiescence toward battering may well positively affect the behavior of men who batter. Furthermore, all of the classic rationales for enforcing laws apply in domestic abuse cases. The interests of standard-setting, deterrence, incapacitation, punishment and rehabilitation will all be fulfilled by a policy mandating the arrest of abusive spouses.

Society Must Stop Abuse

Domestic violence is a pervasive crime in our society with deeply rooted traditions of acceptance. Violence in the home tends to be cyclical and thus perpetuates itself, with children who grow up experiencing the violence against their mothers or themselves being taught that it is acceptable and legal. Society has a clear and pressing interest in stopping this cycle.

Because of persistent notions that wife battering is neither inappropriate nor illegal, police officers have, traditionally, used their discretionary power to refrain from using arrest, thus remaining uninvolved and helping to reinforce outdated stereotypes. Mandatory arrest laws create guidelines for police, batterers and victims, emphasizing that battering is a violent crime and will not be tolerated.

Classifying Violent Acts Against Women as Hate Crimes Would Be Effective

by Lisa Heinzerling

About the author: *Lisa Heinzerling is an associate professor at the Georgetown University Law Center.*

In December 1989, a man walked into the engineering school at the University of Montreal armed with a hunting rifle. He entered a classroom and divided the students he found there into two groups: women and men. Shouting at the women, "You're all a bunch of feminists," he picked them off as if they were ducks in a shooting gallery. By the time his deadly stalk was over, he had killed fourteen women and injured many others. A note found in his pocket after his suicide declared that women had ruined his life.

The man in Montreal killed these women because he hated them—not as individual persons, but as women. U.S. law, however, would not include these murders in the controversial new category known as "crimes of hate."

The Definition of "Hate Crime"

As now defined, "hate crime" refers to an act committed not out of animosity toward the victim as an individual, but out of hostility to a group to which the victim belongs. The 1986 attack in Howard Beach, New York, in which one black man was killed and two were beaten by white assailants, is a notorious example.

As recognition of this category of crime grows, some states have enacted laws to help them respond. California, for example, requires the collection and analysis of statistics on such crimes. In other states, if the "hate" criteria apply, a crime such as second-degree assault is automatically elevated to first-degree assault. Still other states have established a separate crime, such as "ethnic intimi-

Lisa Heinzerling, "A New Way of Looking at Violence Against Women." This article originally appeared in the October 1990 issue of *Glamour* and is reprinted with permission.

dation." The latest "hate crime" legislation is a federal law directing the government to gather statistics on such crimes.

Why are such statistics gathered? Legislators ask for numbers because, in deciding how laws should be fashioned, it's helpful to know the scope of the problem you're confronting. Statistics provide that sense of dimension, especially for a new category like hate crime. Unfortunately, many of the new laws share the same flaw: They do not include gender as one of the motivating factors that can turn an ordinary crime into a crime of hate. The federal law, for example, considers hate crimes to be those impelled by the victim's race, ethnicity, religion or sexual orientation. Other similar laws cite the victim's race, color, creed or national origin.

Thus, if a black man is beaten or killed *because* he is black, that counts as a hate crime. If a woman is beaten, raped or killed *because* she is a woman—as clearly happened to the victims in Montreal—that doesn't count. Women have to ask why.

Gender Bias

"Race, color, religion, *sex* and national origin" has become a kind of refrain in our laws against discrimination. These characteristics invariably appear together as the criteria that must not be applied in allocating (or withdrawing) benefits such as education, employment and housing. And some states—like Connecticut, Minnesota, New Hampshire and California—

> *"Certain acts against women must be recognized as hate crimes."*

have followed this model in the wording of their hate crime legislation. Thus, when other discrimination statutes—including the only existing federal law—do *not* include gender as one of the forbidden bases for conduct, we can only infer that the exclusion was deliberate.

Has sex been excluded here because women in the U.S. do not experience gender-motivated violence? Every woman reading this knows the answer, knows the special risk she faces *because* she is a woman. We've learned to order our lives according to our special danger, so much so that when we refuse to do so—say, by walking in a lonely section of town after dark—we are held as accountable as our aggressor for any injury that results.

Nor can the exclusion be based on the problem of differentiating between hate crimes against women and "ordinary" crimes. Not every mugging of a woman, for example, will fit the new category—but neither will every mugging of a Hasidic Jew. The resulting evidentiary difficulties haven't stopped us from creating the general category of hate crimes; indeed, one of the purposes of the federal statute is to establish a method for identifying which crimes are, in fact, motivated by hate.

103

The truth is, society does not think of crimes against women in the same way that it thinks of racial or ethnic violence. We tend, instead, to treat brutalizing acts against women as isolated cases or, more rarely, as manifestations of racial or ethnic hatred. Many observers have speculated that the young blacks who attacked the Central Park jogger—beating her so savagely that one doctor estimated she'd lost 80 percent of her blood by the time she'd reached the hospital—may have done so because she was white. *Almost none have suggested she was attacked because she was a woman.*

Certain acts against women *must* be recognized as hate crimes. The very act of excluding them may be a symptom of the same pathology that produces such a crime. For if studying such statistics tells our society that these crimes are important—more abhorrent, in fact, than other crimes—then excluding gender as a motivating factor sends an equally important message, one that's chilling indeed: These crimes are heinous, but *not* when they're committed against women; crimes like the murders in Montreal don't really trouble us much. That is a message welcome to none but the misogynist.

Arresting Abusers May Not Be Effective at Decreasing Domestic Violence

by Crime Control Institute

About the author: *The Crime Control Institute is a Washington, D.C.-based organization of criminal justice experts and others concerned with reducing crime in the United States.*

Does the length of time in custody affect the odds of future criminality? This question is central to public policy and criminological theory, yet it remains virtually unanswered. Little enough is known about the individual effects of incarceration for any length of time, let alone for varying times in custody. Yet, at every step of the criminal justice process, there is enormous variation in the length of time each offender is held captive. Given the modern reliance on incarceration as a primary criminal sanction, the ignorance about its dosage-response effects is bewildering. If incarceration was a drug, the Food and Drug Administration would long ago have required animal tests for its toxicity, large-scale randomized trials to demonstrate its benefits, and large-scale user surveillance for allergic reactions.

Arrest Is the Aspirin of Criminal Justice

The question of varying time in custody is especially important at the point of arrest, for several reasons. One is the fact that arrest is the aspirin of criminal justice—the most widely dispensed incarceration "drug" in the United States. Each year, about 56 times more people are arrested than are committed to prison. Another reason is that the range of variation of time in custody is proportionately far greater for arrest than for prison. Although prison terms generally range from about 1 to 25 years, custody associated with arrest often ranges

From the Crime Control Institute, "From Initial Deterrence to Long-Term Escalation: Short Custody Arrest for Poverty Ghetto Domestic Violence," *Criminology*, vol. 29, no. 4, 1991. Reprinted with permission.

from 1 day to 1 week (168 hours). For serious offenses with suspects who cannot make bail, pretrial incarceration can last for months.

Wide variation in arrest time has become an especially important issue for misdemeanor domestic violence. The growth of mandatory arrest laws and policies may be associated with the 70% growth in national per capita arrest rates for simple assault from the 1984 publication of the Minneapolis domestic violence experiment to

> *"Full arrest had no deterrent effect on employed persons, but a criminogenic effect on unemployed persons."*

1989. These laws appear to be premised on a conception of arrest as a homogeneous treatment, a standard pill that has virtually the same effects on everyone. But there is increasing evidence that neither domestic violence arrests nor their effects are homogeneous.

The Minneapolis experiment itself reported a range of time in custody of from under one day to over one week. Since the publication of the Minneapolis results, the National Institute of Justice has funded six replication experiments, of which results from three (Omaha, Nebraska; Charlotte, North Carolina; and Milwaukee, Wisconsin) are available at this writing. Those experiments also showed wide variation in time in custody both across and within cities. One of them, in fact, made such variation an explicit part of the research design. The Milwaukee domestic violence experiment randomly assigned *short* (under 3 hours) and *full* arrests (about 12 hours), as well as no arrest (warning only), to persons eligible to be arrested. This paper reports the varying effects of time in custody found in that experiment.

In other publications, we report the Milwaukee interaction-effect results showing the varying effects of the same dosage of custody on different kinds of people. Full arrest had no deterrent effect on employed persons, but a criminogenic effect on unemployed persons. Similar effects have been found for other indicators of "social bonds." Taken together, these findings suggest that both the content and the consequences of arrest are anything but standard, at least for domestic violence. The results raise major policy questions, not just about domestic violence, but about arrests and other forms of custody in general. . . .

Domestic Violence Arrests

The domestic violence research has prompted new scrutiny of the variation in arrest times for misdemeanors across communities. Our experiment in Wisconsin, for example, led us to research the variation in that state when a mandatory arrest law went into effect after our experiment was completed but before its results were announced. In a mail survey of 39 smaller police departments throughout the state conducted in 1990, over half (8 of 15) respondents said they released suspects arrested for misdemeanor domestic violence within three hours. In Milwaukee, by contrast, the average time in custody for a full arrest is almost 12 hours.

Although communities may differ in the average length of time misdemeanor arrestees are held in custody, there is also substantial variation within communities. Lawrence W. Sherman and Richard A. Berk, for example, reported victim interview data showing that 43% of domestic violence arrestees were released within one day, another 43% were released within one week, and 14% were released after more than one week in jail. Franklyn Dunford et al. reported that official records on total time in custody data were unavailable, although police interviews showed a minimum of one hour in custody would be associated with each arrest. Under 20% of the domestic violence arrestees in the Omaha experiment were released from *custody* within two hours after booking. The mean time to release to another floor for *posting bond* (but not release from custody until bonding was completed) was 15 hours and 46 minutes. Only about half of those released to post bond actually did so; the rest were held until a court appearance.

The Charlotte domestic violence arrest experiment fell between the long and short custody periods for arrest. The median time in custody was 9 hours with 10% of all suspects released within one hour.

> *"Offenders who are released immediately upon booking will have higher . . . incidence of repeat domestic assault."*

Goldstein suggested that time in custody for domestic violence arrest poses a risk to victims when it is very short, as in Charlotte. He hypothesized that in jurisdictions where the suspect is released within an hour or two of arrest (unlike the minimum overnight custody in the Minneapolis experiment), the likelihood of intoxication or anger persisting from the original event would be very high. Under such conditions, he suggested, the odds of immediate recidivism would be very high: The suspect could return to the victim and perhaps commit even more serious violence.

Deterrence

An alternate hypothesis is suggested by Philip J. Cook's (1988) reanalysis of the John E. Berecochea and Dorothy R. Jaman (1981) results. Short arrests could have less deterrent effect than arrests with longer time in custody simply because of less dosage of punishment. Rather than showing the immediate effect Goldstein hypothesized, there could be a long-term effect of differing dosages of time in custody. Classical deterrence doctrine is based on the avoidance of pain or displeasure. A short arrest may simply teach the suspect that the experience of arrest is not painful because it is so short. Having learned that they can easily survive an arrest, with minimal disruption of their life-style or even their employment (when relevant), suspects released shortly after arrest may be less deterred than those who find arrest far more disruptive due to longer time in custody. . . .

Combining Goldstein's anger hypothesis with classical deterrence doctrine, the Milwaukee experiment hypothesized a criminogenic effect of short arrest. The research proposal for the experiment contained the following hypothesis:

> *Jail Time Matters.* For reasons of both deterrence and incapacitation, the reduced recidivism of arrested offenders depends upon the attendant jail time at arrest. Offenders who are released immediately upon booking will have higher short term and long term prevalence and incidence of repeat domestic assault against the same victim, as well as higher recidivism on other measures [compared with the no-arrest suspects].

Theoretically, we posited that punishment causes both *anger* at the punishers and *fear* of repeat punishment. Under conditions of low dosage of custody, the fear may be too weak to overcome the anger—anger against the same victim whose evidence gave rise to the arrest, against any victim symbolically representing that victim, or against society in general. Thus, we expected that a low custody dosage could backfire, causing more crime than no custody, in both the short and the long run.

Experimental Design

From April 7, 1987, to August 8, 1988, we conducted a randomized experiment in arrest in collaboration with the Milwaukee Police Department. The experimental design had been given the unanimous approval of the Milwaukee Common Council (the local legislature) and was subject to a contract with the Crime Control Institute approved by the Milwaukee City Attorney.

The sample consisted of all eligible cases of probable cause to arrest for misdemeanor domestic battery encountered by a special team of 35 Milwaukee patrol officers. . . .

The main difference between the two arrest groups was the time in custody. The mean times of 2.8 and 11.1 hours were computed partly through direct measurement and partly through estimation. The difference was very close to our objective of testing how arrest might work in cities which process misdemeanor battery suspects much more quickly. . . .

"The short-custody suspects clearly took the arrest experience more 'lightly' than the long-custody ones."

Consistent with the deterrence hypotheses, the short-custody suspects clearly took the arrest experience more "lightly" than the long-custody ones. They were twice as likely to say they were not bothered by the arrest or did not care (25 vs. 13%). They were less likely to say they were afraid of what would happen next (31 vs. 39%). They were less likely (29 vs. 42%) to expect the arrest to hurt their future ability to get a job or a loan to buy a car. And they were twice as likely (21 vs. 11%) to expect their friends to be angry with their *partners* for the arrest, not angry with them.

> *"The policy implications of these findings are highly debatable."*

These differences in perception were probably magnified after the jail interview, when the officers personally escorted the suspects through the expedited booking process, often passing other prisoners and going to the front of the line. This procedure was adopted early in the experiment after the booking unit was unable to get the short-custody suspects out much faster than the long-custody suspects. To be released in two hours, the suspects had to be processed immediately at each step in the booking process: fingerprinting, photographing, property identification, and warrant checking. To what extent this experience magnified the suspect's perception of the arrest as a "light" treatment, we can only speculate. . . .

Outcome Measures

Several independent and overlapping data sources were used to measure recidivism in domestic violence by the presenting suspects. The independent sources were the initial and "six-month" follow-up victim interviews. Initial interviews were generally completed from 7 to 30 days after the presenting incident (84%), but 5% were completed after 61 days. Only half of the "six-month" interviews could actually be conducted within 210 days after the presenting incident, and another 42% required over 241 days to locate the victim. Response rates were high for both victim interviews: 78% for the initial and 77% for the follow-up. There were no significant differences in completion rates by treatment groups for either interview, which helps to refute a victim intimidation interpretation of the results.

The overlapping data sources were all official records. They consisted of (1) arrest reports on the suspects involving the same or other victims, (2) offense reports filed by the same victim only about offenses by the same suspect, and (3) hotline records generated by police and recorded by the Sojourner Truth House. These records overlapped in the following ways. Offense reports (filed by victim name) tracked recidivism against the *same* victim, whether or not there was an arrest. Arrest reports (filed by suspect name) tracked recidivism against *any* victim, but not offenses without arrests. Hotline records covered all probable-cause domestic violence cases producing offense and arrest reports, which enabled the hotline to pick up nonarrest offenses against other victims. They were both filed by victim and suspect names.

The most comprehensive official measure was therefore the hotline record, the one measure that tapped offender-absent and offender-present, any-victim domestic violence by the same suspect, both before and after the presenting incident. It was official in the sense that police provided the data for the report; the hotline volunteers merely recorded the data. In a poll taken after the experiment but before analysis or data collection was begun, the experimental officers selected the hotline records as the best data source for evaluating the effects of their actions. . . .

Initial Deterrence

There is good evidence of an initial deterrent effect from short-custody arrest and some evidence of an initial deterrent effect from full arrest. . . . Interview measures show that both short and full arrest reduced the risk of *any* repeat violence—comparable to what was found in Minneapolis—by about two-thirds. The results do not support the Goldstein hypothesis that short arrests increase risk to the same victim in the short run. The prevalence of repeat violence on first reunion (data not displayed) was virtually identical for short (2.2%) and full (1.7%) arrest, and both favorably compared with the 7% of warning group victims who reported being battered again immediately upon the departure of the police. . . .

The magnitude of short arrest's initial deterrent effect was substantial—about a 50% reduction in same victim-reported prevalence and in the

"Arrest can actually increase domestic violence."

rate of any-victim official recidivism per day. This is especially important for the same victim, because total hotline recidivism per day peaked during the initial 30-day period. The continuous official hotline measure, however, showed that short arrest's initial deterrent effect disappeared by the second 30-day period and that a significant criminogenic effect in the third 30-day period was followed by insignificant 30-day differences until the second year.

By the time of the follow-up interviews, none of the measures showed a deterrent effect of either type of arrest, including same- and any-victim tests of prevalence and frequency. Follow-up victim interviews, for example, showed prevalence of any repeat violence for 35% of the full-arrest group, 30% of the short-arrest group, and 31% of the warning group. Hotline prevalence was virtually identical (at 27, 27 and 26%), as were other official measures. However, the period after the first year was marked by short arrest showing a significant criminogenic effect in increasing the mean number of any-victim hotline reports per subject per day. . . .

The most powerful analytic design we employed was the pairwise comparison of before-after changes in official measures of violence in both arrest groups compared with changes in the warning group. This design produced strong evidence of a long-term criminogenic effect of short arrest, but no such evidence for full arrest. Four of eight possible tests of short arrest were significant. . . . None of the tests for full arrest were significant. Moreover, if we limit the official data analysis to the hotline reports as the most comprehensive measure, all four of the possible before-after comparisons of short arrests reveal a criminogenic effect compared with warnings, but full arrests had no effect. (Recall that no before-after frequency rate comparisons are possible with the victim interview data.) . . .

> *"The initial deterrence period may also offer a window of opportunity for new approaches to intervention."*

Although the total frequency of hotline reports per days at risk increased over time in all three groups, it increased about twice as much in the short-arrest group as in the warning group. A similar difference between short arrest and warning, although not as large (46% more), occurred with the frequency of arrests. In contrast, the before-after data for the *full*-arrest group show no consistent criminogenic or deterrent effects compared with warnings. The relative rate of increase is about one-third greater for the full-arrest group than for the warning group in the hotline measure data, but it is about 25% lower in the arrest measure data. . . .

Discussion

The apparent decay of initial deterrence is modestly consistent with some evidence in Minneapolis, Omaha, and Charlotte. The Tauchen's reanalysis of the Minneapolis victimization data found steady decay to the end of the six-month period, by which time any deterrent effect was eliminated. Although those data were plagued by substantial sample attrition, the analytic techniques attempted to take that problem into account. The survival curve for victim-reported injury (but not official measures) in Omaha is also consistent with this pattern: Arrest had a visibly (but not significantly) higher survival rate until the end of the 180-day period, when the differences between treatments disappeared. The decay of initial deterrence is also consistent with the findings of the Charlotte experiment: a small (but not significant) deterrent effect of arrest persisted for only the first three weeks.

The evidence for long-term criminogenic effects from arrest in Omaha and Charlotte is even stronger than in Milwaukee, and it occurs sooner. In Omaha's seven to twelve months follow-up, the criminogenic effects of the arrest treatment clearly increased for both official measures of recidivism (offense reports and arrests). At the end of 12 months, both official and victimization measures showed higher recidivism frequency for the experimental arrest group than for the nonarrest group. The 12-month rearrest frequency was 61% higher for the experimental arrest group, a difference of borderline statistical significance. In Charlotte, where arrest custody was shorter than in Omaha but longer than in Milwaukee, and where over 70% of the suspects were black (vs. 43% in Omaha), the combined arrest and citation groups showed growing criminogenic effects over the first six months. The difference started to grow after week 15, ending in a statistically significant prevalence difference of 13% of informally treated suspects being rearrested compared with 20% of formally treated suspects.

Police Action

These findings are also consistent with observations of decaying initial effects of general deterrence from police patrol crackdowns. Such crackdowns involve sudden increases in numbers of police on patrol or number of enforcement actions taken. Wherever apparent deterrent effects of such increases are found, they invariably decay after varying lengths of time. Whether individual and general deterrent effects can be explained by the same theory is debatable. But as Richard Lempert (1981-82) pointed out, a good deal of what is measured as general deterrence may in fact be specific deterrent effects on persons most likely to offend. . . .

If the pattern of delayed criminogenic reaction is harder to understand because of the initial deterrent effect, recall that our theoretical perspective was premised on the balance of *fear* and *anger*. The consistent pattern of decaying initial deterrence suggests that short arrest produces some fear that wears off quickly. Then sooner (as in Charlotte and Omaha) or later (as in Milwaukee) anger takes over, and the memory of the previous arrest may become a challenge to prove how "hard" a man the suspect is in his willingness to use violence. There is no law of social science that says humans have to be consistent, and no reason why the same stimulus cannot have contradictory effects as time elapses.

> *"Short arrest increases suspect anger at society without increasing fear of rearrest."*

These findings should, however, be considered with several cautions in mind. Most important, the short-arrest treatment may have been contaminated by the special treatment necessary to process suspects within two to three hours, and it may not be generalizable to jurisdictions in which every misdemeanor arrestee is released that quickly. Another caution is that the before-after tests have not been subject to replication, although the after-only official recidivism results are arguably consistent with findings from Charlotte and Omaha. A third caution is that we conducted many significance tests and that one possible interpretation is that the small number of significant effects could be found by chance alone. . . .

Policy Changes Should Be Considered

Assuming that there is a long-term, and definitely not a short-term, criminogenic effect of short arrest, we can draw two conclusions about our hypotheses. One is that the Goldstein hypothesis of short-term danger from short arrest is clearly contradicted by these data. The other is that short arrest, over the longer term, apparently did something that full arrest did not do to provoke more violence against intimates. Goldstein's concern about the use of short arrest, then, appears to be warranted, but for very different empirical reasons than he suggested.

> *"A little jail time can be worse than none."*

The policy implications of these findings are highly debatable, because they produce a moral dilemma between short-term victim interests and long-term control of domestic violence. For the victim who wishes to avoid the 7% risk of a repeat attack as soon as police leave, short arrest is clearly preferable to no arrest. Even with a 2% risk of repeat violence upon the suspect's return home, short arrest nets the same victim two-thirds lower odds of repeat violence in the short run. Yet, the long-term cost of that choice is to increase the total violence committed by that suspect against all potential intimate victims. This long-term effect does not clearly develop with full arrest, which may justify its continued use as a policy. But in order to avoid the long-term escalation of recidivism from short arrest, such policies or laws would have to specify 12-hour minimum times in custody.

Moreover, many would argue that a proper policy analysis of arrest would include other effects, such as unemployment by the suspect and the impact of arrest on the domestic relationship. Others might argue that the criminal justice model of "victim" and "suspect" used in this experiment is inappropriate for what are arguably situations of mutual conflict more properly labelled "disputes." Still others would argue that arrest is appropriate as a just desert, regardless of its effects on recidivism.

Effects of Arrests

An additional policy consideration not discussed here, but also raised by Sherman and Berk, is the varying effects of arrest on different types of offenders. No discussion of either policy or theory should ignore the finding that some arrest has very strong, early-on, and persistent criminogenic effects on certain types of offenders. Indeed, full interpretation of the differences and consistencies of findings across sites must also take these interactions into account in examining the long-term criminogenic effect of arrest.

To the extent that mandatory arrest policies are founded on a premise of long-term specific deterrence, then, the current experiment clearly refutes that premise, at least in ghetto poverty areas like Milwaukee's. As the third experiment to reach that conclusion out of four reported to date, the current analysis is the first to conclude (though not to show evidence) that arrest can actually increase domestic violence. This should give considerable pause to advocates of mandatory arrest who flatly assert a deterrent effect from arrest no matter what the time in custody, no matter what the population arrested.

Two other findings tend to call into question the deterrent value of mandatory arrest. One is the relatively low percentage of the victims (24%) and suspects (19%) interviewed who were aware of the city's mandatory arrest policy, which was over one year and 5,000 arrests old for most of the experiment. This finding suggests, but does not demonstrate, a lack of general deterrence from a mandatory arrest policy. The second finding is the very rare occurrence of any serious injury in the recidivism against the same victims. The total of 28 serious injuries reported in 921 follow-up interviews suggests that mandatory arrest is hard to justify on the grounds of a high probability of serious violence in the near future.

We find no reason in these data to challenge Sherman and Berk's recommendation against mandatory arrest laws, but good reason to challenge their recommendations of presumptive arrest policies regardless of time in custody. This paper suggests that such laws or policies may be harmful when they are implemented through short arrest, at least with urban underclass populations. Other kinds of legal innovation may be far more useful, such as nonarrest strategies to forestall violence immediately after police leave. The initial deterrence period may also offer a window of opportunity for new approaches to intervention, either by police or others.

Perhaps the most important theoretical and policy implication of these findings is the difference that dosage apparently makes. The results are consistent with, but do not directly test, the hypothesis that short arrest increases suspect anger at society without increasing fear of rearrest. The less criminogenic effects of full arrest could be explained by its higher cost to suspects in custody time. What this hypothesis does not explain is why short arrest should provide stronger evidence of an initial deterrent effect than full arrest. Nor does it explain why the escalation effect should take so long to appear.

Yet, if the number of hours in custody affects underclass recidivism for this offense, what about for other offenses? Dosage might even make even more—or less—difference for suspect populations with lower prevalence of prior arrests. Given the recent growth of arrests for drug possession and other charges routinely dropped, U.S. police now make over 14 million nontraffic arrests each year, many with short-custody dosage. Policymakers and criminologists should therefore consider the possibility that a little jail time can be worse than none.

Classifying Violent Acts Against Women as Hate Crimes Will Be Ineffective

by Patt Morrison

About the author: *Patt Morrison is a staff writer for the* Los Angeles Times *newspaper.*

To the list of motives for hate crimes, gender has at last been added. Attacking another person on the basis of gender can turn a misdemeanor into a felony and can tack another three, maybe seven, years onto a prison term.

On the Basis of Gender

But let's drop the neutral language and admit it: *On the basis of gender* means a woman victim. Assemblywoman Lucille Roybal-Allard sponsored the bill after the L.A. city attorney found that the bulk of hate crimes are committed not against gays or religious and ethnic minorities but against women.

Ask what a hate crime is, and you will likely hear about the classic, vicious, often anonymous offense—writing "rice ball" on an Asian family's fence, burning a cross in a black family's yard.

Women Are Terrorized

But add gender, and something changes. Hundreds of women are terrorized, intimidated, beaten, raped and murdered simply because they are women. Their killers and abusers are not crazy; they are haters who rage at all women by defiling one. Smash a fist into a woman's face? Nothing personal, bitch.

Consider the volume dealers. George Hennard murdered 23 people in a Texas cafeteria in the fall of 1991. He hated his mother—hated women, period. Fifteen of his victims were women. He picked them out, table by table. This was a hate crime as surely as if he'd taken pains to aim his Ruger P89 at black faces or brown ones.

Hate crimes grow from the soured soil of fantasy and power. Medieval Arabs and Jews were killed because Christians imagined they were spreading the plague; modern homosexuals are attacked for supposedly spreading AIDS.

In the days before Hennard toted his arsenal into that cafeteria, he took a shine to two young women. He scarcely knew them, yet he watched them and followed them and, like a playwright, fantasized entire lives for

> *"This is a country where people think Judge Wapner sits on the Supreme Court."*

them. He gave them names of his choosing, Stacee and Robin, and he wrote a long letter telling them that other women were "vipers" but that both of them were virtuous.

The retail haters rarely make the front page. A man's wife or girlfriend leaves him to establish her own life, and he cannot abide that. He breaks into her house, her apartment, *her* new space. One of three things happens next: He holds a gun or a knife on her and kills her; he kills her *and* kills himself; or he kills her and the police kill him. Once in a while, he lives to go to trial. Once in a rarer while, she lives to tell about it.

Tolstoy, of course, never read the newswire when he declared that unhappy families are each unhappy in their own way. These tales vary only by caliber. If we write about them at all, it is briefly and rendered in headlines as MAN SHOOTS EX-WIFE, SELF.

A Hate Crime

Someone will tell me this is not a hate crime, only love gone askew. I don't buy it. So far as human variables can be reduced, this *is* the formula for a hate crime. When a man depersonalizes a woman, she is no longer a woman but *Women*. He has to reclaim his power; he must resume the relationship or finish it on his terms.

And he does. The Encino man who shot his bride because she wore slacks and left the house, both against his orders, did. And so did the Texas man who fatally shot three in-laws and kidnaped his estranged wife when she wouldn't get back together with him. And so did the North Carolina teen-ager who abducted his ex-girlfriend, then stabbed her to death in front of classmates after she said she didn't want to talk to him.

Those Who Hate Will Ignore the Law

Adding gender to the hate-crime list is commendable. Its omission cried out for remedy, says Roybal-Allard. But the law directs its message to people who can't hear it. This is a country where people think Judge Wapner sits on the

Supreme Court. To expect that they will understand this legal refinement, much less fear it, is asking a lot. Whether his fury is for women or blacks or homosexuals, three more years on a prison sentence will not stay a bigot's hand.

In the offices and courthouses that keep track of these matters, file cabinets will be filled, more file cabinets will be ordered and they too will be filled. Men will go to prison and stay there longer. And the women they kill will stay dead forever.

Chapter 4

Does Pornography Promote Violence Against Women?

CURRENT CONTROVERSIES

Chapter Preface

The ongoing debate over whether pornography promotes violence against women has taken a constitutional turn. Many legal scholars and other experts contend that the First Amendment right to free speech includes even hardcore pornography. They fear that not only would attempts to suppress pornography open the door to further censorship, but they would also undermine freedoms won by the women's movement. For example, they point to antipornography laws that have been used to ban explicit birth control and safe sex information. They also fear that laws prohibiting pornography will be used to restrict women's right to produce "erotica"—sexual images, including those of women, produced for women to view. Leonore Tiefer, a psychologist and associate professor at Montefiore Medical Center in New York, argues that "there will be no sexuality for women at all without freely available sexual information and open talk about sexual possibilities and experience." For many people, then, restricting or prohibiting pornography is a free speech issue.

But others, including some feminists and many moral conservatives, argue that pornography is not a free speech issue. They point out that "speech" that poses a clear danger (such as yelling "fire" in a crowded theater) is not protected by the Constitution. Pornography, they believe, encourages violence against women, and thus poses a clear danger. According to Patty McEntee of Morality in Media, Inc., the Supreme Court has clearly proscribed "obscenity," the legal term for hardcore pornography. She states, "Throughout our history, the Supreme Court, no matter whether characterized as conservative, moderate or liberal, has held that obscenity is not protected by the First Amendment. In 1973, the Court stated: 'We hold that there are legitimate state interests at stake in stemming the tide of commercialized obscenity. . . . These include the interest of the public in the quality of life . . . and, possibly the public safety itself.'"

The debate over whether pornography is a free speech issue will continue to rage. It is one of many controversial debates that have sprung from the clash between those who believe that pornography promotes violence against women and those who believe it does not.

Pornography Contributes to Violence Against Women

by Franklin Mark Osanka and Sara Lee Johann

About the authors: *Franklin Mark Osanka holds a Ph.D. in sociology from Northwestern University in Evanston, Illinois. Sara Lee Johann holds a J.D. from the University of Wisconsin Law School in Madison. Both authors have spoken extensively about the negative effects of pornography on society. Besides* Sourcebook on Pornography, *from which this viewpoint is excerpted, they have coauthored a book on battered women who kill.*

The case histories of pornography victims and perpetrators that follow present overwhelming documentation that pornography serves as a catalyst for sexual abuse and violence and other physical abuse of women and children and sometimes men. While evidence of pornography-related abuses abounds, little, if any, evidence exists to demonstrate any value of or justification for pornography. We found close to five hundred different offenders in our limited files whose acts of sexual abuse, violence, or physical abuse were pornography related. Unfortunately, many of these offenders victimized multiple victims. Few professionals who are in positions to document pornography-related abuse ask the right questions of abuse victims and offenders; therefore, most pornography-related offenses go undocumented. . . .

The Relationship Between Pornography and Abuse

In July 1985, a representative of Washington County (Minnesota) Human Services, Inc., completed a survey designed by Sara Lee Johann as part of the background material compiled to support antipornography legislation in Wisconsin. The survey concerned the relationship between pornography and abuse, battering, sexual assault, and exploitation of persons. The results, based on six years of experience with the program and 2,380 sexual assault victim and offender clients, were interesting. The representative estimated the following:

1. Abusers often used pornographic material portraying women, children, and men involved in all sorts of sexual activity from intercourse to bestiality, child molestation, rape, and group sex. This material included depictions of violence such as torture, pain, humiliation, mutilation, bleeding, bruises, beatings, physical injury, whips, chains, and ropes.

> *"Pornography serves as a catalyst for sexual abuse and violence and other physical abuse of women."*

2. In 68 percent of the 2,380 cases, the abuser beat or sexually abused the victim or someone else after looking at pornographic material.

3. Fifty-eight percent of the abusers pointed out pornographic pictures or articles to their victims.

4. Forty-seven percent of the victims were upset by someone, often the abuser, trying to get them to do what he or she had seen in pornographic materials. (Such materials were used as a preconditioning to abuse.)

5. In 23 percent of the cases, the abuser was influenced to act in a violent manner from viewing pornography.

6. In 14 percent of the cases, the abuser took pornographic photos of the victim or someone else. . . .

Death from Pornography

People have died as a result of pornography-related crimes. . . .

In early June of 1985, five large bags of human bones, some charred, were collected from shallow graves at a remote cabin site in Calaveras County, California, about 140 miles northeast of San Francisco.

It was alleged that Leonard Lake, 39, and Charles Chatt Ng, 24, "acted out and videotaped sexual torture fantasies." According to Calaveras County Sheriff Claud Ballard, "The best evidence we have are movies of a woman pleading with Lake and Ng to give her back her baby, and being abused and forced at gunpoint to engage in sex acts with them." It was believed that up to twenty-five men, women, and children may have been victims. . . .

The remains of a child, woman, and man were previously found on the three-acre site used by Lake. Police also found jewelry, clothes, handcuffs, and "pornographic photographs and videotapes showing scenes of sexual torture involving Lake, Ng, and women victims." Also confiscated were Lake's diaries. These detailed his daily activities since 1983, giving an account of his practice of "keeping women in captivity as sexual slaves." The torture apparently took place in a cinder-block bunker with a secret chamber, mattress, and two-way mirror.

According to Calaveras County Sheriff Claud Ballard, one of Lake's diaries had fifty pages of his philosophy "that God meant women for cooking, cleaning house and sex and when they are not in use, they should be locked up." The *San Francisco Chronicle* reported the diary had detailed scripts of up to one dozen videotapes showing the torture of victims.

The killings were thought to be linked to "fantasies of sadistic sexual domination, war games and survival." There were videotapes of women being threatened with death. Ng appears in one allegedly slashing a woman's clothing with a knife. . . .

Use of pornography has been linked to other major crimes, including those of mass murderer Ted Bundy, who was interviewed by Dr. James C. Dobson, psychologist, hours before Bundy's execution in Florida in 1989. Among other things, Bundy said:

> My experience with pornography that deals on a violent level with sexuality is that once you become addicted to it—and I look at this as a kind of addiction—I would keep looking for more potent, more explicit, more graphic kinds of materials. Until you reach the point where the pornography only goes so far. You reach that jumping-off point where you begin to wonder if maybe actually doing it will give you that which is beyond just reading about it or looking at it. . . .

In the cases cited [here], the harms from pornography were fatal to innocent victims. We believe that these and other deaths show that the risks of harm from pornography are greater than its value (which, we believe, is none).

Wives, Prostitutes, and Other Victims

We have uncovered dozens of cases in which pornography played a known role in the abuse of wives by husbands. We believe that if battered women shelters, police, doctors, social workers, attorneys, psychologists, and other professionals who work with domestic abuse victims were to ask victims whether their abuser used pornography and whether pornography played any role in their abuse, the response would be overwhelmingly affirmative. We encourage professionals to begin investigating, in an organized fashion, the relationship between pornography and the abuse of women and children.

"People have died as a result of pornography-related crimes."

Ms. P. testified at the 1983 Minneapolis hearings [on Ordinances to Add Pornography as Discrimination Against Women, Minneapolis City Council Government Operations Committee]. She said her husband read pornography like a textbook. Most of the scenes they enacted were the exact scenes he read in the magazines. Finally, they divorced. Ms. P. said:

> I could see how I was being seasoned to the use of pornography and I could see what was coming next. I could see more violence and I could see more humiliation and I knew at that point I was either going to die from it, I was going to kill

myself or I was going to leave. And I was feeling strong enough that I left. . . .

A former prostitute, Terese, referred to as Ms. Q. in the hearings report, described the connection between pornography and prostitution when she spoke on behalf of a group of women who were all former Minneapolis prostitutes at the Minneapolis hearings. Terese also testified before the Attorney General's Commission on Pornography, Chicago, July 1985.

> We were all introduced to prostitution through pornography, there were no exceptions in our group, and we were all under 18. Pornography was our textbook. We learned the tricks of the trade by men exposing us to pornography and us trying to mimic what we saw. I could not stress enough what a huge influence we feel this was. Somehow it was okay. These pictures were real men and women who appeared to be happy and consenting adults, engaged in human sexuality. . . .

We found numerous case histories of adults who were victimized by adult pornography users. For example, a 19-year-old female was offered a ride home by a 19-year-old man she knew. He took her to the country and demanded a sex act. She refused. He had piercing or stabbing magazines in his car. She was sexually assaulted by every possible means and stabbed fifty-seven times. . . .

A California man was sentenced to prison for eleven years for kidnapping two young women and sexually assaulting one. In his car, police found a gun, rope, knives, a syringe and needles, pornography magazines, and a catalog of bondage devices. A man suspected in twenty-five or more Austin, Texas, rapes took pictures of his victims during the attacks. Officers found a pornography magazine, a Polaroid camera, and a nude photo of one of his victims in his car. . . .

Helen Gualtieri, a social worker, told the Attorney General's Commission on Pornography of the abuse one of her clients suffered as a result of pornography. The client, a 29-year-old foreign woman, had accepted a mail-order marriage proposal from a man she had corresponded [with] for six years. He showed her pornographic video films and told her to perform the acts she had seen portrayed with the men. She refused to prostitute herself. He beat her for days until she escaped. . . .

People who have been used in pornography sometimes fear the future dissemination of the pornography. As one victim told the Attorney General's Commission, "I know the men who made it. I know where they are, and there is nothing I can do about it. I live knowing that any time it could surface and could be used to humiliate me and my family [and] ruin my professional life in the future. . . ." Many other witnesses told the commission that they had to seek medical and mental assistance because of injuries they attribute to pornographic materials.

These case histories of victims and perpetrators of pornography demonstrate that pornography serves as a catalyst for sexual and other physical abuse of human beings. We firmly believe that if the perpetrators had not been exposed to or involved in creating pornography, many of the victims whose stories were detailed in this viewpoint would not have been killed, raped, or otherwise abused.

Pornography Must Be Censored

by Cal Thomas

About the author: *Cal Thomas is a columnist for the* Conservative Chronicle, *a weekly newspaper of political and social opinion.*

ABC Television broadcast a special, *Men, Sex and Rape*, in May 1992 that was, as *New York Times* reviewer Walter Goodman noted, full of "pretension to virtue."

After the obligatory tabloid-television approach featuring "swelling breasts and buttocks, mostly amid the sands of Palm Beach," as Goodman summarized it, the program attempted to move to the brain for some serious discussion of a troubling subject. The approach had the moral impact of going to confession after a long-planned orgy.

First Amendment absolutists have resisted every attempt to control the huge levels of immoral effluent that have turned our society into a toxic waste dump. Then they create programs like the one broadcast on ABC in which they wring their hands and decry what they have helped to create. It would be like the tobacco industry criticizing the growing number of lung-cancer deaths.

Violence and the Media

Women are being raped in record numbers—as many as 1,871 per day if one rape victims rights group is accurate.

One does not have to be a social scientist to see a connection between these increased incidents of rape, and other acts of violence against women, and the way women are treated in the popular media. One quick look at MTV offers a sample of the diet on which many young people feed at an early age.

A new Michael Jackson video called *In the Closet* features Michael and a woman thrusting their pelvises at each other. Michael sings, "There's something about you, baby, that makes me want to give it to you."

This video is followed immediately by another called *Baby's Got Back*, in which women are shaking their behinds at the camera, various fruits and vegetables shaped like body parts are shown, and the rapper says he likes women's buttocks and feels like "sticking it" to them.

> *"Rape is linked to the tolerance and promotion of pornography."*

Pornography is worse, of course, but this stuff is what might be called beginners' material for the raping of the young American mind.

Andrea Dworkin, the feminist writer who has crusaded for tougher anti-pornography laws, wrote a profound letter to the *New York Times* in which she told of her own sexual abuse. She believes rape is linked to the tolerance and promotion of pornography and sexual images that give cultural permission for men to treat women as objects, not fellow human beings.

To the purists who will not tolerate any controls on "speech" or pictures, Dworkin wrote: "Freedom looks different when you are the one it is being practiced on. Those sexy expletives are the hate words he uses on you while he is using you." Dworkin added that men "act out pornography. They have acted it out on me." She correctly indicted men who hide behind the First Amendment so they can traffic for profit in women's misery. "They eroticize inequality in a way that materially promotes rape, battery, maiming and bondage; they make a product they know dehumanizes, degrades and exploits women; they hurt women to make the pornography, and then consumers use the pornography in assaults both verbal and physical."

For networks (or movie and magazine publishers) to claim that there is no connection, or that they are not responsible if there is a connection, between pictures and words and the brutalizing of women is a lie. Do they tell their advertisers there is no connection between consumer behavior and images of soap, cars and beer? Not if they want to sell ad space and commercial time. For advertisers, they make the opposite claim.

Images and Aggression Are Linked

Chris O'Sullivan, a social psychologist who is writing a book on group sexual assault on college campuses, sees a link between sex crimes and visual images. In a letter to the *New York Times*, he wrote: "There is a higher level of aggression, sexual and nonsexual, among those who most often expose themselves to depictions of sexual and nonsexual violence than among those who do not."

Were such a connection established, or even likely, in any other field, government would quickly move to do something about it. Kentucky Republican Sen. Mitch McConnell is trying to take a small step toward cleaning up the mainstream of some of this filth in his bill that would compensate victims of sexual assault who could link the assault to pornography. Most of the media establishment has written editorials and lobbied against the bill.

Yet, it is a bill and an idea deserving of support. Women deserve as much protection against rape as it is possible for society to offer. As Dworkin wrote: "A photograph shields rape and torture for profit. In defending pornography, as if it were speech, liberals defend the new slavers. The only fiction in pornography is the smile on the woman's face."

If rape is a terrible crime, and it is, and if there is a connection between pornography and the cultural permission it gives those already predisposed to perform these acts on women, then government has an obligation and duty to control its proliferation.

Censoring Pornography Would Reduce Rape

by Ernest van den Haag

About the author: *Ernest van den Haag, a former John M. Olin professor of jurisprudence and public policy at Fordham University in Bronx, New York, is a distinguished scholar at the Heritage Foundation, a conservative public policy think tank in Washington, D.C.*

Most trials leave no doubt that a burglary, a murder, a robbery was committed; the court must decide only whether the accused did it. With rape, however, trials often hinge on whether a crime even took place. The defendant will often insist that the sexual act occurred with the consent of the alleged victim, for if she consented no crime was committed. This defense, of course, is seldom persuasive in stranger rape: the man who jumped out of the bushes or broke into an apartment will have a hard time convincing the jury that the victim agreed to have sex. Any additional crimes committed (e.g., robbery) can provide further evidence for lack of consent. But "acquaintance rape" and "date rape" are more problematic. Consent is less unlikely, and typically there are no witnesses. Under such circumstances it is hard to find anyone guilty beyond a reasonable doubt.

Consent and Refusal

Juries have thus been reluctant to convict, even when presented with evidence that force has been used. They might blame the victim for giving the rapist opportunities or "leading him on." Yet, opportunity—or the silliness or seductive behavior of the victim—neither excludes nor excuses rape. Some legal progress has been made, particularly in the inadmissibility of the victim's sexual history. It never was relevant; a woman can be raped even if she is promiscuous or a prostitute.

But, in practice, consent and refusal are not as clear-cut as the law presumes. Genuine misunderstandings are possible; so is ambivalence. The victim may consent to sexual play but resist going all the way. She may communicate (or *make*) her decision only at the last moment. Her partner may feel that the liberties she permitted implied her consent. She may feel that she made her unwillingness clear, but that clarity may emerge only in retrospect. The idea of some feminists that anything but an explicit verbal statement must be taken as a refusal is patently absurd. Genuine willingness or unwillingness can be conveyed by non-verbal means, and is usually not hard to discern. But sometimes the man cannot be certain, because his partner is not; relationships are far more ambivalent than contracts and laws. (Of course, not even contracts and laws are always clear; otherwise there would be fewer lawsuits.)

> *"Pornography depicts women as fungible means for the gratification of sexual desire."*

Still, a woman should be able to be alone with a man without fearing that he will assume *eo ipso* that she is willing to have sex. On the other hand, a man should not have to fear that being alone with a woman will automatically expose him to a claim of rape. Yet some risk of actual or claimed rape is unavoidable, as long as people want privacy. And, without privacy, how will they find out whether they care for one another, or are attracted? The very situations that make rape and claims of rape possible are indispensable to developing intimacy.

Women as Property

In the past, rape was thought wrong for largely material reasons. The rape of a virgin radically reduced her value on the marriage market, while the rape of a wife violated the husband's property rights. Violation of the woman's will was not taken seriously; women were usually married to men they hadn't chosen. No, rape was wrong because it violated the will of parents or husbands. So seduction—sex with a consenting unmarried woman or someone else's wife—was regarded as no better than rape.

Today, rape is thought wrong because it violates the victim's right to make her own choices freely. To be sure, other crimes, such as robbery, violate the victim's will, but a rapist does not take an object, as a robber does: he takes the very intimacy the victim wishes to reserve for someone else. She is forced to submit to the use of her body to satisfy the rapist's desire to humiliate her—for, in rape, sex is a means, not an end. After all, sex is available at affordable prices to anyone who cares to buy it. Prostitutes, too, may be patronized by men who feel a need to exercise power, but at least the women volunteer, which makes the humiliation less blatant.

The wish to overpower is more central to acquaintance rape than to stranger rape. At first glance, this may seem odd. But stranger rape is committed largely by impulsive men; just as a robber takes a shortcut to obtain jewelry, the man who rapes a stranger takes a shortcut to obtain sex. Either could get what he wants by legitimate means: money can be earned, things bought. But the short-cut seems easier.

On the other hand, the man who rapes an acquaintance thinks: Here is a girl who trusts and likes me enough to invite me up or to come to my place. Why should he want to overpower her, then? Because she likes him, but not enough. The rapist finds it outrageous that she is unwilling to surrender totally. How dare she resist him? Obviously, only because she does not realize what she actually wants. Just as Karl Marx thought that workers who do not share his view of their own objective interests suffer from "false consciousness" (they do not realize that they need a Marxist dictatorship), so the rapist believes that his victim suffers from false consciousness (she thinks she does not want sex with him). The rapist feels that he must force his victim to do what is in her objective interest, as he defines it, even if she does not realize that it is. Ultimately the rape (or the revolution) will convince victims that they were wrong to resist. They will be grateful to have had the realization of their objective interest forced on them.

Most people relinquish their childish fantasies of omnipotence and irresistibility as they grow up. They may hold on to minor aspects of these fantasies, but generally become sufficiently aware of reality not to act on them. Yet some people retain undiluted an infantile refusal to acknowledge reality. Unceasing attempts to seduce, to exhibit, to be approved of, are the least harmful ways they find to support their fantasies. Rape is the most antisocial way of doing so.

Why Rape Has Increased

As sexual mores have loosened, rape has become more, not less, frequent. This is not as paradoxical as it may appear. When sex is greatly restricted by law and custom, a man's fantasies of irresistibility are not often impaired by rejections. Men do not expect non-marital, non-commercial sex. Nor is prostitution regarded as an admission of amorous incompetence, as it is now. However, when non-marital, non-commercial sex is readily available, as it is now, rejection stings. It may be perceived as a personal offense, an insult, by those who are insecure, and have compensatory fantasies of irresistibility. The rejected person feels a greater need to punish those who impair his self-image or, worse, confirm it.

> *"If the number of rapes is to be reduced, a willingness of courts to restrict pornography may be required."*

Is there nothing to be done to reduce the frequency of rapes (more than 130,000 in 1991)? It is not certain whether rape is on the rise or whether it's simply being reported more often, but either way there is too much of it.

The wish of some males to assert themselves by humiliating women by compelling sex has deep psychological roots. Pornography depicts women as fungible means for the gratification of sexual desire, implicitly denying that sex is more than the utilization of women for that purpose. Although statistical proof is hard to come by, common sense tells me that pornography encourages those predisposed to assert themselves by raping women.

Pornography has generally not been considered protected speech under the First Amendment, but courts have been reluctant to enforce anti-pornography laws. If the number of rapes is to be reduced, a willingness of courts to restrict pornography may be required. Fears that such restrictions are a slippery slope to the curtailing of political or cultural freedom are not borne out by historical experience; I know of no case where limitations on, or the banning of, pornography has led to fascism, Communism, or even censorship proper. Courts are capable of distinguishing between pornography and non-pornography, and have a compelling interest to act on their ability to do so.

Pornography Does Not Promote Violence Against Women

by Leanne Katz

About the author: *Leanne Katz is executive director of the National Coalition Against Censorship (NCAC), an alliance of artistic, professional, educational, religious, labor, and civil rights groups that works to inform the public about the dangers of censorship and about how to combat it.*

A division among feminists is intensifying over questions of social policy involving women, censorship and "pornography." Disagreements begin over what we are even discussing: the word "pornography" is not used in U.S. law, and certainly there is no common understanding of its meaning. Recently, the word has begun to be used by certain feminists as though sexually-explicit expression is inherently "subordinating" or "degrading" to women, as though these terms are themselves not subject to disagreement—or as though, even if we were to agree, the response should be, must be, suppression.

Sexually-Explicit Material

Our society contains a vast body of sexually-explicit writings and images, new and old, "high" and "low" culture, lesbian and gay and heterosexual, designed, variously, to educate, disgust, entertain, sexually arouse, shock, inspire, and much more. Texts, images and humans are all complex; even women who are close friends can disagree on whether a sexually charged movie scene is valid and important or simply titillating and exploitative; whether and how it is anti-woman, and what kinds of effects it may have. To many, it is terrifying to contemplate turning over the power of making such judgments to any group, or any government authority.

Leanne Katz, "Same Old Censorship," *CrossRoads*, March 1993, revised by the author for inclusion in the present anthology. Reprinted with permission.

In this country and others, many women's lives are deeply affected by racism, poverty, violence, economic discrimination and by sexual oppression in its innumerable manifestations. Pro-censorship feminists, personified by Andrea Dworkin and Catharine MacKinnon, argue that admirable passion and stick-toitiveness but with dubious analysis: that "pornography"—as they *very* broadly define it—is central to women's oppression, that it is action not speech, that its very existence violates women's rights and that according to their legal theory, the state, through its legislatures and courts, will give power to women to restrict and control sexually-related expression which "harms," "subordinates," "degrades" and "lies about" women. They speak and write as though all must agree (and they simultaneously revile and claim they are victimized by those who *don't* agree); as though fantasy is reality; as though we *are* what we see, and all we *see* is "porn," which is, they claim, always violence. To some, this may seem like a vision, but many women see it as a nightmare.

New Theories, Old Censorship

A large and growing number of women—especially feminists who are writers, artists, scholars, critics and intellectuals—are scornful of suggestions that censorship is the remedy for violence against women, or for discrimination against them. More and more, they see old censorship in "new" theories. They understand that suppression brings the same old efforts to control women's bodies, women's sexuality, women's lives.

In seeking new theories to remedy old injustices, those feminists who support anti-pornography campaigns choose a path—censorship—which has been often tried, and always found wanting. The censor acts on behalf of the status quo: the established religion, the established political, economic, social and sexual order. And his or her remedy for many ills is *more* control. Clearly, this is against women's interest in social change.

Moreover, every group which seeks social change needs the strongest possible system of free expression, in order to express grievances, and to speak and agitate for change. As the feminist journalist Ellen Willis has said: "When will oppressed groups learn that if you give the state enough rope it will end up around our necks?"

> *"Feminists . . . are scornful of suggestions that censorship is the remedy for violence against women."*

Pro-censorship feminists are supported—in their rhetoric and in their campaigns—by the same right-wing groups which attack art as "pornographic" if it is not heterosexual and in every other way "decent" and "moral" (attacks never opposed by pro-censorship feminists). These groups assail today, as they have in the past, every effort to change or ameliorate the conditions of women's lives. The same conservative forces, symbolized by Anthony Comstock, in the past brought us the persecution and jailing of Margaret Sanger for the "immoral" act of telling women they could decide when—or if—to have children; today, they demand the banning, especially from young people, of *Our Bodies Ourselves*, Judy Blume novels, and sex education in our schools, and even in our colleges. The neo-Puritan feminists profess a different agenda, yet welcome these allies. Together, they want to tell us what ideas, fantasies, words and images are right, for them and for each one of us.

> *"[Pro-censorship] campaigns promote the false messages that women are degraded by sex."*

Today's news in the controversy over "pornography" and censorship is that so many women are now determined to make clear that they don't want, don't need, and won't accept efforts to use law to suppress sexually-explicit expression.

During the 1991-92 session of Congress, many feminists—together with others, including major lesbian and gay groups—opposed a misnamed Pornography Victims Compensation Act. It would have permitted lawsuits against writers, artists, book and video store clerks, and filmmakers (among others!) if a plaintiff alleged that a sexual assault against her was "caused" by the assailant's exposure to a sexually-related book, or picture or recording. It was favorably reported by the Senate Judiciary Committee and adopted by the Republican Party into its platform; only the rush to adjourn prevented Congressional action.

False Messages

Feminists who oppose censorship believe pro-censorship campaigns invariably exploit sexual fears, ignorance and uncertainties, not a difficult task. The campaigns promote the false messages that women are degraded by sex, and that women's sexuality is dangerous and must be controlled.

A growing number of women are angry at claims that women can benefit from censorship. They refuse the offer of censorship in exchange for "protection" as a terrible bargain which has, in any case, never worked. Again and again, such campaigns have led to attacks on sexually-related art and literature, on education, entertainment and intellectual inquiry. Women's interests are invariably hurt, but it should be no surprise when those who are less powerful are most injured by censorship. Some years ago it would have seemed unthinkable for a Gag Rule to be imposed on medical professionals to prevent their informing women who depend upon government for their health care about abortion. And it would have seemed unthinkable as well that such a Gag Rule would be upheld by our highest court.

Leonore Tiefer, a psychologist and associate professor at Montefiore Medical Center in New York, has said she believes—"as a feminist and psychologist who specializes in research and clinical work on sexuality . . . that women are in more danger from the repression of sexually-explicit materials than from its expression."

In Tiefer's opinion, "there will be no sexuality for women at all without freely available sexual information and open talk about sexual possibilities and experience, and there will be no open sexual talk if every seedling effort is met by knee-jerk congressional defunding, and knee-jerk feminist outrage."

About arguments that "pornography causes violence against women," Judith Becker, a dissenting member of the Meese Commission, has stated: "Pornography is an insignificant factor, if any factor at all, in the development of deviant behavior."

Becker's entire research career has been devoted to studying sexual abuse and sexual violence. In 1992, she wrote: "It is essential to state that the social science research has not been designed to evaluate the relationship between exposure to pornography and the commission of sexual crimes; therefore, efforts to interpret the current data into proof of a causal link between these acts cannot be accepted."

Censorship Hurts Women

To speak out and inform the media and the public, especially women, about how censorship hurts women, a Working Group on Women, Censorship, and "Pornography" was recently formed in the National Coalition Against Censorship. It is composed of prominent feminist authors, educators, journalists, scholars from many disciplines, attorneys, and activists. They oppose the old moral guardians and the neo-Puritan feminists, both determined to police every aspect of sexual expression by or about women.

Pornography Should Not Be Censored

by Marcia Pally

About the author: Marcia Pally, a writer, lecturer, film critic, and author of Sense and Censorship: The Vanity of the Bonfires, *is co-founder of Feminists for Free Expression, a nonprofit anticensorship organization.*

Censorship in the United States today is sold as an elixir of safety. Just as the traveling salesmen of a century ago promised that their tonics would cure what ails ya', today's proponents of book banning (and movie, magazine and music banning) suggest their remedy will cure violence and social upset: Get rid of bad words, and one is rid of bad acts. This is the great soothing appeal of censorship, and one reason so many people of good intentions are lured to the bonfires.

Hate Speech and Censorship

The most frequent rallying cry is that sexual words are the root of what ails us, and so their elimination will bring an end to society's woes. Although non-sexual speech has increasingly become the target of censorship efforts—conservatives attack alleged blasphemy; liberals attack the so-called "hate speech" that they believe promotes racism, sexism, homophobia and the like—it is still sexual material that draws the fire of book-banning legislation, judicial rulings and private campaigns.

Witness: Judy Blume—the most-banned author in the United States, according to the American Library Association—is attacked for mentioning menstruation and masturbation in her novels. Playwright Holly Hughes saw her National Endowment for the Arts grant revoked because she writes frankly about female sexuality. Groups who a decade ago said they objected only to the "really gruesome horrible stuff" of hard-core pornography now launch national campaigns against such mainstream television programs as *Married . . . With Children* and

Marcia Pally, "The Soothing Appeal of Censorship," *1993 Writer's Handbook*. Reprinted with the author's permission.

Murphy Brown. These shows are attacked not for on-screen depictions of sex, but because their scripts address the secondary, but still sexually related, topics of divorce and single parenting. The TV specials *Absolute Strangers* and *Our Sons* (with Julie Andrews and Ann-Margret) were targeted for discussing abortion and AIDS, respectively. The rap band 2 Live Crew was indicted for obscene lyrics. During the [1992] presidential primaries, Republican hopeful Patrick Buchanan directed slash-and-burn ads against the experimental film *Tongues Untied*, based on the poetry of black gay men. And book banning has increased threefold since 1979, according to ALA [American Library Association] statistics. (For an excellent review of literary censorship, see Edward De Grazia's *Girls Lean Back Everywhere: The Law of Obscenity and the Assault on Genius*, published by Random House.)

Blaming Pictures, Not People

Image blaming—whether the image is created through words or graphics—provides an easy solution for society's problems: Whatever the trouble, it's the book's fault. Image blaming relies on the flattering notion that without invidious outside forces, people would be good.

The promise of benefit through the banning of sexual imagery is advanced by an odd coalition of religious ultra-rightists and right-wing feminists. Both groups propose that ridding society of sexual words and images will reduce rape, incest and battery. Right-wing feminists would add sexual harassment to the list; religious fundamentalists would add interracial sex, homosexuality, AIDS and feminism.

Even moderate liberal groups sometimes resort to image blaming. The National Coalition on Television Violence distributes a list of objectionable books that includes the words of Stephen King, Robert Ludlum, Frederick Forsyth, Mario Puzo, James Clavell, Helen MacInnes, John le Carré and Leon Uris. The coalition also objects to the animated movie *Lady and the Tramp* and the Christmas ballet *The Nutcracker Suite* for its "battle between soldiers and mice."

> *"Violence and sexism flourished for thousands of years before the printing press and camera."*

At times these political camps censure the same material, such as *Playboy* or the cassettes found on the adult shelves of video stores. They teamed up in 1985 to pass precedent-setting restrictions against sexual material in Minneapolis and Indianapolis (statutes later struck down by a female trial judge and the US Supreme Court). Today, the camps find themselves supporting a nearly identical bill before the Massachusetts state legislature. They also back the Pornography Victims' Compensation Act (PVCA) introduced in the US Senate.

The PVCA would allow victims of sexual crimes to sue the publishers, distributors, exhibitors or retailers of any book, magazine or movie that victims believe triggered the crime that harmed them. It requires no conviction of the alleged perpetrator (a rapist may leave the courtroom a free man while a bookstore owner who sold him a magazine may not) and sets no limit on the amount of money a publisher or distributor may be fined. This bill's nickname is "the Ted Bundy bill," recalling the serial killer who, when his

> *"The idea that sexual images or male arousal is degrading to women is curious."*

insanity plea was denied, switched to the defense that he'd committed his murders under pornography's sway. The bill is also called the "porn-made-me-do-it" excuse and "book banning by bankruptcy."

By any moniker, PVCA advances the argument that words and pictures about sex unleash violent desire at women's bodies (if the feminists are talking) or at the body politic (if the fundamentalists are). The cure seems simple and has the lure of peace in our time. Yet, as it targets words and graphics rather than the substantive causes of violence, PVCA bolsters none of the legal and social services that aid crime victims, such as rape crisis centers, family counseling, or special training for lawyers and police who confront domestic violence and sexual abuse. Finally, this image-causes-harm idea is mistaken because it misunderstands both sexual imagery and harm.

Don't Blame Gutenberg

The argument ignores the fact that violence and sexism flourished for thousands of years before the printing press and camera. Most of history's rapists, batterers and child abusers read no sexual material whatsoever; certainly, they saw no movies and heard no rap. Countries where no sexual material or Western music is permitted even today, like Saudi Arabia and Iran, do not boast social harmony or strong women's rights records. Teenagers manage to get pregnant without the aid of Judy Blume or rock. In their book *Intimate Matters: A History of Sexuality in America* (Harper & Row), John D'Emilio and Estelle Freedman write that up to one third of births in colonial America occurred out of wedlock or within eight months of hurried marriages. Homosexuals (considered a problem by the religious right) have lived and coupled in every society, . . . whether or not homosexual imagery is available.

In light of the historical success of violence and sexism, it is unlikely their cause lies in such Johnny-come-lately products as pornographic books and magazines.

Some image-blamers argue that commercial sexual venues have changed men's attitudes about women. They cannot mean changes from those happy pre-pornography days when women could not vote, sign contracts, retain control of earned income or custody of their children or appear in public without permission of fathers or husbands—the days when it was legal to beat one's wife with a stick and, when, to use Ann Snitow's pointed words, "rape was unreportable because it was unremarkable."

No reputable research today finds a causal link between sexual imagery and violence, family unhappiness or marital instability—including the much-misinterpreted Meese Commission on Pornography and Surgeon's General Report, issued in 1986. When the Meese Commission, ignoring its own research, recommended restrictions on sexual material, two commissioners—both women—issued a dissenting report saying, "No self-respecting investigator would accept conclusions based on such a study." One dissenter, Dr. Judith Becker, then director of the Sexual Behavior Clinic at New York State Psychiatric Institute, told the *New York Times*, "I've been working with sex offenders for 10 years and have reviewed the scientific literature, and I don't think a causal link exists between pornography and sex crimes."

Correlation studies in this country, Europe and Asia find no rise in violence with the increased availability of sexual material. The only factor correlating positively with crime is the number of men between the ages of 18 and 84 living in a given area. Studies by the University of Copenhagen show European countries that liberalized their obscenity laws in the mid-'60s saw violent sexual crime rates remain constant or *decline*. Japan, where pornography frequently relies on themes of bondage, violence and rape, saw a 45% *drop* in rape rates between 1964 and 1974 and today has one of the lowest rates of sexual violence of any country.

Blaming Images, or Women?

Some image-blamers respond to such research by making the provocative case that sexual words and images may not cause the harm, but in fact *are* the harm. By objectifying and degrading women, they are problem enough. Although purportedly radical, this review relies on traditional notions of female purity and the good-girl/bad-girl sexual double standard.

The idea that sexual images or male arousal is degrading to women is curious. To believe it, one must believe sex degrades women, that being sexual or arousing men is something good girls don't do—that only bad girls "turn men on." If we follow this reasoning, we must believe that *sexual activity is bad for women because it turns them into bad women.* This is the sexist's

> *"First it was the devil that made them do it, now it's Madonna."*

view of women; it is the batterer's excuse for battery—she deserved what she got. It excuses the batterer and promotes female shame, not feminism.

The notion that pornography objectifies women is equally curious. Those who promote it cannot mean that no woman was the object of male desire before mass-market printing. And can it be said that objectification is always an evil? Being an object of sexual desire is demeaning only if that is *all* one is. As part of life, as a piece of experience, it is a boon. No one gets dressed up on a Saturday night to be ignored. At times, one wants to be desired by total strangers, one wants to grab the attention of a room. This is quite different from wanting to be loved for all one's aspects; at times one wants the buzz of lust.

> *"Censorship has always been more problem than solution."*

What of the theory that sexual imagery teaches men that women are solely sexual objects to be used and discarded? This theory lives only in the minds of those who thought it up. All human beings have powerful, frequent, three-dimensional experiences of women being many things, beginning with one's mother. It is perverse to think that words or two-dimensional pictures, sexual or otherwise, could wipe out this reality. And yet, censors give credence to any voice that blames words or images for the actions men take.

Beneath image blaming runs a strong current of woman-blaming. Men used to get away with rape and assault using the "tight sweater" excuse. A skirt too short, a neckline too low made rape the woman's fault. Image blaming still faults the woman—if not the woman in the sweater, then the woman in the book. If not the woman on the street, then the woman on the screen, magazine or wall. This porn-made-me-do-it reasoning may be anchored by long tradition: First it was the devil that made them do it, now it's Madonna.

Identifying the Real Evils

If sexual words and graphics do not cause violence, public attention should turn to what does. Leading feminists and the US Commission on Civil Rights suggest that violence against women begins with educational and economic discrimination, including a sex-segregated labor market and devaluation of traditional "women's work." Men learn to consider women burdens, stiflers and drags on their freedom. Women in turn do not have the economic independence and access to day-care that would enable them to leave abusive settings.

To reduce violence in life, one must look at the life experiences that teach children where and how to deploy aggression. Fear and anger may always be a component of sex; men may forever be a bit angry at women, stemming from the days when mom—font of affection, food and warmth—could not, however devoted, meet all of her child's infantile needs. But how will men act on that anger?

Real-life violence is learned in the nonfantasy, three-dimensional pedagogy of family and community. In every nuance and gesture, one generation instructs the next in the sorts of contempt and violence that are acceptable and expected. However popular and convenient it is to blame two-dimensional media, research continues to show that basic values about men and women, race, religion, sex, money, work and the mores of violence are learned early, and learned at home.

The pedagogy of violence is taught in four areas. These are what we must address:

• Boy training that makes bullying and violence not only an acceptable response to fear and frustration, but a manly one—not only accepted, but expected. It teaches boys that the thrill of dominance is their due.

• Girl training that teaches girls nervous, ingratiating self-presentations that make them dismissible, easy targets for contempt and violence, and that teaches girls an overreliance on pleasing others at the expense of self-respect and authority. When a woman thinks she must be nice to others at all costs, it will cost her.

• Adjustments in work and family so that men care for newborns and children 50% of the time, making the emotional template less sexist.

• The subtle patterns of sexism taught daily in the home: not only the man who slaps his wife around, but also the man who walks away while she's still talking or who spits out "Aw, shut up."

The Allure of Activism

A question still nags: Why does image blaming feel so right? Why does banning sexual texts seem like the right solution to so many troubles? It offers the allure of activism. Sexual imagery is visible, tinged with the illicit, and books are far easier to expunge than deeply rooted injustices. Well-meaning citizens believe they can fight it, beat it and win. For feminists exhausted from fighting a sexist economy and politics and sexual violence, and for average Americans alarmed by what they perceive as rapid changes in gender, family and race relations, the "decency" movements are a comfort that allows them to feel in control.

Ironically, image blaming has the same appeal as the fantasies it assails. It provides a devil that is frightening but beatable; it pledges a happy ending. Like monster movies and pornography, image blaming is a fantasy that sells.

Would that the cure to society's troubles were a matter of eliminating bad words and pictures. Would that it were so easy. Censorship has always been more problem than solution. It purges society of books, movies and music, leaving hate, racism, sexism, poverty and violence to flourish as they did before the printing press and camera. It flatters us into thinking we have done something to improve life while we ignore what might be done.

Evidence Proves That Pornography Does Not Promote Rape

by Berl Kutchinsky

About the author: *Berl Kutchinsky is a professor at the Institute of Criminal Science at the University of Copenhagen in Denmark.*

In the war against pornography which has been raging for a quarter of a century, the idea that pornography may be the direct cause of rape was originally expressed primarily by Christian/Conservative moralist politicians and police authorities. Senator Estes Kefauver (1960) and J. Edgar Hoover (1965) in the U.S.A., and Mary Whitehouse and Lord Longford (1972) in England are well-known examples, as was the minority report of the U.S. Presidential Commission (U.S., 1970). In the academic world, among psychologists, psychiatrists, educationists, and behavioral scientists, the pornography-causes-rape theory was generally rejected, and, accordingly, this was the viewpoint expressed by official commissions dominated by these professions. Most famous among commission reports is that of the U.S. Commission on Obscenity and Pornography which had sponsored and scrutinized several reviews and empirical studies of the relationship between pornography and sex crimes, but "found no evidence . . . that exposure to explicit sexual material plays a significant role in the causation of criminal behavior." This conclusion was challenged by three members of the Commission (a Christian/Conservative minority). Nine years later it was essentially reiterated by the Committee on Obscenity and Film Censorship.

Attempts to Prove the Theory

Since the mid-1970s the Christian/Conservative fight against pornography was joined by feminist groups and authors; leading figures were Susan Brownmiller,

From Berl Kutchinsky, "Pornography and Rape: Theory and Practice." Reprinted with permission from the *International Journal of Law and Psychiatry* 14 (1991): 47-64, Pergamon Press Ltd., Oxford, England.

Laura Lederer, R. Morgan, D.E.H. Russell and Andrea Dworkin who formed alliances under the slogan: "Pornography is the theory, and rape is the practice."

The feminists' claim that a growing availability of increasingly more violent and misogynic pornography was the direct cause of increasing numbers of rapes and was a major inspiration to a new wave of research, *"Sex offenders generally reported . . . rigid conservative attitudes toward sexuality."*

mainly in the U.S.A., trying in various ways to demonstrate such a connection. Apparently these efforts have been so successful that the combined conservative Christian and feminist views of pornography now seem to be influencing legislative action in several countries (e.g., in Canada, the U.S.A., Great Britain, Norway, and Sweden). Moreover, judging from the literature, it appears to have penetrated deeply into the ranks of behavioral and social scientists.

While qualified skepticism regarding the pornography-causes-rape hypothesis has existed all along, its currency has been comparatively weak. Recently, however, a number of reviews and articles have appeared which are not only skeptical, but in fact highly critical of the new wave research on pornography and rape.

We shall first briefly review the evidence regarding the postulated causal link between pornography and rape, with an emphasis on the more recent research. We shall then present the recent criminological evidence.

Experimental Studies

The most severe point of criticism against the 1970 Report of the U.S. Commission on Obscenity and Pornography was that it had not sufficiently investigated the long term effects of aggressive pornography. One might have expected, therefore, that the new research would have taken up precisely that challenge. This, however, is not the case. On the contrary, the bulk of the new research studied effects of the shortest possible nature (typically reactions immediately following a few minutes of exposure). The reason for this is probably that the new research did not depart from the criticized Commission studies, which had in fact combined experimental laboratory elements with some field elements and at least tried to assess effects over a certain period from weeks to months, although mostly using nonviolent pornography; violent pornography was not very common in the late 1960s when research sponsored by the Commission was carried out.

The inspiration for the new research came from the laboratory experiments on the effects of nonsexual violent depictions, particularly the studies by L. Berkowitz. In the new studies the nonsexual aggressive portrayals had been replaced by depictions of sexual aggression; but these studies had also inherited the fundamental weakness of the original aggression studies, namely that both the stimulation is administered and the reactions measured under extreme laboratory conditions which are far removed from real life situations.

In a study, the short film clippings have been replaced by five feature length movies combining or juxtaposing sex with aggression against women; these films, which included *Texas Chain Saw Massacre* and *I Spit on Your Grave*, were shown to the same subjects on five consecutive days. In the earlier short term experiments, E. Donnerstein and his coworkers had shown that male subjects viewing clips from sex-aggressive films would tend to become desensitized or disinhibited in a way which appeared to facilitate aggression against a female if the subjects had been angered before watching the film, or if the models in the film appeared to enjoy being raped. In the new studies, apparent effects of desensitization and disinhibition (as measured in the reactions of the subjects to a video taped mock rape trial) were obtained through multiple viewing of such films. Although this new design removes some of the shortcomings of the earliest laboratory studies, there are still a number of basic problems when it comes to generalizing from the results of these studies to the commission of rape in real life.

Artificial Situations

First, the subjects have not themselves chosen to see these movies, let alone to see five of them in one week. When it comes to extremely violent movies, as those used in these experiments, this is no doubt an exceptional situation. Second, the subjects knew they took part in an experiment and they could hardly be completely unaware of what was expected of them; this would seem to facilitate a strong experimenter effect (i.e., subjects will tend to comply with experimenter's expectations).

"Reactions to pornography have no bearing on past or future behavior relating to coercive sex."

Third, while it does seem plausible that repeated viewing of such objectionable fiction in some persons may lead to reduced sensitivity as a result of reduced anxiety, and that this more relaxed state may carry over to, for instance, a less punitive reaction to a mock rape trial, it is still most uncertain that it would similarly carry over to real life situations, for instance influencing real jury members' reactions to a real rape trial, bystanders' reactions to a real rape situation, or—even further removed—a person's inclination to actually rape a woman. For one thing, aftereffects of media exposure appear to be short-lived; for another, in these situations, one would think, the cognitive, emotional and motivational impacts of real life would strongly overshadow whatever influence there might remain from the fiction. The apparent ease with which the insensitivity resulting from viewing these horrible films is removed through the debriefing following the experiment suggests that it is not a very powerful effect likely to turn a decent man into a monster.

Then again: perhaps many men are already half monsters, and a relatively weak influence such as the one accumulated through repeated exposure to sex-aggressive movies (or even nonaggressive pornography) is enough to push them over the line. Perhaps. Perhaps not. These experiments, when they are best, pose an intelligent question—they do not answer it.

Pornography and the Rapist—Is There an Answer?

Some believe the answer can be found in the experience, the possession, and reactions of rapists to pornography. The rationale is that if one cannot study long term effects of pornography currently, one can at least try to assess these effects through retrospective studies of the role of pornography in the history of rapists. The U.S. Commission on Obscenity and Pornography sponsored several studies of these kinds, comparing sex offenders with nonsex offenders and control groups of nonoffenders.

The results were discouraging. Sex offenders generally reported sexually repressive family backgrounds, immature and inadequate sexual histories, and rigid conservative attitudes towards sexuality. During adolescence they had had less experience with erotica than other groups. As adults, sex offenders seemed to catch up with other categories, but did not use pornography more frequently than others; and sex offenders did not differ significantly from other adults in their reported arousal or reported likelihood of engaging in sexual behavior during or following exposure to pornography.

The problems with these studies was, of course, that they had to rely on the subjects' own reports about their reactions to pornography, and they did not particularly study experience with and reactions to aggressive pornography. Both of these shortcomings were overcome by a number of researchers in the late 1970s who, applying modern sexological laboratory techniques, were able to measure erectile responses in convicted rapists and normals who were watching, listening to, or reading depictions of sexual activities including consenting as well as coercive sex. The first results seemed very promising. While normals showed greater arousal to scenes of mutually consenting sex than they did to similar scenes involving coerced sex, rapists appeared to be equally aroused by the consensual and the coerced scenes.

G.G. Abel et al. wrongly concluded from these studies that rapists actually preferred forced sex over consenting sex. This was clearly not the case. But the very finding that rapists were apparently not particularly inhibited by the coercive element in sexual encounters seemed to fit in neatly both with the results of the experimental sex-aggression research of N.M. Malamuth, Donnerstein and others and with the common sense notion that rapists, unlike other men, are not turned off sexually

> *"The rapist is not, as a rule, a sexually deviant person."*

by the victims' serious resistance to advances or her expressions of pain and agony. Unfortunately, even this finding turned out to be false. Subsequent large-scale replications have shown that among a group of rapists, arousal to forced sex was significantly lower than it was to consenting sex; moreover, the rapists did not differ in this regard from groups of ordinary men. Back to square one.

The Nature of Rape

Militant feminists might claim that these studies showed no difference between men who are convicted of rape and men who are not, simply because, as L.M.G. Clark and D.J. Lewis state, all men are "real or potential rapists." A more meaningful conclusion is that reactions to pornography have no bearing on past or future behavior

> *"Pornography relates to fantasy not action."*

relating to coercive sex—it has neither diagnostic nor prognostic value. First, this conclusion coincides with the negative results of many other attempts that have been made to construct simple tools of diagnosing or prognosing crimes and criminals. Second, it agrees with our knowledge about the nature of rape and of rapists: that rape is an extremely complex act with complicated and differing patterns of motivation which cannot be reduced to simply a matter of sexual arousal; and that the rapist is not, as a rule, a sexually deviant person who should for that reason be expected to react deviantly to pornography. Finally, this conclusion agrees with our knowledge about the nature of pornography and its relation to behaviour: pornography relates to fantasy not action.

It is not possible, then, to find a valid answer to the question of causality between pornography and rape? I believe it is—at least to the extent causality in this connection is meant to be a substantial empirical fact and not just an expression of emotional and ideological dissociation from two equally detestable phenomena. It is possible to test the necessary consequence of a substantial causal relation between rape and pornography, namely that the appearance and growing availability of increasingly hard-core pornography, including aggressive pornography, coincided with or was followed by a growth in the number of rapes. Not that the finding of such a temporal correlation in itself would be sufficient proof of a causal relation. Many social problems have grown these years without being directly related (e.g., theft and pollution). But a temporal correlation is a *necessary* condition for accepting the assumption of a causal connection. Without it, we shall have to discard this assumption.

To test the hypothesis of a substantial causal connection between pornography and rape, we shall look at the incidence of rape in four different societies where pornography, including the aggressive varieties, has become widely available. Denmark, Sweden, and West Germany are the only countries to have legalized pornography (in 1969, 1970, and 1973, respectively). In the United

States pornography has not been legalized, but is easily available at least in all major cities (in shops, arcades, "studio" theaters, and cinemas) and through mail order. In these four countries as a whole the period of rapid growth in quantity and variety of hard-core pictorial pornography was from the late 1960s to the mid-1970s, although since the late 1970s the video has increasingly become a favorite medium. A 20 year period would therefore be sufficient to trace any influence of the "porno wave" on the rape statistics. . . .

Comparing the Incidence of Rape

Although one should always be cautious when comparing crime statistics from different countries, it can safely be said that the only country in which there has been a marked increase of officially recorded incidents of rape during this period is the U.S.A. (where, on the other hand, neither of the plateaus in the mid-seventies and since 1979 is easily explained with reference to pornography). In West Germany the level has remained remarkably steady throughout the period. In Denmark and Sweden there are moderate increases from or after the mid-seventies. In both cases, it is likely that at least some of the increase is due to increased reporting and registration of rape, as a result of growing awareness of the rape problem among women as well as the police.

"Rape is an act of aggression rather than a sexual act."

As a matter of fact there are strong indications that even in the U.S.A. the increase of rape since the mid-1970s may be due to increased reporting/registration. . . .

Rape cannot be considered as an isolated social phenomenon. For a criminological appreciation of the development of reported rape over time, it is necessary to compare it at least with the development of other crimes during the same period. Since forcible rape is, by legal definition, both a violent crime and a sex crime, a comparison with nonsexual crimes of violence and with nonviolent sex crimes would seem reasonable. Such a comparison has been made for each of the four countries—to the extent accessible data permit.

Figure 1 compares the development of forcible rape with that of aggravated assault in the U.S.A. Although rape increases slightly more than assault during some of the period, the similarity between the two curves is striking. This suggests that the two developments are related and should be explained in the same terms, a suggestion which is compatible with the dominant viewpoint in most of the recent U.S. research and theory about rape (i.e., that rape is an act of aggression rather than a sexual act). That pornography should be the common explanatory factor in the development of both sexual and nonsexual violence (the latter being more than nine times as frequent and directed primarily against men) makes little sense. Moreover, the almost perfect correlation between the two developments is not a recent phenomenon.

Unfortunately it has not been possible to compare assault and rape in the U.S.A. with nonviolent sex crimes, since the UCR [Uniform Crime Report] do not include these types of offences. Such a comparison has been possible for the three other countries. The similarity of development patterns for rape and assault found in the U.S.A. is not repeated in Denmark, Sweden, and West Germany. In all three countries, assault has been rather strongly increasing during 1964-84 (in fact, at rather similar rates, all being between 225 and 300%), whereas rape has increased more modestly or, as regards West Germany, not at all.

Analyses of crime statistics not presented here suggest that the developments of nonsexual violent crimes in these countries are roughly similar to those of the overall crime patterns, which are of course strongly dominated by property crimes. Apparently, in these European countries, rape is not clearly part of either the general crime pattern or the pattern of violent crimes in particular. Rather, the developments of the violent sex crime of rape lie in between the developments of nonsexual violent crimes (assault) and those of nonviolent sexual crimes. . . .

Frequency of Aggressive Themes in Pornography

This study of the hypothesis that pornography causes rape would be incomplete without a closer look at the independent variable: pornography—more

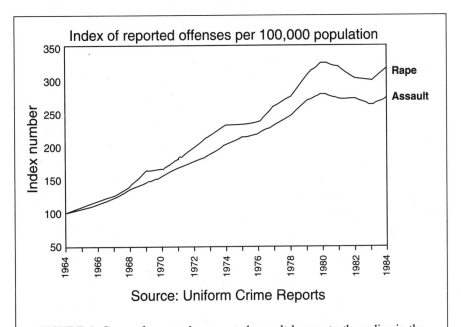

FIGURE 1. Cases of rape and aggravated assault known to the police in the U.S.A. 1964-1984. Indexes of offences per 100,000 population. Index 100: Rape = 11.2; aggravated assault = 106.2. Source: Uniform Crime Reports, various years.

precisely: violent or aggressive pornography.

As indicated earlier, it can be presumed that, in the four countries in this study, during the 20 year period in question, visual material combining explicit sex with aggression and/or explicit dominance moved from a stage of considerable scarcity to one of easy availability. Not only is aggressive/dominant pornography relatively easily available to any adult person in these countries who may want it (e.g., to be bought in shops or through mail order or viewed in movie theaters or arcades), it also appears to be available at reasonable prices and in sufficient variety so as to satisfy a steady demand for such material.

> *"Pornography constitutes a modest proportion of all entertainment mass media."*

This does not necessarily mean that aggressive pornography has become available and used in excessively large quantities relative to nonaggressive pornography or nonpornographic entertainment mass media on the whole. Both of these proportions have been grossly exaggerated by feminist writers as well as new-wave pornography researchers.

Violent Pornography

Thus, Andrea Dworkin claims—without documentation—that the pornography industry is "larger than the record and film industries combined," and describes their products in these terms: "Real women are tied up, stretched, hanged, fucked, gang-banged, whipped, beaten, and begging for more." D.E.H. Russell and L. Lederer report that "pornography usually combines some sort of violence with sex." According to K. Barry, "the most prevalent theme in pornography is one of utter contempt for women. In movie after movie women are raped, ejaculated on, urinated on, anally penetrated, beaten, and, with the advent of snuff films, murdered in an orgy of pleasure." And Susan Griffin reports that "inevitable" moments in pornography are those "in which most usually a woman, sometimes a man, often a child, is abducted by force, verbally abused, beaten, bound hand and foot and gagged, often tortured, often hung, his or her body suspended, wounded, and then murdered."

N.M. Malamuth and E. Donnerstein write—without any documentation or reference—that "some have estimated that the yearly profits from pornography exceed those of the general movie and record industries combined." And W.L. Marshall and H.E. Barbaree contend that "there have been dramatic increases in the amount of violent sex in both soft-core . . . and hard-core pornography . . . available in Western societies." Similar contentions are made in numerous places in the Meese Report. The fact is, however, that pornography constitutes a modest proportion of all entertainment mass media and that aggressive pornography constitutes only a small proportion of all pornography.

As far as Denmark is concerned, it has been estimated that even at its highest level, in 1969, the sale to the Danes of hard-core pornographic magazines of all varieties constituted no more than two percent of the total volume of entertainment magazines sold including women's magazines, family magazines, hobby magazines, comics, etc. Similarly, the amount of hard-core sadomasochist pornography produced or sold in Denmark after 1967 appears to have been "less than 2% of all available material, even when aggressive pornography was most readily to be had." There is every reason to believe that the situation is similar in other countries. Thus, the total production of pornographic magazines (including soft-core) in several countries appears to be remarkably constant relative to the population, namely about one copy per year per capita. . . .

No Evidence of Snuff Films

In his historical survey of pornographic movies, J.W. Slade points out that unlike the mainstream film culture around it, "the hard-core film . . . rejected violence almost entirely." Slade also explodes the myth of the "secret circulation of 'snuff films', i.e., reels that depict actual intercourse climaxed by the literal murder of the female:"

> To date, despite a thorough investigation by the FBI, despite a large reward posted by the publisher of the sex tabloid Screw, and despite frenzied searches by collectors of the bizarre, no authentic snuff film has come to light.

Slade's conclusions about violence in the hard-core pornographic film have been corroborated by the most careful content analysis to date of pornographic videos. A total of 150 movies rented from 43 different video outlets in the Vancouver area were analyzed along a variety of parameters by five coders (three females and two males). Among the 92 videos which were classified "triple-X," equalling what Slade—and the present author—would call "hard-core pornographic films," only 6.4% of the scenes were rated as sexually aggressive despite the fact that according to T.S. Palys, "a significant proportion of the triple-X were sampled in an effort to find the 'worst' pornography available in this area."

Sixty percent of these movies were rated as showing "positive affect" in the participating models, whereas 35% were rated as "neutral/mechanical." Only 5.3% were rated as "negative" and 0.4% as "very negative." Aggressive themes were found slightly more often in the "adult movies" (i.e., soft-core pornographic videos), but even then only 10% of the sexual depictions were perceived as "negative" or "very negative." Based on the recent concern about sexual violence in pornography

"No authentic snuff film has come to light."

which had prompted the study by the Canadian Department of Justice for the Fraser Committee on Pornography and Prostitution, Palys had expected to find a high degree of violence or degradation in the material, however,

149

what we find is largely sexually explicit material—incredibly graphic, often somewhat tasteless a celebration of a "sex is fun" mentality, but little else.

Palys concludes that as far as sexual violence is concerned, "this material has apparently decreased in frequency." However, at this point, he is arguably mistaken, for aggressive themes have never been abundant in pornography.

No Proof for Allegation

We have looked at the empirical evidence of the well-known feminist dictum: "pornography is the theory—rape is the practice." While earlier research, notably that generated by the U.S. Commission on Obscenity and Pornography (1970) had found no evidence of a causal link between pornography and rape, a new generation of behavioral scientists have, for more than a decade, made considerable effort to prove such a connection, especially as far as "aggressive pornography" is concerned.

The first part of the viewpoint examines and discusses the findings of this new research. A number of laboratory experiments have been conducted, much akin to the types of experiments developed by researchers of the effects of nonsexual media violence. As in the latter, a certain degree of increased "aggressiveness" has been found under certain circumstances, but to extrapolate from such laboratory effects to the commission of rape in real life is dubious. Studies of rapists' and nonrapists' immediate sexual reactions to presentations of pornography showed generally greater arousal to nonviolent scenes, and no difference can be found in this regard between convicted rapists, nonsexual criminals and noncriminal males.

"Pornography does not represent a blueprint for rape."

In the second part of the viewpoint an attempt was made to study the necessary precondition for a substantial causal relationship between the availability of pornography, including aggressive pornography, and rape—namely, that obviously increased availability of such material was followed by an increase in cases of reported rape. The development of rape and attempted rape during the period 1964-1984 was studied in four countries: the U.S.A., Denmark, Sweden and West Germany. In all four countries there is clear and undisputed evidence that during this period the availability of various forms of pictorial pornography including violent/dominant varieties (in the form of picture magazines, and films/videos used at home or shown in arcades or cinemas) has developed from extreme scarcity to relative abundance. If (violent) pornography causes rape, this exceptional development in the availability of (violent) pornography should definitely somehow influence the rape statistics. Since, however, the rape figures could not simply be expected to remain steady during the period in question (when it is well known that most other crimes increased considerably), the development of rape rates was compared with that of nonsexual violent offences and nonviolent sexual offences (in so far as available statistics permitted).

The results showed that in none of the countries did rape increase more than nonsexual violent crimes. This finding in itself would seem sufficient to discard the hypothesis that pornography causes rape. In fact, in three countries, Denmark, Sweden and West Germany, rape increased less than nonsexual assault, and in West Germany rape did not increase at all. There are no indications that a significant increase of actual cases of rape could hide behind these official figures; on the contrary, there are strong indications that at least some of the increase (or lack of decrease) in reported figures reflects increasing willingness of victims to report offences and of police officers to register reported offences.

Differences Between Europe and U.S.

The fact that, in Denmark, Sweden and West Germany rape increased less than nonsexual assault or not at all, suggests that, in these countries, rape is not clearly an integrated part of the general trend of violent offences. Rather, the finding that in all three countries the trend of reported rape is situated in between that of nonsexual violence and nonviolent sex crimes, with features resembling each of these curves, suggests an interpretation of this development in line with the traditional view of rape as both a violent crime and a sexual crime. In the U.S.A. on the other hand, rape and nonsexual assault follow exactly the same pattern. As we have seen, this exceptional resemblance between the two developments goes back to the 1930s. This finding is more in line with the newer suggestion that rape is essentially an act of violence rather than a sex crime.

In sum, the aggregate data on rape and other violent or sexual offences from four countries where pornography has become widely and easily available during the period we have dealt with would seem to exclude, beyond any reasonable doubt, that this availability has had any detrimental effects in the form of increased sexual violence. Especially the data from West Germany are striking since here the only increase in sexual violence takes place in the form which includes the least serious forms of sexual coercion and where there may have been increases in reporting frequency. As far as the other forms of sexual violence are concerned, the remarkable fact is that they decreased—the more so, the more serious the offence.

This finding is not so strange. Most other research data we have about pornography and rape suggest that the link between them is more than weak. And our knowledge about the contents, the uses and the users of pornography suggests that pornography does not represent a blueprint for rape, but is an aphrodisiac, that is, food for the sexual fantasy of persons—mostly males—who like to masturbate.

151

Chapter 5

How Can Violence Against Women Be Reduced?

Chapter Preface

Many of the efforts to reduce violence against women concentrate on changing society, especially society's fascination with violence. A major goal of those who work to reduce attacks against women is to abolish the glorification of violence. "In the last 30 years," charges David Gelman in *Newsweek*, "Americans have developed a culture of violence surpassing in its pervasiveness anything we experienced before." Todd Gitlin, writing on sadomasochism in the movies, notes that "movies are not alone in their delectation of ingenious ways to blow people apart. Heavy metal and rap sound vicious notes. Newspapers, local television news and syndicated crime shows, music videos, popular fiction—all fill with gore."

Many believe that this societal glorification of violence has real-world effects. "The consensus among social scientists is that very definitely there's a causal connection between exposure to violence in the media and violent behavior," says University of California professor of psychology Daniel Linz, who has spent much of his career researching the subject. And Carole Lieberman, chair of the National Coalition on Television Violence, notes that "there are close to a thousand studies on all kinds of entertainment—TV, movies, video games, war toys, comic books, music—that show a 95 percent causal link between violent entertainment and subsequent harmful behavior." For example, Lieberman believes the increase in reported rapes is connected with a trend to associate sex with violence in movies; viewers learn, she says, that it is "cool" to treat women in a violent sexual manner.

Others believe that the media do not cause violence so much as provide an accurate reflection of a violent society—one in which violent crimes increased by 500 percent from 1960 to 1990, according to the FBI, while the population increased only 41 percent. "It's a chicken-and-egg problem," says Stanford University department of communication chairman Donald F. Roberts. But whether media images are cause or mirror, most observers find disturbing such incidents as the ones Susan Faludi reported in her book *Backlash* about viewer reactions to the movie *The Accused*. The movie was based on the true story of a young woman gang-raped at a bar while a crowd of men watched and refused to intervene. Many young men watching the film, reports Faludi, "hooted and cheered the film's rape scene. And clearly," she adds, "a society in which rape rates were skyrocketing could stand some reeducation on the subject."

The authors of the following viewpoints examine a variety of options for reducing the incidence of violence against women. All of them recognize, though, that the larger goal is simply the reduction of violence against anyone.

Therapy for Couples Can Reduce Domestic Violence

by Eve Lipchik

About the author: *Eve Lipchik, a clinical social worker, is codirector of the therapy practice ICF Consultants in Milwaukee and clinical supervisor of the Milwaukee Women's Center.*

Recently, I was giving a workshop on my approach to spouse abuse—brief, solution-focused therapy—when one therapist in the audience raised her hand and asked, in tones of barely concealed outrage, how in good conscience I could go on using my profession to reinforce the oppression of women. There was muttered agreement from several others in the room, and three women walked out in a huff. Unfortunately, this response is not unusual. Often my challengers don't bother disguising their hostility, accusing me of being unethical, incompetent, and insensitive to women's safety by treating abusive couples together from a systemic point of view. I've even heard people admit that they came to my workshop to "chop off [my] head," and "crucify" me for presenting these ideas.

A Commitment to Stopping Violence

Ironically, this intense, even violent, reaction comes from trained professionals so emotionally overwrought by what they think I'm saying that they don't hear me say I'm as committed as they are to stopping abuse and violence. Many seem to believe that treating the spouses together with short-term, systemic therapy is tantamount to implicitly condoning the abuse. Therapists sensitive to gender-related issues often doubt that couples therapy for an abusive relationship is ever appropriate. They argue that systemic thinking implies that each spouse participates with mutual complementarity in the relationship, which reinforces the spurious notion that men and women have equal social and economic power either within or outside of marriage.

Eve Lipchik, "Spouse Abuse: Challenging the Party Line," *The Family Therapy Networker*, May/June 1991. Reprinted with permission.

This view has its roots in the feminist movement of the '60s, which first made the public aware of the thousands of women being criminally assaulted by their own mates. Its mission—rescuing and protecting the battered woman, helping her leave the batterer, and eventually, providing services to rehabilitate him—gradually became the implicit mandate for feminist therapists, who automatically advocated for the women, thus becoming adversaries of the men. The rationale for this therapeutic approach rested on the not unreasonable fear that the abused woman might be killed if she stayed in the relationship, and the belief that the man was probably seriously disturbed, if not psychopathic, and in need of major rehabilitation. Feminist therapists also tended to give more value to the woman's point of view to counterbalance the way society, including many mental health professionals, automatically assumed that she had provoked the abuse and was somehow to blame for it in the first place.

> *"My priority is always the prevention of further violence."*

Arrest of Abuser Is Standard

By now, this once path-breaking approach has become standard practice in the therapeutic community and has become a basic tenet of government policy as well. During the last few years, the majority of states have mandated the arrest of persons for spouse abuse, and several, including Connecticut, Colorado, New York, Texas, and Minnesota, are buttressing this judicial innovation by legislating the use of state funds to support abuser-education/treatment programs. Other states, like California, Florida, Massachusetts, and Pennsylvania, are developing legislative standards to make treatment programs eligible for state funding and court referrals. In other words, the general drift of opinion and policy has not changed much since the problem of spouse abuse was "discovered" in the late '60s. The implicit goal is to separate the spouses, rescue the woman from the abusive union, and send the abuser to state-sanctioned group punishment, treatment, education, and/or rehabilitation. Couples counseling is actively discouraged, even though there is no evidence to suggest it is less effective than other methods or leads to more recidivism. The Wisconsin Department of Health and Social Services issued a discussion paper on programs for batterers, recommending cognitive-behavioral group education and treatment programs for abusers, even while admitting that "due to the limited amount of research available and the methodological problems with the current studies, no conclusive data is available to support the effectiveness of abuser treatment."

Even more startling, the authors of the Wisconsin discussion paper tacitly admit that the approach they recommend for spouse abuse rests upon incorrect assumptions. The current paradigm—separate the spouses, save the woman, rehabilitate the man—depends upon the widespread but quite unfounded perception that abusers and their spouses are easily identifiable types of people, responsive to a single treatment formula. The authors of the paper report that neither abuser nor victim fits any predictable and identifiable profile and cite evidence to demonstrate that there are no "characteristics or psychological differences that distinguish battered women from non-battered women," and that "batterers are a heterogeneous population," requiring "different treatment methods." What is all

> *"The batterer . . . must come to recognize his complete and total responsibility for the abusive behavior."*

too clear, however, is that many couples, even after the recommended interventions, tend to repeat the cycle of violence.

Altogether, the monolithic quality of the current model, reinforced by movie and television renditions of the most brutal of wife-beaters and their terrified, helpless spouses, fails to take into account the multitude of differences in personality and experience of both victims and perpetrators, as well as the particularities of their relationships. Both husbands and wives in many of the couples I see, for example, want not only to stop the violence, but to remain together and improve their marriages. But there is very little fit between that desire and the orthodox interventions they can expect from the therapeutic and legal systems.

Unique People, Unique Problems

Just as addiction specialists have learned that there are as many patterns to drug and alcohol abuse as there are abusers, so my own case records of abusive couples reveal a heterogeneous population of individual personalities, in particular relationships, under a wide variety of circumstances. George and Sally, for example, are pillars of their community. He is a high-profile, white politician who beats his wife once or twice a year. After the last fight, when he gave her a concussion, she made the ultimatum that unless he went with her to treatment, she would take their 10-year-old son and leave.

Roger is a Native American parolee who has spent much of his life in jail. He frequently beats his girlfriend, Betsy, even though he has been through several batterers programs. His parole officer reports that they "absolutely" want to stay together.

Lawrence and his girlfriend, Linda, are a young, black couple who have been together for six years and have three children. On probation for battery, he requested couples counseling because he and his girlfriend had begun fighting again after her mother moved in. He has been through a batterers program and alcohol treatment.

Kumara and Milind are an Indian couple from Bombay. Kumara is threatening to leave because Milind is beating her and unduly restricting her freedom. His older brother interviewed and hired me to treat them, and is paying the bill, out of a sense of familial obligation in the absence of their parents, who would normally counsel the couple.

William and Denise used and sold cocaine until two months ago, when he was jailed for hitting her. This was not the first incident of physical abuse. She is divorced, with a seven-year-old son, living on alimony and child support. William wants to marry her and stay clean; she has not forgiven his battery and unfaithfulness when they were both using.

All these couples are as different from one another as any other random group of troubled couples. They have been referred for treatment by employee assistance programs, probation and parole officers, the District Attorney's office, battered women's centers, or they have come on their own initiative, either individually or together. Nonetheless, according to the conventional wisdom, I should insist on the same approach for them all—separate the spouses while referring all the men to education/treatment groups, and all the women to individual or group therapy—as if good therapy could ever be done by formula. Never mind that more than half of these couples have already gone that route one or more times without success!

In spite of its political appeal, an unchanging and orthodox treatment approach is seldom in the best interests of individual clients. And, contrary to the criticism that I am championing togetherness for couples at the expense of safety and self-determination for the women, my main goal is to prevent recidivism and help both partners find the resolution that suits them best individually and together. Helping one couple decide reasonably and calmly to separate with a mutually satisfactory sense of closure can be as successful a therapeutic outcome as improving the relationship of another couple.

A Focus on Solutions

I have found that the solution-focused approach I use, as well as systemic models in which the therapist acts as an observing part of the system—as a collaborator rather than an outside expert—have the flexibility to fit the needs of the most varied clients and situations. Rather than emphasizing the clients' defeats and failures, with which they are already too familiar, solution-focused therapists look for the exceptions to the problems—times when they have gotten along well, or resolved disagreements without violence—and reinforce clients' existing strengths and resources. Instead of feeling confirmed in their despair and punished

"Other abusive couples are clearly not ready for couples counseling, and may, indeed, be better off apart."

for their inability to get along, they begin to perceive themselves as potentially healthy and capable. This growing sense of hope fosters the motivation to change. This approach allows the therapist to drop the adversarial stance with

157

one or the other spouse and focus on the individual responsibility of both clients for the future of the relationship.

My priority is always the prevention of further violence, so my initial work with the couple is directed to finding out what must happen to assure the safety of the woman and help the batterer control himself. My first step is to meet with both partners for a joint session and then meet with each partner individually. In the individual session with the woman, I assess her safety and provide her with the necessary information she may need to protect herself. With the man, I gauge his attitude, intentions, and degree of self-control. While some people might think it more logical to do the individual sessions first, I have found that the unexpected, positive, accepting climate the couple experiences during the first joint session is a powerful deterrent to further violence. It also allows for a much more productive individual session with each partner: the men seem to deny less and be less defensive knowing I will not judge them, and the women are more open because they know their partners don't feel threatened by me. If there are any police records accompanying the referral, I let the couple know that I will formulate my own opinion of the case before reading them. I have found that this reassurance greatly reduces the couple's denial.

> *"Some couples with very rocky relationship histories turn out . . . to have surprising inner resources."*

My first, seemingly naive, question is, "Do you want the violence and controlling behavior to stop?" If one or the other answers "no" (and this has happened), couples treatment comes to a speedy conclusion, and I make recommendations for legal control, education, and/or therapy for the batterer, as well as separate treatment for the woman. True, many offenders initially lie, answering as they think the therapist wants them to. But my colleagues and I have found that respectfully accepting, rather than challenging, their answers creates a kind of self-fulfilling prophecy, and makes enough of a difference in the abuser's attitude to prevent further violence.

The Likelihood of Success

During the individual sessions, I also test the likelihood of successful couples therapy by probing each spouse's explanation for the situation—what causes the violence, how frequent and intense it is, where the responsibility lies for the conflict—and their willingness to focus on their own behavior in the relationship and how they might change. I ask them to describe good things about being together, seek out evidence of coping skills and information about what interventions may have helped them before. Finally, I try to determine whether alcohol and drug use, as well as overall physical, mental, and emotional status, are related to the fluctuations in the relationship. In no way does this approach let the batterer off the hook; he must come to recognize his complete and total responsibility for the abusive behavior, regardless of what he believes she may or may not have done to "cause" him to hit her.

In short, I do not proceed with treatment until I feel certain that the woman is safe, that the partners are more than objects of self-gratification for each other, and that there is motivation to change. There must be signs of bonding and personal caring from each, some feeling of healthy satisfaction from the relationship and a sense of responsibility for what happens next. If these qualities are missing, even though the couple reiterates that they want to stay together, I continue to see each separately, asking more questions, encouraging them to think more deeply about the relationship, what they want from it, what they are willing or unwilling to do to strengthen it, and how they imagine the future without the other. This work tends either to increase the sense of individual responsibility in each spouse for the relationship, or it clarifies the desirability of separating.

An Advocate for the Relationship

During the joint interview, I watch the couple's verbal and nonverbal interaction and ask them to come up with at least one mutual goal toward which to begin working. I always make certain that both partners know that I am open to the position of each at all times and that I am advocating for the relationship, not for the victory or defeat of one or the other. This is a steadfast position, even in the face of the potential or actual recurrence of vio-

"Sociopolitical issues must be addressed in some way in all cases."

lence. When abuse is threatened or happens again (rare, in my experience), I immediately separate the couple and take an advocacy stance with each one separately—with the woman, to help her protect herself and rethink staying in the relationship; with the man, to help him stop acting on impulse and instead weigh the consequences of his behavior. I ask the woman if she thinks it is safe to go home, where she can go if she doesn't think so, and what strategies she has to keep her partner at bay until he cools down. I ask the man what he needs to do to calm down when he feels on the verge of violence, and where he can go to get some distance from his partner, as well as the advantages of handling conflict without losing his temper. This stance allows for the resumption of couples work when the danger is past without the abuser feeling that the therapist has rejected him personally, and found him to be "the bad guy" who can no longer be trusted or expected to contribute to a renewed effort at joint therapy.

I expect the consequences of further violence to be determined by the criminal justice system. This therapeutic framework allows a dependable but flexible response to a heterogeneous assortment of violence-prone couples, and, in fact, was the basis for the different choices I made about therapy with all the cases briefly mentioned above.

George and Sally, the well-established, white, community political leader and his wife, seemed at first questionable candidates for couples therapy. George was clearly used to being in charge, wielding unquestioned authority over both his career and his family. He was defensive and belligerent in the individual session and angry with Sally for forcing him to choose be-

> *"Self-referred cases involving spouse abuse have the highest chance for success."*

tween going to therapy or seeing his marriage end. Sally, who had suffered a concussion during the last fight, wanted to stay with her husband as much for financial security and social advantage as for personal attachment, but no longer thought the benefits were worth the once- or twice-yearly beatings. Further, when the 10-year-old son came in for an individual session at my request, I found him so uncomfortable and fearful of talking about family relationships that I got practically no useful information. All this suggested that this couple might not be the best prospect for couples counseling.

On the other hand, George's attitude softened considerably when I assured him that I understood how difficult it must be for a man in his position to be pressured into therapy, and how much he really must care for his wife to subject himself to it. After testing my response to him a few more times, he broke down and cried, telling me that he had been beaten badly by his own father, and felt terrible that he was repeating the pattern with his wife and child. He said he'd had individual therapy previously to deal with his anger, but it hadn't worked. Now he seemed intensely anxious to learn how to respond differently to Sally, to give up his compulsion to control the way she lived her life.

When I asked Sally whether there were ever fights when she did not feel abused, controlled, or frightened, she realized she felt better when she waited a bit for George to cool off and he was ready to listen to her opinion. There was no alcohol or drug abuse clouding the issue of this couple's interaction, and in the joint assessment interview both agreed that they would like to learn to live together without violent fighting. Therefore, I decided to see them together as a couple on a session-to-session basis, and, if there was no change or the situation worsened, I would see Sally and the boy separately from George.

Better to Separate

Other abusive couples are clearly not ready for couples counseling, and may, indeed, be better off apart. William and Denise, the white, unmarried couple who both dealt cocaine, had been referred by a parole agent two months after William had been jailed for hitting Denise during a fight. Until that time, both had used and pushed cocaine, which had caused William to be fired from his job as a commercial artist. In the first joint session, the couple gave some evidence of a mutually satisfying relationship and set a goal of learning to listen better to each other. However, in the individual session, Denise expressed intense anger at William for his battery and chronic unfaithfulness, and, except for sex, could not recall one positive aspect of the relationship because, as she put it, "until two months ago we were always high."

William admitted he had done things to hurt Denise when he had been on drugs, but said he now wanted to stay drug-free and marry her. His only positive memories of the relationship were the times he had been able to make Denise feel good, like when he taught her to play pool and to roller skate. He did seem motivated to change, and swore that he would leave rather than hit her and go to jail again.

When I saw them for a joint session, they refused to respond to a positive focus and fought so much that I separated them to discuss safety with her and control of his anger with him. I decided against couples counseling for the time being, and offered individual therapy to both so they could decide what they wanted for themselves, as well as for the relationship.

Couples Counseling

Some couples present a more ambiguous picture. On first impression, Roger, the Native American parolee, and Betsy, his girlfriend, seemed a good bet for couples counseling. Roger's parole officer had said that the two "absolutely" wanted to stay together, Roger swore that he was committed to spending the rest of his life with his girlfriend without violence, and Betsy insisted that she, too, wanted to work on the relationship. They were able to define clear, mutual goals and describe some positive aspects of their relationship.

But certain things were troubling about this case. Roger spoke about his violence as if it were totally out of his control, something he could not help, and by implication, something for which he could not be held accountable. Betsy insisted that her only desire was to "make things better" between them, but there was something hesitant, ambivalent, and anxious about the way she spoke. Because she was unwilling to entertain any question about her absolute belief in the relationship, I focused on her safety and coping strategies in the individual session,

> *"The professionals and politicians committed to keeping women safe from abuse should encourage, rather than ignore, innovative treatment alternatives."*

and directed her to some community resources. Most disturbing, during the joint assessment, Roger exhibited sudden, inappropriate flashes of anger that subsided as quickly as they appeared. He agreed to undergo a psychiatric evaluation, and I decided to see each partner separately until I received the results and could make a further assessment.

Some couples with very rocky relationship histories turn out, upon deeper investigation, to have surprising inner resources. Lawrence and Linda, the young, black couple who had been together for six years and produced three children, had spent most of their relationship drinking heavily and fighting violently, aided and abetted by their extended families who fanned each partner's jealousy of the other. But about nine months earlier, three months after Lawrence was put on probation for battery, they had made a promise to put each other first, above all others, and not allow themselves to be manipulated into fighting. He went into a batterers program and sought treatment for alcohol abuse, and the two had gotten along beautifully ever since. That is, until six weeks before coming to see me.

At that point, Linda's mother moved in with the couple, and almost immediately filled the house with her noisy friends. This placed Linda in the position of divided loyalties between her mother and her boyfriend, who was angry and disturbed by all the commotion. But this time, when the couple fought, Lawrence left the house rather than risk losing his temper. However, his attempt to avoid violence by leaving aroused Linda's insecurity, mistrust, and jealousy. The growing tension culminated in Linda's threatening Lawrence with a knife to keep him from leaving, whereupon he moved out and said he had to end the relationship. His sister had critically wounded him with a barbecue fork several years before, and he did not want to put his life on the line again. Linda then asked her mother to leave.

> *"We must avoid forcing real people into oversimplified categories."*

In the joint session, I asked the couple how they had managed to turn their relationship around successfully for nine months after five years of fighting. They were very clear that commitment had made the difference. They agreed that their sobriety and Lawrence's decision to leave rather than fight had made their latest argument different from earlier ones. This time, it was Linda who had become violent, and Lawrence who had asked for a referral for couples counseling. This couple seemed to be a good bet for couples counseling, not only because of their tenacious desire to stay together, but also because of the positive nature of their bond and their ability to understand their own responsibility toward making their relationship work.

Different Cases

The mistake of forcing all couples in which abuse has occurred into a single mold is nowhere more obvious than in cases dealing with couples from other cultures. For example, Kumara and Milind, the couple from Bombay, were, by some American standards, an almost hopeless case of male domination and female oppression. Milind insisted that everything had been fine, and he'd had no problems with Kumara at all back in India, where she had behaved exactly as a good wife should and obeyed him as was her duty. Now, since coming to America, he said, she had developed new ideas about what they had both thought was proper in marriage. While he admitted she was still basically a good wife, he was disturbed by her recent attempts to defy his authority, which he felt justified his use of physical force against her. Kumara, on the other hand, felt that, since moving to America, her expectations for marriage had changed; she wanted some of the freedom and privileges that American wives took for granted, and had even threatened to leave the marriage.

On the other hand, both described the relationship in more positive than negative terms. They shared an interest in music and collecting art and enjoyed their sexual relationship immensely. Further, both felt that divorce would not only disgrace them in the eyes of their families and culture, but in their own eyes as well.

This couple felt enough pressure to save the marriage to be willing to compromise, and I decided to work with them together. I also suggested a batterers group for Milind as a way to learn about male/female relationships in our culture, as well as the legal ramifications of spouse abuse.

This referral to a group for Milind is consistent with my belief that sociopolitical issues must be addressed in some way in all cases. I would like to see everyone in a violent relationship attend an educational group (separate for men and women) which addresses gender issues, social injustices, the legal rights of women and consequences for offenders, regardless of whatever other interventions are made. Nevertheless, I believe that it is better to keep therapy and education separate since it takes considerable skill to know how and when to address sociopolitical issues without damaging the cooperative relationship with both partners.

As with all therapy, self-referred cases involving spouse abuse have the highest chance for success. Couples who come voluntarily to solution-focused therapy report the same rate of satisfaction for both partners a year after therapy as other voluntary clients—about 80 to 85 percent. For couples legally mandated to treatment, the success rate is about 65 percent. There is less attrition and fewer no-shows among mandated cases referred by a District Attorney (these cases usually involve abuse that is less chronic) than among the couples sent by parole and probation boards. My approach to assessing and treating couples who want to stay together, or get back together, is just one example of an alternative to the monolithic approach which is being standardized throughout the country. The professionals and politicians committed to keeping women safe from abuse should encourage, rather than ignore, innovative treatment alternatives that address the full range of relationships in which abuse takes place. We must avoid forcing real people into oversimplified categories and expand therapeutic options in confronting a mental health problem that was ignored for too long.

Physicians Must Act to Reduce Domestic Violence

by Antonia C. Novello et al.

About the author: *Antonia C. Novello was surgeon general of the U.S. Public Health Service from 1990 to 1993.*

Domestic violence is an extensive, pervading, and entrenched problem in the United States. It is an outrage to women and the entire American family.

Health care providers must take an active, vigorous role in identifying this serious recurrent public health problem. This is not just a "minor dispute" between spouses or loved ones. It is a violation of our criminal laws and a callous disregard for human life. If we do not help to break the cycle of abuse, it will reflect itself in the next generation.

Statistics on Abuse

Estimates suggest that at least 2 to 4 million women each year are physically abused. Six out of every 10 married couples have experienced violence at some time during their marriage, according to one survey. Domestic violence may touch as many as one fourth of all American families.

One study found violence to be the second leading cause of injuries to women, and the leading cause of injuries to women ages 15 through 44 years. That study, conducted for a 1-year period by the Philadelphia Injury Prevention Program, examined injuries to women resulting in emergency department visits or death.

The authors found that falls were reported to be the leading cause of death overall, and that rates of falls were highest among young women 25 through 34 years of age. Such high rates of falls among young women should make health care providers suspicious that some of these so-called "fall injuries" are actually sustained in beatings—after all, other studies have determined that fall injuries are highest in the elderly, not in able-bodied women.

Antonia C. Novello et al., "From the Surgeon General, U.S. Public Health Service," *JAMA*, June 17, 1992. Reprinted with permission.

Violence often occurs at the hands of people the victim knows well. According to the Uniform Crime Report of the Federal Bureau of Investigation (FBI), 30% of women killed in the United States die at the hands of a husband or boyfriend. In 1990, more than 800 women were killed by their husbands; 400 more were killed by their boyfriends.

In 1990, the National Crime Survey estimated that, for the years 1979 through 1987, at least 626,000 violent victimizations of women were committed by husbands or boyfriends each year.

Prevention of the abuse of women must not focus solely on legal marriages; to do so will miss abuse that occurs during dating, abuse that happens in nontraditional relationships, and abuse that happens in relationships that have been terminated through separation and divorce. For example, one study conducted in Atlanta found that more than one fifth of intimate violence incidents involved prior or estranged partners, and more than one fifth involved nonspousal partners.

Defying Prediction

What is the profile of the abuser? Unfortunately, the causes of abuse are complex and sometimes defy prediction. Yet, in many cases the perpetrator is a male intimate, often one who feels threatened or alienated in some way. Alcohol and/or illegal drug use are often involved, and guns and other weapons are frequently present.

Pregnancy does not exempt women from being abused. From 4% to 8% of women going to prenatal clinics were abused during pregnancy. Patterns of abuse seem to vary. For some women, battering begins or is exacerbated during pregnancy, whereas, for others, it stops altogether.

Sadly, domestic violence may be underreported. Many women fail to report acts of violence. Often there are strong social or familial pressures to abstain from reporting, not to mention fear of reprisal, or denial.

One essential solution is for physicians to increase their awareness. More than half of the victims of assaults by intimates are seriously injured. At least 25% report receiving medical care. One in 10 is treated in a hospital or emergency department. It is estimated that 35% of women who visit hospital emergency departments are there for symptoms of ongoing abuse. Unfortunately, as few as 5% of the victims of domestic violence are so identified.

"There are chances for physicians to intervene before domestic violence reaches life-threatening levels."

We must recognize not only that abuse is common, but that it escalates in severity within relationships. This means that there are chances for physicians to intervene before domestic violence reaches life-threatening levels. As a profession, we have not produced a sterling record of success in this area. We must overcome our own denial and apathy.

It is known that if women are asked about violence directly and routinely, in a way that isn't threatening, they will discuss their abuse, particularly if they feel safe and if they feel the health care provider really wants to know. Therefore, we should ask about psychological or physical abuse in the home in order to make referrals to appropriate agencies or to professional counselors.

"Women must be able to live their lives free from violence."

We must also work with other health care professionals, community leaders, and government officials to standardize protocols to screen trauma patients in the hospital emergency department. This technique has been found to substantially increase the ability of health care personnel to correctly identify battered women. I commend the Joint Commission on the Accreditation of Health Care Organizations for recently passing accreditation standards for the care of abuse victims.

In addition, the Public Health Service (PHS) has developed a framework for actions to deal with domestic violence, one that involves developing guidelines to assist communities in implementing programs aimed at preventing violence, and aiding communities to design and implement multifaceted community violence prevention programs. The PHS is also conducting scientific research to evaluate specific preventive interventions. The PHS is also training staff, community leaders, and health professionals in violence prevention.

Physicians Must Lead the Community

Finally, physicians must step forward and help establish broad-based community coalitions to enhance awareness of domestic violence. We must assume the leadership role that is incumbent on us as professionals and compassionate citizens of this country.

As health professionals, we must make every effort to end domestic violence. Women must be able to live their lives free from violence, both inside and outside the home. Our awareness, our intolerance of violence, and our active intervention can greatly diminish the license for domestic abuse. As professionals, we can make a remarkable difference.

Churches Must Work to Reduce Violence Against Women

by Christine E. Gudorf

About the author: *Christine E. Gudorf is a theology professor at Xavier University in Cincinnati, and the author of* Victimization: Examining Christian Complicity.

Have you ever heard a sermon on sexual violence—or heard the church include rape, child incest, sexual harassment, child sexual abuse, or conjugal battery in the litany of sins to be avoided?

Most people never have, though these sins are common. Everyone has a relative, friend, co-worker, or neighbor who has been sexually victimized, whether we know it or not.

Every grade-school class, even in parochial schools, contains: one or two sexually abused children, some children who have seen daddy hit mommy, very often a girl incestuously abused by her father or stepfather—as well as other children destined for rape, sexual harassment, conjugal battery, and other forms of sexual violence.

These things do not just happen to public-school kids, non-Christians, poor people, members of the working class, or racial minorities, as one may like to think. Sexual violence occurs in all religions, races, and economic classes. Yet the church has been long silent about the problem of sexual violence.

The Problem: The Biblical Context Itself

In the fall of 1992 the National Conference of Catholic Bishops broke its silence on sexual violence by releasing a pastoral statement on conjugal violence, "When I Call for Help: Domestic Violence against Women." With this state-

Christine E. Gudorf, "Sexual Violence: It's Sinful to Remain Silent." Reprinted with permission from *Salt* magazine, May 1993, published by Claretian Publications, 205 W. Monroe St., Chicago, IL 60606.

167

ment, the bishops finally respond to the many requests to them to address conjugal battery, which they acknowledge is only one aspect of the larger problem of sexual violence.

For the most part, the bishops' statement offers appropriate and useful guidance for pastoral and school staffs, for abused women, and for batterers themselves. It is an excellent start—with one exception.

When the bishops turn to the church's response to conjugal battery, they say, "As a church, one of the most worrying aspects of the abuse practiced against women is the use of biblical texts, taken out of context, to support abusive behavior. Counselors report that both abused women and their batterers use scripture passages to justify their behavior."

The bishops go on to say, "As bishops we condemn the use of the Bible to condone abusive behavior. A correct reading of the Scriptures leads people to a relationship based on mutuality and love."

What the bishops fail to acknowledge is the extent to which the church—its bishops, pastors, and teachers—are responsible for this misuse of scripture. It is not accidental that victims and abusers use the Bible to justify their behavior.

The bishops' implication—that only by reading biblical passages "out of context" could one use them to support abuse—is not fully honest. While the bishops are right in saying that the example of Jesus in the gospels stands over against sexual violence and abuse, both the Old Testament and the epistles of the New Testament can be (and have been) used by the church itself in ways that lay the groundwork for sexual violence and abuse.

Mutuality

Take a look at the epistles of the New Testament, for example. Their insistence on the headship of the husband in the family, on the submission of the wife, on the obedience of children, on the duty of fathers to keep order in the home, and on the need for women to keep silent in church all work directly against the bishops' claim that a correct reading of scripture leads people to relationships based on mutuality and love.

Where is mutuality in the passage of 1 Corinthians 11, which proclaims, "the head of every man is Christ, the head of every woman is her husband, and the head of Christ is God"?

"Sexual violence occurs in all religions, races, and economic classes."

In the Old Testament, men own their wives and children. They have the right to sell them into slavery, even the right to decide whether they live or die. The stories of Abraham preparing to sacrifice Isaac (Gen. 22), of Abraham exiling Hagar and Ishmael into the desert to die (Gen. 21), and of Jepthah sacrificing his only child to keep his vow (Judg. 11) are all portrayed as being in accordance with God's will and plan. Lot offers his daughters (Gen. 19)—and the Levite his concubine (Judg. 19)—to two separate, violent mobs threatening harm to male visitors. In neither story is this behavior censured or punished; rather, it is supported by the action of the stories.

The law that gives these characters this power lists no limits on the power of husbands and fathers. The section of the Mosaic Law on incest (Lev. 18:6-18), for example, forbids a man to have sexual congress with his parents, sisters, grand-daughters, aunts, sisters-in-law, or daughters-in-law—but does nothing to ban sexual relations with his own children, whom he owned. Like most of the Old Testament, the command regarding incest understands sexual rights as primarily based in male ownership and not in respect for personal dignity and rights.

The Problem of Patriarchy

The problem with sex in scripture is not taking texts "out of context," as the bishops propose. The problem is the biblical context itself, which is permeated by patriarchy. Patriarchy is the normal biblical ground; those stories and state-ments in scripture that rise above the prevailing patriarchal sexism are wonder-ful but exceptional.

The church's failure to point out the moral inadequacy of much of scrip-ture regarding sexuality allows scrip-tural sexism to retain authority. None of the bishops' recommendations in "When I Call For Help" point to the need to teach scripture in ways that make clear that biblical sexism is sin-ful and not normative.

> *"The church's silence about the problem of sexual violence . . . sends a cruel, untrue message . . . that [victims] do not belong in the church."*

The bishops' suggestion that (a) educators and catechists use teachings and texts free of sexual stereotyping and that (b) they use inclusive language in liturgy, "as authorized," fail to mention biblical texts. And, even if these sugges-tions *were* to cover Bible texts, their application would simply exclude offen-sive texts. Exclusion does not deal with the central issue—the necessity of teaching that not all biblical texts are directly revelatory.

What needs to be taught is that the revelatory capacity of some biblical texts rests in their falsity and moral offensiveness. That is: even biblical communities of faith had blind spots—misunderstanding God's will in areas such as sexual-ity—and should serve to alert us to our own capacity for misunderstanding God.

Look at Abraham, for example. This is a man who, out of love for his wife, Sarah, resisted his own culture's pressure to either put Sarah aside because of her barrenness or take a second wife. Nevertheless, Abraham still succumbs to exercising his male cultural prerogative when it comes to exiling Hagar and Ishmael into the wilderness of Beersheba. If Abraham is unable to overcome the limitations of his culture, then we also should beware the power that cultural sexism exerts over us.

The church's silence about the problem of sexual violence—and its failure to teach scripture in ways that prevent it from becoming a support for that violence—sends a cruel, untrue message to victims of sexual violence: a message that they do not belong in the church, that such things do not happen to church members.

> *"We need to teach that sexual activity both requires mutual consent and must intend mutual pleasure."*

So, victims of sexual violence frequently drop out of the church. They feel unworthy, that they no longer belong, that church people could not possibly understand. The church, which should embody God's comfort and support to victims, actually isolates victims and increases their suffering.

And the suffering involved in sexual violence far exceeds the dead bodies, the broken bones and lacerations, the momentary pain and terror. Subsequent self-destructive attitudes and behavior are frequent, including drug and alcohol abuse, dangerously indiscriminate sex, and depression leading to suicide.

Research shows that victims of sexual violence, especially child-incest victims, often become victims of sexual violence in later life. The most common explanation is that they have learned to value themselves so little—and understand abuse as so ordinary and inescapable—that they fail to implement ordinary measures of self-protection. Most common among sexual-abuse victims is an inability, often lifelong, to trust others enough to develop close, intimate relationships. Victims of sexual violence frequently need months—sometimes years—of struggling, aided by therapy, to reclaim control of their lives.

Major Changes That Are Necessary

Ending church silence on sexual violence entails not only comforting victims, but also preventing sexual violence. If the church is to be effective in comforting victims and in preventing sexual violence, it must undertake some major changes in its life and teaching. Six of the most central of these changes are:

1. Validate the dignity and equality of women. This entails rejecting images of women as dependent, as being appropriately classed with children. It means rejecting the notion that women are natural victims who need men's protection and guidance.

This effort will involve critical attention to those biblical stories in which women or children are subordinate, are the property of men, or both. It will also mean some serious attention directed to why certain New Testament injunctions—such as those ordering women to keep silent in church, demanding them to cover their hair, and offering them salvation through childbearing—are not authoritative.

But the theological tradition of the church is just as problematic as the Bible. Christians need to hear the church formally reject the hatred, fear, and suspicion of women that runs through the theological tradition of the church up to the present.

Understanding women in terms of their reproductive differences from men—not in terms of the rationality they share with men—and the consequent tendency to understand women

> *"It is much easier to blame innocent victims than to live honestly in a sinful world."*

as more carnal, and therefore more sinful, laid the ground for the clerical tendency to treat and teach women as sinful seductresses, as symbols of evil. Women have been equated with the very temptations from which celibates—and all men—must be protected. Such attitudes are closely related to sexual violence against women. . . .

Only large numbers of women in leadership roles in church and society can effectively teach the dignity and worth of women.

2. Humanize the image of men. Similarly, the church does not discourage sexual violence when it presents men as aggressive, insensitive, and incapable of nurture.

Papal insistence on sexual complementarity has had tremendous effects on traditional piety. That teaching of sexual complementarity consists of two parts: depicting women as gentle, compassionate nurturers who maintain a family refuge amid a harsh and inhumane world; and portraying men as rational, aggressive, insensitive, and unrelational workers and providers for the family.

The tendency to attribute headship to men providers and parenting to nurturing mothers, whose nurturing is understood as "irreplaceable" in the family, is profound.

It is also dysfunctional, in that real communication—much less intimate bonding and mutuality—is impossible between men and women who do not have shared traits and values. Furthermore, contrary to the implication of papal teaching, these complementary stereotypes are not natural or inevitable, but learned.

Societies exist in which men are not aggressive and dominant, societies in which women are not the exclusive nurturers—societies that are much less violent than ours, societies in which sexual violence is virtually unknown.

Male/Female Roles

If men and women are to grow out of the all-too-common roles of female victim and male aggressor, men need to be depicted as capable of nurture and women as capable of rational and responsible leadership. Training girls to play with dolls and baby-sit—and boys to play football, cut grass, and sell lemonade—sets society up for exclusively male instrumental roles and exclusively female nurturing, supportive roles.

One basic demand is to re-eroticize male nurturance. As Beverly Harrison and Carter Heyward have pointed out, our society has eroticized male-dominant/female-submissive interactions. Thus, virtually everyone—men and women alike—sees male nurturance as wimpy, as behavior that is less than manly. In other words: however much I may want my husband and sons to be able to nurture, when they *do*, I will need to be reassured of their masculinity by a show of dominance in another area. This is one reason why far too many women are attracted, time after time, to violent and abusive men: many men and women have learned that the exercise of domination—even when violent— is erotic.

A New View of Jesus

The church must help us break this pattern. One necessary piece is for the church to take a lead in replacing the model of Jesus that is currently at work: replacing a gentle-but-asexual Jesus with a Jesus who is more masculine, more powerful, less masochistic, but still gentle and nurturing.

This re-imaging of Jesus and the eroticizing of masculine nurturance should be linked to teaching ministry as nurturing service, not rule. The church needs to offer and encourage training programs in cooperative decision-making for both men and women.

> *"Sexual orientation is not chosen and therefore cannot be sinful."*

All parish decision-making should be examined regularly to assess the degree of integration, cooperation, and collaboration between the sexes. In fact, programs that help spouses learn cooperative models of decision-making or that help parents interact more cooperatively and less autocratically with children would be of great help in younger parishes. Every parish needs to periodically examine its interactions—between the laity and the clergy, within the lay parish organizations themselves—to determine their adequacy.

3. Sexuality, especially the sacramentality of marital sex, must be explicitly taught in the church. The church has been so long preoccupied with the moral dangers in sex that it has failed to teach the laity to understand the grace that spouses can derive from their sexual life. That grace offers strength and sustenance in dark times.

When sharing sexual pleasure in marriage reminds the spouses of their love for each other, of the history and still-enduring strength of that love, it acts as grace that carries them through the ordinary and the extraordinary sufferings and disasters in human life.

If the church had done a better job of teaching how marriage is sacramental—and how central sexual pleasure in marriage is to the spiritual life and growth that characterizes the vocation of marriage—the sinfulness of sexual violence would be much clearer than it presently is. For in the context of sacramental sex—sex that deepens intimacy, strengthens the bond between the partners, and makes love expand to include even more persons—sexual violence is obviously monstrous, repellant, and impossible to justify.

We need to teach that sexual activity both requires mutual consent and must intend mutual pleasure. We need to teach that mutual pleasure in the presence of trust and commitment creates and deepens intimacy and bonding.

> *"Too often victims are made to feel like offenders so that others can feel safe."*

The sacramentality of marital sex depends upon its being mutually pleasurable. Such pleasure acts as a reward to both partners for risking openness and vulnerability, for giving themselves to each other without reservation. Their shared pleasure becomes a bond between them and creates a space in which physical intimacy encourages emotional and spiritual intimacy as well.

The absence of consent, however, makes sex violent. The absence of mutuality in pleasure, even *with* consent, robs sex of its sacramental symbolism, making it vulnerable to abuse.

4. Address sexual violence openly, without blaming victims or defending sexual offenders. Victims need to hear that the rapist, the batterer, the harasser, and the abuser sinned. Most victims have become so accustomed to hearing that they "asked for" the punch, the rape, the violation of their body, that they feel guilt and shame and are ready to share the blame—if not take all the blame.

Guilt and Shame

This guilt and shame often prevents them from feeling God's love and support. It makes healing much more difficult and prevents some people from healing at all. Victims of sexual violence need to hear that fixing a bad dinner, jogging alone, accepting a date, going to a bar, or even talking back or attempting to leave a relationship are never justification for sexual violence.

Too often victims are made to feel like offenders so that others can feel safe. I do not like to fear that my husband could hit me, that my children could be abused, that my sisters are at risk of rape or battery.

I can feel safe—and feel more sure of the safety of those I love—if the woman who got raped was stupid enough to leave her door unlocked and the woman who got battered back-talked and the child who got abused comes from a trashy family in which others have been abused.

If all the victims were complicit in their own victimization, then I, and those I love who are not complicit, are not at risk. It is much easier to blame innocent victims than to live honestly in a sinful world, where even the innocent are at risk. We in the church need to deal openly with the reality of sexual violence. We need to resist the strong temptation to blame the victims. We are at risk, all of us. That is the nature of sin: it frequently punishes the innocent.

At the same time, people—but especially Christians—have a discomfort with conflict, with division, which often leads us to push for premature forgiveness as the path to community or family reconciliation. Premature forgiveness is always done at the expense of both the victim and the offender.

Forgiveness is premature when the offender is not contrite, not repentant. When the offender is not sure that he or she is an offender, does not know exactly what he or she did wrong, and is not yet ready to ask sincere forgiveness of the victim, it is not appropriate for anyone to demand that the victim forgive and be reconciled with the offender.

To do so is unjust to victims in two ways: it puts them at risk of being victimized again by the same offender, and it leaves victims no one to blame—to be angry at—but themselves.

Premature forgiveness also fails to support the offender in reaching true contrition and thus increases the risk of continuing to sin. Especially in families, there is often pressure for spouses and children to forgive their offenders in order that reconciliation occur. But without repentance by the offender, there should be no reconciliation.

Eventually, victims reach a point in the healing process where they put their victimization behind them in order to be fully healed and go on with their lives. But that "forgetting" is not reconciliation, and should not be. Some reconciliations may only take place on Judgment Day—and some, perhaps, not even then.

The Church Community Must Help

5. Make local resources for sexual victims well-known in your church. Pastors, lay ministers, and teachers should all know local support groups for victims and for offenders. Churches should keep a file of references to therapists who work with victims of sexual violence and of medical, criminal-justice, social-service, and other agencies that offer support.

Churches should also have some idea of the adequacy of these persons and agencies and should never see referrals as exhausting church responsibility to minister to victims.

In many places, for example, shelters for battered women and children are not only full but able to accommodate only half or less of those who request shelter. The church community needs to accompany victims who appeal for help—throughout not only the period of crisis, but throughout the recovery as well.

> *"Our loving, compassionate God did not create anyone . . . to be victims."*

There are still great variations in the degree of training and sensitivity displayed by police and hospital personnel to victims of sexual violence. The quality of therapy offered to these victims differs as well.

A responsible referral is one in which: (a) the church has checked that the persons or organizations they turn to for referrals will treat victims with dignity, will take seriously the great injury done to them, and will encourage them to begin the healing process toward full recovery; and (b) there is pastoral contact throughout the recovery period.

6. Forcefully condemn violence against gays and lesbians and affirm their basic human rights. Make it clear that sexual orientation is not chosen and therefore cannot be sinful—and that God alone has the right to judge the justice of each of us. Dispel the common myths about homosexuality. Make explicit the connections between homophobia and sexual violence in general.

Homosexuality is perhaps the sexual issue on which it is clearest that the church has been the chief support of injustice, persecution, and discrimination. Christianity is still the most common legitimator of homophobia in this nation and in much of the world.

Where guilt is greatest, so should responsibility be.

In the Catholic Church today the scandals around priest pedophilia are aggravating inherited homophobia. Tragically, the scandals only serve to mistakenly confirm for many that homosexuals are child molesters.

The bishops were inexcusably long in admitting the problem of pedophilia and implementing guidelines for dealing with it. If the failure of many diocesan newspapers to print pedophilia stories—sometimes even after local, daily papers have run them—has lowered the trust level of many laypeople, then so have the details of irresponsible transfers of priests, the people cover-ups, and the pay-offs that often accompany pedophilia incidents.

The bishops know that a great many of their priests are homosexually oriented, as does the laity. The bishops therefore have a responsibility to protect the church's ministry, as well as to defend victims of violent prejudice, by teaching what is well proven: that homosexuals are no more likely—and even slightly *less* likely—to molest or seduce children and adolescents than are heterosexuals.

The overwhelming majority of children who are sexually molested are molested by heterosexuals, and that minority molested by homosexuals is smaller than the proportion of homosexuals in the population. . . .

Our loving, compassionate God did not create anyone—not women or children, not gays or lesbians—to be victims. Nor did God create a class of victimizers. It is a cop-out to blame God or human nature for our collective unwillingness to resocialize our society, for our unwillingness to encourage more just and cooperative interactions and less violent, sexual ones.

Jesus called his followers to participate in a discipleship based on equality and a leadership based on service. This call should prevail in all areas of life, including sexuality.

Reducing Societal Violence Will Reduce Violence Against Women

by Victoria Mikesell Mather

About the author: *Victoria Mikesell Mather is an associate professor of law at St. Mary's University School of Law in San Antonio, Texas.*

During the 1970's, public attention in the United States and Great Britain was drawn to the problem of the battered and abused spouse. People gradually became aware that the fairy tale story of romance, of meeting your prince and living happily ever after was exactly the opposite experience for large numbers of women, including many members of the upper economic and social classes.

In the late 1970's and early 1980's, the attention of the legal and psychological community specifically focused on the issue of the battered woman who killed her abuser, arguably in self defense. At least twenty appellate court cases decided during 1989-1990 involved a battered woman who killed her abuser. During the period 1987-1989, four books were published on this subject: *Terrifying Love*, by Lenore E. Walker; *Justifiable Homicide*, by Cynthia K. Gillespie; *When Battered Women Kill*, by Angela Browne; and *Battered Women Who Kill*, by Charles Patrick Ewing.

Reducing Violence

Most of the writing by legal and other scholars in the area tends to focus on the end result: What do we do with the batterer who abuses his mate, and what do we do with the battered woman who has killed her abuser? Some of the earlier scholarly efforts dealt with attitudes and institutional policies of police, prosecutors, judges, social workers, juries, and the general public in dealing with battered women and abusive men. Substantial changes in many of these

From Victoria Mikesell Mather, "A Scary Tale: Battered Women Who Kill Their Abusers," 18 *Ohio Northern University Law Review* 601 (1992). Reprinted with permission.

policies and attitudes have resulted. However, the focus remains on cleaning up the mess after the situation is out of control, perhaps even after someone is dead, rather than on preventing the abuse in the first place. This is a far more difficult problem to grapple with, since it is not capable of resolution by a change in a legal test or standard of proof, or even by mere enforcement of existing laws.

> *"The battered women's movement is a feminist cause and has long been identified as such."*

This focus on the end result tends to be true of the feminist scholarship in this area. The battered woman's movement is a feminist cause and has long been identified as such. This makes sense, since it is basically a woman's issue in that it disproportionately affects women and, indirectly, children, and that it was not treated as a serious or important problem until very recently. However, it is interesting that most of the literature in this area focuses almost exclusively on the male-female dichotomy in law and society and virtually ignores the pervasive effect of violence. Violence, I think, is the other half of the equation. In fact, some studies show that women may be abusive to men almost as often as men are abusive to women, although the physical consequences of abuse tend to be less severe for men than for women. Also, women tend to physically abuse their children more than men.

All four books (the Ewing book is somewhat distinctive) take a feminist, or at least revisionist, approach in their recommendations for the legal system in dealing with battered women. . . . In general, it is my view that although the feminist or revisionist approach is useful, it is only one facet of what we should be evaluating when we deal with family violence issues. . . .

Fighting Violence with Violence

In recent years there has been a lot of attention focused on the specific issue of the battered woman, and the battered woman who eventually fights violence with violence. This is with good reason, since it is a widespread, serious problem for our society. [Many] authors . . . struggle with notions of male dominance, experiment with legal tests, and manipulate the instruments of law enforcement in an attempt to figure out exactly what to do with, and for, these people in abusive relationships. However, as the authors themselves sometimes indicate, the problem is so much deeper in our culture that these issues just scratch the surface.

In our society, violence is almost completely acceptable as entertainment in a wide variety of situations (e.g., sports, television, movies) and as an appropriate form of punishment both within and outside of the criminal justice system. Weapons are commonly found in our homes. In fact, in many cases where a battered woman kills her abuser, she does so with a gun that she finds or is readily accessible to her.

Studies tend to show that violence has a spillover effect. Repeated exposure to violence in the media can lead to a more casual or jaundiced attitude toward violence in real life. The authors of one study on spousal abuse in the military found the abuse encountered was more severe and frequent than what was found in comparable civilian relationships. The authors hypothesize that the "military effect, a term meaning the total impact of the military indoctrination/ socialization experience . . . legitimizes a pervasive sense (and expectation) of violence." The authors even found some evidence of a spillover violent effect into the community where military bases dominated the area.

As Richard Gelles and Murray Straus, two prolific writers in the area of domestic violence, point out, violence is essentially a political question, not a legal one. Why are people violent? Why are parents, spouses, and children abusive towards their own family members? Gelles and Straus say it is because society lets them. Individuals are violent and abusive because they can be. We as a society decide what is an acceptable level of violence and what is an acceptable level of interference with individual privacy. We as a society decide what is "deviant" violence. As a result, the question is political, an issue of public policy. The answers to what is an acceptable or appropriate level of violence vary across economic, racial, social, professional and religious, as well as sexual, lines.

Attitudes Toward Parental Violence

When dealing with the problem of child abuse, the question shifts the debate from issues of family privacy to more general, but still important, questions of what societal consensus is and should be on our tolerance of parental violence towards children. Gelles and Straus give the example of Sweden's ban on the spanking of children. Sweden only changed its criminal code, not its penal code, so there is no punishment for parents who spank their children. However, the authors point out that the purpose of the law is to demonstrate a moral objection to certain kinds of conduct and that it is enforced by internal and social, not necessarily legal, controls. Sweden also prohibits corporal punishment in schools, has abolished capital punishment, and strictly controls television and movie violence, particularly for children. This attitude is in stark contrast to the American view, where a large majority of those surveyed in one study believed that parents have not just the legal right, but the moral obligation to spank or slap their children.

> *"In our society, violence is almost completely acceptable as entertainment."*

Many feminists would agree with Gelles and Straus in principle, but they believe the political view is almost entirely shaped by gender-related discrimination, both past and present. In the eyes of many, feminism is a seamless web where all issues affecting women are related by concepts of male dominance and female oppression in our culture. As a result, the feminists tend to distrust a "political" (male-dominated) solution to what they see as an inherently feminist problem of male violence against women. Personally, although I can see the vital feminist component of this issue, I tend to believe the problem is a combination of societal attitudes about women *and* attitudes about violence.

> *"Repeated exposure to violence in the media can lead to a more casual or jaundiced attitude toward violence in real life."*

Aren't these concepts related? Certainly. However, I tend to agree with authors like Gelles and Straus who point out that the focus should be on the vulnerability of the victims of violence, and that this vulnerability is not exclusively linked to sexism in the system, legal or social. We need to change the way we view women, and the way we treat women. Part of that change will in fact be accomplished through the revision of legal rules, consciousness-raising, and education. But the sea of change will have to come about through deeper, tougher, and more fundamental revision of our thoughts about violence.

Many American liberal thinkers become very threatened when we talk about changing fundamental attitudes about something as subjective as violence. The very idea seems to tread on traditional civil liberties because it smacks of censorship, big brother, or thought control. The debate about control of pornography is a good example of this type of fear. This is where feminist thought and scholarship can come back into play. Feminism asks the key question—civil liberties for whom? Civil liberties should be a part of everyone's rights, including children, the old, the infirm, as well as women, to be free of violence and terror in their own homes, particularly from members of their own families. Any sort of protection of the right of a parent, a man, or a stronger person to abuse another human being because of a "privacy" interest is abhorrent. If we try to protect such rights, it should make us question our values.

Methods of Reducing Violence

On the other hand, the change in society need not, and probably should not, come exclusively from strictly legal sanctions, which are a form of violence in themselves. We, as a society, could do many things, both within and outside of the legal system, to reduce the amount and severity of violence and abuse in the culture. Some progress has been made in the area of family violence in the past several years. For example, mandatory reporting requirements for suspected cases of child abuse appear to have increased public awareness of the problem. There is some evidence that quick, no-nonsense intervention and arrest in spousal abuse cases decreases further incidents of abuse. Other, more general, proposed actions include: Abolition of capital punishment, elimination of corporal punishment from the school system, strict gun control legislation, and regulation of violent toys and television programming for children. Another alternative that exists is to boycott violent films, plays, sports, or other forms of "entertainment." A variety of educational programs could be conducted through public school systems or through church and community organizations. Possible topics include parenting, dealing with stress in relationships, marriage, and conflict resolution. Alcohol and drug information, education, and counseling could include more information on the connection between the use of drugs and possible violent behavior. More ambitious plans might call for a complete prohibition of corporal punishment, or any act that physically hurts or intends to hurt any person, not just a child.

Sexual Equality Prevents Violence

In the broadest sense, researchers seem to agree that family violence would decrease in many quarters if society would work on several general issues. To return to part of the feminist agenda, researchers have found both child and spousal abuse to be more common in male dominant families. This is attributed to the fact that the man, as head of the family, may feel that he has the definitive word in all decisions. If the man, as head of the family, does not get the final word, he may use force as the last resort. Straus and another researcher, Christine Smith, state: "One cannot emphasize too strongly the preventative value of sexual equality, both within and outside the family." One of the most interesting conclusions of Gelles and Straus' research on family violence is that women who are housewives are more violent toward their children than women who work outside the home. The authors hypothesize that working mothers spend less time with their children and therefore are less at risk for abusive conduct. Straus and Gelles also believe that employment outside the home gives women more status, power, and control within the family structure.

Researchers also mention the importance of poverty programs. Families in stress tend to have higher levels of violent behavior. If employment opportunities, health care and other support are available, it is believed that stress, and hopefully the resulting violence, can be reduced.

In my Family Law class, we cover the notions of punishment versus child abuse. I usually tell the class about the Swedish idea of spanking as an improper form of punishment. The typical reaction is either one of incredulity or of amusement. Class members sometimes become angry when I discuss some other proposals

"We as a society should decide what is 'deviant' violence."

for controlling exposure to violence and to instruments of violence. I do not mean to pick on the students, but I think their attitude is typical of the kind of prejudice that advocates of non-violence encounter. This opinion emerges from an educated, comparatively young, and relatively open-minded group of people.

In summary, I believe the feminist approach is not the ultimate solution to the problem of family violence. Although the feminist view has done a valuable service in opening our collective eyes and making us aware of the hidden problem of spousal abuse and of helping many women who were and are in truly desperate situations, I do not think it goes far enough. Prevention is the key, and this will affect both men and women. Sexism in the family, in the social system, and in the legal system must go, but so must violence.

Creating a Just Economy Will Reduce Violence Against Women

by Patricia Horn

About the author: *Patricia Horn is an editor of* Dollars & Sense, *a progressive monthly economics magazine.*

Fleeing a boyfriend in San Francisco who had almost choked her to death, Susan arrived at her brother's apartment in Boston with $15. She left behind friends and, equally important, her job.

"I was terrified," Susan recalls. "If I had said 'I am leaving you,' he would have beat the shit out of me."

Kathy, 52, another battered woman, also lost her job because of a husband who battered her. She had worked as a dispatcher at an alarm company for eight years. Her husband, who had beaten her for several years, pressured her to leave her job. When she wouldn't, he harassed her and her co-workers so frequently with obscene phone calls she finally decided to leave because she couldn't take the pressure and embarrassment.

"They were very good to me, but what could they do?" says Kathy about her employer and co-workers. "They needed those lines open."

Consequences of Domestic Abuse

Susan and Kathy are just two of the millions of women who suffer the devastating economic, as well as physical and psychological, consequences of domestic abuse. Many Americans wonder why women stay in abusive relationships, and why those that leave for a while often return. One reason—frequently ignored by governments, law enforcement agencies, and therapists seeking solutions to woman battering—is that women often cannot afford to support them-

Patricia Horn, "Beating Back the Revolution," *Dollars & Sense*, December 1992. Reprinted with permission. *Dollars & Sense* is a progressive economics magazine published ten times a year. First-year subscriptions cost $16.95 and may be ordered by writing *Dollars & Sense*, One Summer St., Somerville, MA 02143, or by calling 617-628-2025.

selves and their children. For them, choosing safety is choosing poverty.

The current recession and over a decade of social spending cuts have further narrowed battered women's options. Supporting a family on two incomes can be difficult enough. But with women segregated into low-paying occupations and paid less than men, with affordable housing and child care still rare, and with unemployment high, supporting a family on their own may seem impossible. Instead of wondering why battered women don't leave, we should be surprised that so many do.

> *"Husbands, partners, and boyfriends batter three to four million women a year."*

"I am in awe of women who leave," says Lisbeth Wolf, executive director of Women Advocates in Minnesota, who has worked with battered women for 20 years. "It is so much harder than 20 years ago."

Power, Control, and Economic Distress

Statistics vary on the extent of domestic violence, and few comprehensive national surveys of its incidence have been conducted. The FBI calls battering one of the nation's most underreported crimes, since many women are still reluctant to admit to abuse. The most widely held estimate is that husbands, partners, and boyfriends batter three to four million women a year.

These women come from all races, educational levels, and types of family background. They are lawyers, mothers on welfare, computer programmers, and carpenters. They live in mansions in East Hampton, New York; in poverty-ridden *colonias* in south Texas; and in suburbs of Portland, Oregon. They are white, Latina, black, and Asian.

"Violence is not greater in poor communities," says Dr. Lisa Dodson, a public health expert who's worked with battered women. "But the options to get away are a lot less. Money buys safety."

Battering is not only a punch or a slap. It is any of a range of actions—physical, emotional, sexual, and financial—designed to assert a man's power and control over a wife, lover, or girlfriend. A man may hit, kick, rape, hammer, and throw "his woman." He may not allow her to do paid work. He may put her on an allowance and then withhold the money. He may isolate her from family and friends, limit her sleep, and tell her how and what to cook. And he may accuse her of imaginary sins and berate her for them until she believes herself worthless.

Staying in a battering relationship is hell for the woman, but leaving may kill her. A batterer is most dangerous when the woman leaves. In a spate of domestic abuse murders in Massachusetts, many of the women killed had just left their batterers or had taken out a restraining order. In general, 75% of battered women who are killed lose their lives after separation. Many stay in abusive relationships because they quite reasonably fear severe injury or death if they attempt to leave.

Sociologists and other researchers are still exploring the causes of battering. Most agree that the unequal power men hold in U.S. society is a root cause. Men learn when young that women need not be treated as their equals at home, at school, or in the workplace. Battering, according to the National Woman Abuse Prevention Project, is the extreme expression of the will to continue this domination. Physical domination, in particular, works for men, and, not surprisingly, a woman often obeys a man who beats her. Until recently, these men suffered few consequences for their actions.

Economic distress, such as that caused by unemployment, can also trigger violence, say University of Rhode Island sociologist Richard Gelles and his longtime collaborator Murray Straus, director of the Center on Family Violence at the University of New Hampshire. In two national surveys they conducted in 1975 and 1985, they found that men who are unemployed or working only part time are at least twice as likely to beat their partners as those employed full time.

If a man has lost his job, his social identity, [and] his income, [has] become dependent on [his wife], can't find a job, can't get a source of income, he will be at a greater risk to be violent, says Gelles.

> *"Violence is not greater in poor communities, but the options to get away are a lot less. Money buys safety."*

In Massachusetts, reports of domestic abuse have soared as the economy has sunk. Since announcements of layoffs became daily news, calls to battered women's hot lines, requests by victims for restraining orders, and reported murders of women (and family) by their husbands/fathers/partners have all markedly increased. The frequency of such murders in Massachusetts climbed from once every 22 days in 1989 to once every 8 days in 1992.

Florida women faced a similar upsurge in domestic abuse in the wake of Hurricane Andrew. After Andrew tore through south Florida ruining homes and businesses, calls to Miami's Domestic Violence Hot Line more than doubled, the *New York Times* reported, and requests for police protection rose in a Dade County Circuit Court from fewer than 10 a day to about 20 a day.

Why Women Stay

More women stay in battering relationships when unemployment is high and the economy sour because they then have fewer options for survival. "They know it takes longer to find a job, and they know there are no housing subsidies, affordable child care, or job training," explains Bonnie McFarlane, executive director of the Support Committee for Battered Women. "'If I leave, I will be homeless.' We hear that all the time."

One out of every three homeless individuals identifies domestic violence as the reason for his or her homelessness, according to a 1989 statewide study of Pennsylvania homeless shelters by that state's Coalition on Homelessness and the Institute on Policy Studies at Temple University. A similar study by the Philadelphia Health Management Corporation found that 43% of the families, almost all of which were headed by women, in the city's homeless shelters had sought shelter because of domestic violence.

Leaving a batterer also means trying to make it in an economy that is particularly unfriendly to single women—especially those with children, those who are older, or those who have not worked in a few years. Women earn less income—only 60% of a man's average annual income. The median annual full-time earnings of a white male are close to $29,000, of a white woman about $19,000, of a black woman just over $17,000, and of a Latina woman only about $6,000.

A Lower Living Standard

When a woman leaves her abuser, she usually takes along her children, whom she must then support—usually on significantly less than the couple earned. In the first year after divorce, a woman's standard of living typically drops substantially, while a man's improves. And women's jobs are less likely to offer adequate health care coverage for either the woman or her family. Women are twice as likely as men to have limited health-care coverage and high co-payments and deductibles. In addition, if a woman wants to move to a different apartment, she must have the substantial savings needed to pay the first and last month's rent, plus a security deposit.

For a middle-class or affluent woman with a job and her own bank account, leaving usually does not mean poverty; but it does generally mean a substantial decrease in her standard of living. But even a wealthy woman will start out poor if her batterer has had total control of family finances.

"In most situations, both of you are trying to keep up the bills. So you know you can't afford to live with you and your kids out there alone," says Sarah, who stayed in an abusive relationship with her daughter's father because she was not working. "What do I do? What can I do?" She eventually left when the abuse began to harm her daughter emotionally.

More than half of all battered women do try to leave: Estimates run from 50-90%. Straus and other researchers, such as sociologist Ed Gondolph, have found that the amount of economic resources available to a battered woman is the best predictor of whether she will permanently separate from her abuser. If a woman has a job that can support her and her children, and has transportation, child-support payments, and other financial resources, she is

> *"Economic distress, such as that caused by unemployment, can trigger violence."*

more likely to make a final break. "If I had daughters," cautions Wolf of Women Advocates in Minnesota, "I would make sure they got a career."

But many women do not have a career other than homemaking. They must

> *"Leaving a batterer also means trying to make it in an economy that is particularly unfriendly to single women."*

rely either on jobs that pay poorly or on welfare. So, many victims return home. "We see women who leave two, three or four months down the road, are facing years on welfare and living in a condemned building with no financial hope or future," says Andrea Mullin, executive director of battered women's services in Lebanon County, Pennsylvania, a rural area where many women do not finish high school. "If the batterer is doing the 'I'm sorry, I'll never do it again, I'll get counseling' routine, [returning] starts to look like a source of hope."

Living in Shelters

Kathy, the dispatcher, lived at a battered women's shelter for more than six months. She was lucky: Most shelters can only allow women to stay for up to eight weeks. From her years of abuse, she has suffered nerve damage, has had to have her spleen removed, and may face additional surgery. She had left her husband several times before, but came back each time because she loved him and believed "I had nowhere else to go." She is currently trying to recover physically and piece her life back together.

Although Kathy enjoyed working, she can no longer work at all because of her many emotional and physical scars. Many battered women face similar difficulties.

Domestic abuse costs women, employers, and the U.S. economy a great deal. A woman's job performance often suffers because of her fear, lack of sleep, and injuries. The Department of Justice estimated that in 1981 domestic abuse cost the nation 175,500 lost days of paid work, probably a low estimate. And battering brings significantly increased health-care and insurance costs, which are passed on to all of us. A 1985 study showed that battering accounts for 20% of all medical visits by women and 30% of those to emergency rooms.

Obstacles

A battered woman who does choose to leave faces more obstacles to achieving economic independence than do women who separate from non-abusive partners. If instead of taking out a restraining order, she flees her home, she usually leaves everything behind. "I didn't stay and pack everything," says Sarah, who now lives in a shelter with her daughter. "I waited until I knew it was a safe time—it was 3:00 am. You don't stick around and wonder 'What am I going to lose?' You just go."

Abandoned batterers often decide to wage financial warfare. If a man's first action isn't to kill his former partner, it is often to empty their joint bank accounts. In addition, "he will drag every divorce, every custody, every separation, and every property disagreement through the courts to cost her as much as he possibly can in legal fees," reports Mullin. "He will take all the money he can, he will destroy the furniture, he will sabotage the house, he will have the electricity cut off, he will do anything he can to make it financially difficult or impossible for her to stay away from him."

For instance, when Kathy was in the hospital, she took out a court order on her husband requiring him to leave their apartment and stay away from her. He did leave—taking everything with him, including all her clothes and furniture. And because only his name was on their Section Eight lease, he also stole her right to their federally subsidized apartment, which would have allowed her to live on her own. This subsidy would have pegged Kathy's rent at only 30% of her income.

Seeking and ensuring the arrival of child support payments in full is another difficult task for battered women. "I've had one [a child support order] since 1984," says Sarah Buel, a former battered woman and now an assistant district attorney specializing in domestic abuse for Norfolk County in Massachusetts. "But, I can't collect a dime. The federal government tells us that $18 billion is owed by absent parents in child support. So what do we want battered women to do? They don't have access to the lawyers that can even get them the initial child support order." Moreover, workers in battered women's shelters report that many of their clients choose not to seek alimony or child support in order to avoid dealing with their abuser and giving the father some custody rights.

> *"Women must have the economic resources they need to leave men who beat them."*

Economic Warfare

Society offers little help to the victims of economic warfare. In the last 20 years, federal and state governments have scaled back their social support programs: welfare, general assistance, disability payments, housing assistance, affordable housing projects, job training, and education assistance. At the same time, the costs of housing, tuition, and child care have risen faster than the general rate of inflation.

"There were far more safety nets when I left than there are today," says Buel. "In 1977, when I left, I was able to leave and get on welfare. Through a CETA program, I got a job in a legal services office. I was also able to get Section Eight housing assistance—which has virtually been eliminated by the Reagan and Bush administrations—and I was able to get Title 20 day-care assistance."

Chapter 5

Battering women is not new. The familiar phrase "rule of thumb" originated in a U.S. modification of English common law. It allowed a husband the right to whip his wife, provided he used a switch no thicker than his thumb. Until the 1970s, spouse abuse continued as an unacknowledged problem in the United States. Society considered what happened within the confines of a family's home a private matter.

The women's movement changed that. As women gathered in the late 1960s to discuss their histories and concerns, they slowly began speaking about the violence in their own homes.

In the next 20 years, the battered women's movement organized and dramatically changed the public response to the once taboo subject. In the early 1970s, no battered women's shelters existed; today over 1,400 exist, along with many hot lines and safe-home networks offering a haven and advice to millions of women.

The battered women's movement has forced other changes as well. Because all 50 states now identify domestic violence as a criminal act, women can seek civil protection through the courts. In addition, police more often arrest batterers, instead of simply taking them out for a "cool down" walk. And doctors who used to ignore signs of abuse are being urged by their profession and by the government to discuss abuse with women patients. Many states and the federal government earmark funds, though far too little, for battered women's services.

But these efforts will not eliminate battering. The 1,400 shelters simply cannot serve the 3,000 counties in the United States. Hence they must turn away thousands of women each year, 11,000 in Pennsylvania alone, a state with one of the best funded networks in the country. And eight weeks at a shelter is far too little time for a woman to turn her life around. So, complete funding of shelters, hot lines, and networks would help enormously. Battered women say that these services are the most effective of any available services they contact.

But more funding for services can't provide women affordable housing, health care, and child care, a job that pays an adequate wage, and assurance that their child support payment or alimony check will arrive in the mail every week. It also can't fund adequate police protection so women won't have to escape from their own homes.

Social and Economic Roots

To stop the beating, we must destroy its deep social and economic roots. Making batterers pay a price will prevent some violence, but it will not end battering. Women must also have the economic resources they need to leave men who beat them. And that will take a strong commitment from society to establish a just economy. It will also take men and women learning to live as equals in a world that must become far less addicted to violence as the means to an end.

Human Rights Measures Can Reduce Violence Against Women

by Jane Roberts Chapman

About the author: *Jane Roberts Chapman is the editor of* Response to the Victimization of Women and Children *and a prominent authority on violence against women and other aspects of gender bias. Founder and director of the Center for Women Policy Studies, a nonprofit public interest organization, she has also worked as an economist with the U.S. Department of Labor and as an independent consultant on laws and public policies related to violence against women.*

There is widespread violence against women around the world, based on considerations of their sex alone. There is also a high degree of official and social tolerance of violence against women. This widespread violence and tolerance of it constitute a major human rights problem which has been largely ignored or unacknowledged as a human rights issue. The situation exists in part because of official propensities to, at best, conceive the problem as a series of individual complaints and, at worst, to tolerate it as the rightful consequences of being female. Violence against women is an ancient story recounted in art, literature, and personal accounts, but not in history books. The modern chapter of this story concerns its transformation into a public issue, first national and now global.

A Global Problem

Since 1985, a movement has been under way to move women onto the world's human rights agenda. Because violence against women is global, has severe short- and long-term effects, and is partly a result of official actions or bias, it is an essential element of that agenda.

The thrust of this viewpoint is not to argue whether violence against women

Jane Roberts Chapman, "Violence Against Women as a Violation of Human Rights." Reprinted by permission from *Social Justice*, vol. 17, no. 2, Summer 1990.

constitutes a human rights abuse. The incidence, severity, and universality of such violence have been sufficiently documented. When bodily and psychic harm of an extreme nature is done to millions of people around the globe, and the factor that puts them at risk for maltreatment is their gender, who are we kidding? Of course there is a human rights problem. The purpose of this viewpoint is, rather, to present three aspects of the efforts to eradicate violence against women which have been used locally and nationally, and to examine their potential in the recently developing effort to incorporate the problem into the agenda of the international human rights community. These three aspects are: legal reform, an interdisciplinary conception of the problem and its remedies, and locally based initiatives.

Extent and Severity of Violence

All evidence suggests that violence against women is universal, occurring in all cultures and countries. A study of 90 cultures around the world found family violence in almost all of them, with violence against women the most prevalent form of family violence.

Data on the incidence of violence against women is complex and piecemeal, and has not been collected according to a single international standard. What data there are, however, consistently show high levels of violence by men against women. A United Nations [U.N.] study, *Violence against Women in the Family*, concludes that women, in great numbers around the world, are murdered, assaulted, sexually abused, threatened, and humiliated within their own homes and that this behavior does not seem to be considered unusual or uncommon. The very absence of national data on crimes against a group that represents over half the global population is in itself telling, because despite all indicators of magnitude and seriousness, the problem remains to a large degree unacknowledged and unaddressed internationally.

Major surveys of the incidence of violence against women have been done for the United States, the United Kingdom, and Canada. Fewer are available for developing countries, but they are increasingly being undertaken. A study by the Papua New Guinea Law Reform Commission found that up to 67% of women suffered marital violence. Police statistics are considered to represent only the tip of the iceberg, but they show that violence against women, from assaults to homicide, represent a significant source of crime all over the world. Homicide statistics in the United States and all other countries show that large numbers of murder victims are women killed by husbands or boyfriends. One statistic hints at the magnitude of violence against

> *"Violence against women is an ancient story recounted in art, literature, and personal accounts, but not in history books."*

women: a study in Peru found that 70% of *all crimes* reported to police are of women being beaten by their partners.

Identifying the multiplicity of forms of violence against women suggests the universality of the problem. Such violence takes a great many forms around the world, reflecting cultural and social differences. The following list, which includes some (but by no means all) forms of violence against women, is an indication of the variety and the severity of abuse: battering, rape, incest, suttee, foot binding, infibulation, clitoridectomy, dowry death, selective malnourishment, emotional abuse, bride burning, child sexual abuse, female infanticide, daughter neglect, gang rape, date rape, forced boxing, forced prostitution, international sexual trafficking and slavery, homicide, sexual harassment, sexual degradation, party rape, circumcision, child prostitution, widow abuse, violent pornography, child pornography, human sacrifice, mutilation as discipline (i.e., cutting off noses or hands).

Many would argue that these are not separate problems but parts of a single problem rooted in the structure of society. Wife beating, for example, is not a family problem or caused by an individual psychosis but, instead, reflects the unequal distribution of power between the sexes. Thus wife beating, far from being a rupture in the social order, is, in fact, "an affirmation of a particular social order," [according to L. Lerman in *The Harvard Women's Law Journal*, 1984]. When viewed in this conceptual framework of structural inequality, the commonality of the various forms of violence emerges.

> *"Violence against women . . . represents a significant source of crime all over the world."*

Sexual violence is a widespread and severe form of the abuse of women. Many women experience fear of rape, and this threat is claimed to keep some women from more openly protesting their oppression. Violence is used as a form of control against women who break social norms. In one chilling example, in Bangladesh there is a growing practice of men throwing acid on women who break *purdah* [the traditional seclusion of women from public view].

Legal Systems Are Part of the Problem

Rape is generally considered to be a crime, but legal systems in some countries are part of the problem. Jail guards, police, hospital aides, etc., rape the women under their supervision. Eighty percent of refugees are women and children. Considerable abuse is incurred by them, including rape by guards. In the China Sea, over 2,400 women on refugee boats have been raped by pirates.

Social surgery refers to sexual mutilation that is done for social rather than medical reasons. It has severe short- and long-term effects and, even though widely outlawed, is no less common now than it was 10 years ago. It affects over 70 million women in Africa alone.

Sexual exploitation. Extensive poverty among women makes them vulnerable to sexual exploitation, including prostitution. Prostitution is not controlled by the women who participate in it but by others, with violence and coercion permeating the system. International trafficking in women (the transport, exchange, and sale of humans) is extensive, and takes several forms:

> *"Wife beating . . . reflects the unequal distribution of power between the sexes."*

1. Female prostitutes are sent to another country and have no say in the move;

2. Girl children are sold into prostitution by their families (who may believe they are selling the child into domestic service); and

3. Poor women are recruited under false pretenses (such as a marriage bureau or the promise of jobs in domestic service).

Dowry abuse refers to abuse of a woman by her husband and his family, often to the point of death or suicide, and has been described as a particularly serious problem in India where it is estimated that a dowry death occurs every 12 hours. Although India has outlawed the custom of dowry in order to reduce such abuse, the practice has continued and even the apprehension and punishment of perpetrators of bride burning has proved difficult. A study by Indian researcher C.L. Kundu (1990) reported on the link between dowry abuse and suicide.

The Human Rights Concept

Violence can be more easily carried out against women because of their lower social, economic, and legal status. Women make up over half the world's population and perform two-thirds of its work, but receive one-tenth of its income and own less than one one-hundredth of its property. Not only are women denied equality but they are also often denied personal dignity as a result of violations of their physical and mental autonomy.

The majority of the world's poor are women. The poverty of women and their inability to participate fully in development are linked to the violence against them. Violence and abuse are factors in keeping women from functioning independently in the world. Women are prone to multiple disabilities in economic activity—wage discrimination, legal constraints, and poor access to education. Untold millions of women (far more than men), according to the U.N., suffer from malnutrition and anemia. These factors severely compromise their ability to function effectively and put them at continuing risk for exploitation and abuse. Taken as a whole, the law and practice which exploit women's labor and deal with women as chattel have been referred to as a form of "structural violence" by the Joint U.N. Information Committee/Non-Governmental Organization Programme Group on Women, 1988.

Scholars and activists alike have argued for the incorporation of violence against women, as a human rights infraction, into existing international conventions and standards. The applicability of human rights machinery to the abuse of and violence against women was first seriously addressed internationally at the U.N. Mid-Decade Conference on Women held in Copenhagen in 1980. The conference found that "domestic violence was a complex problem and constituted an intolerable offense to the dignity of human beings." Five years later, the U.N. Conference on Women, held in Nairobi, included a recommendation on violence against women in its final report:

> Violence against women exists in various forms in everyday life in all societies. Women are beaten, mutilated, burned and sexually abused and raped. Such violence is a major obstacle to the achievement of peace and the other objectives of the Decade and should be given special attention. Women victims of violence should be given particular attention and comprehensive assistance. To this end, legal measures should be formulated to prevent violence and to assist women victims. National machinery should be established in order to deal with the question of violence against women within the family and society. Preventive policies should be elaborated, and institutionalized forms of assistance to women victims provided (*Report of the World Conference*, 1985: para 258).

The international community has manifested concern for the human rights of women in a number of other meetings, including the Seventh Congress on the Prevention of Crime and the Treatment of Offenders held in Milan in 1985 which adopted Resolution 6

"Eighty percent of refugees are women and children."

on the fair treatment of women by criminal justice systems. In November 1985, the General Assembly of the U.N. adopted Resolution 40/36, a domestic violence provision which called for strong multidisciplinary measures to deal with the problem as well as the reform of justice systems to eliminate bias.

Gender-Based Violence

The Universal Declaration of Human Rights, the first and overarching U.N. document on human rights, makes explicit references to equality for women, not only in its "Preamble" but also in several Articles. It does not, however, identify gender-based violence as a distinct problem.

The international instrument considered most central to the concerns of women is the Convention on the Elimination of All Forms of Discrimination against Women. It forbids discrimination in a number of specified areas, including political and public life, employment, education, health, marriage, and family. Although it does not include a specific provision on violence, several provisions in effect provide sanctions for violence directed at women. Furthermore, the U.N. Committee on Discrimination against Women (CEDAW), whose purpose is to implement the Convention, resolved at its Annual Session in Vienna in 1989 that violence was clearly an item for its agenda.

One hundred and one countries have ratified this U.N. convention; the United States is not among them. Although a number of U.N. conventions are relevant to the human rights of women, the convention on women, according to the chair of CEDAW, has the greatest potential for "making the human rights machinery effective for women."

The international movement to secure human rights for abused women is small, but growing, and incorporates several distinct features of national movements: a focus on reform of the law, increasing consideration of interdisciplinary approaches, and strong links with locally based activist projects.

The Law and Violence Against Women

The U.S. social change movement on behalf of abused women is entering its third decade. From the outset, it has been important to raise public consciousness about the significance and severity of maltreatment of women. The ultimate goal has been to put the issue of legal reform on national and local agendas. In the United States, state and local law enforcement and judicial systems did not—and often still do not—adequately protect female victims. Violence against women was seldom considered to be criminal activity, and, therefore, not the responsibility of law enforcement or the judiciary. A woman beaten by her husband was involved in a "domestic dispute," a gang-raped student had "asked for it."

Thus, it has been a priority with activists and concerned practitioners and policymakers to have legal institutions treat violence done to women as criminal behavior. A significant approach taken in the United States has been to press the system, at every level, to consider violence against women as a criminal offense, regardless of the relationship between victim and perpetrator. That is, a person who assaults another person should be arrested and appropriately charged, prosecuted, and sentenced even if married to, domiciled with, or known socially to the victim.

"Violence and abuse are factors in keeping women from functioning independently in the world."

But the law is a double-edged sword for women. On the one hand, it is essential to criminalize the violence; otherwise it continues, grows, and impairs women in their efforts to achieve equality and independent lives. On the other hand, legal systems around the world are themselves a source of mistreatment of women, ranging from biased treatment to outright abuse.

Nowhere in the world do women enjoy the same legal or constitutional rights as men. In most countries, there are several legal avenues theoretically available to women who have experienced violence: through domestic law (divorce or separation); through civil suits; and through criminal law. In a number of countries other law reforms have been added specifically for wife abuse. Unfortu-

"The law is a double-edged sword for women."

nately, having "good" laws on the books does not, in and of itself, guarantee a solution. Laws must be properly enforced throughout the criminal justice and judicial systems.

Reports in the literature and from activists suggest that at every level, enforcement and interpretation of the laws are problematic for female victims of violence. Studies of gender bias in the courts are underway in a majority of states in the United States, as well as in many other countries, to uncover and correct this bias, particularly as it applies to processing of rape, battering, and abuse cases. These studies confirm that throughout the world, in varying degrees, there is a reluctance to prosecute assailants of women. A U.N. report has pointed out the legal systems' "current failure to respond adequately" and cites a number of underlying factors, particularly the reluctance of legal institutions to "interfere" in the family and the tradition of dominance of male authority in the family.

Law Officials as Perpetrators

In addition to the failure to provide equal protection under the law to women, legal systems play an even darker role as perpetrators of violence. In a review of the status of women in international law, B. Elder (1987) noted that the U.N. Commission on the Status of Women Study Group's examination of communications on human rights violations in 1983 "identified one widespread and horrendous trend: physical violence against women while in official custody. Cases of rape, sexual abuse, and violent treatment of pregnant women were reported." Official abuse of women in detention has been further documented by Amnesty International. Both men and women in custody can suffer conditions that violate human rights standards, but women are more likely to endure ill treatment or torture which includes various forms of violent sexual abuse. Children are used in psychological torture of women. "Many women have had to endure having their own children or the children of female friends and political comrades tortured in their presence," [states X. Bunster, 1984].

It has been essential to bring violence against women under the rubric of criminal law, and in many countries, activists are still struggling to have such violence treated as criminal behavior. However, concentrating so strongly on legal issues can result in a narrow view of the problem. The criminal justice system involves prosecution of specific criminal incidents and, when it operates properly, it serves abused women in this specific way. Policymakers often prefer to view problems narrowly, focusing on a particular set of practices that can be remedied with a tightly drawn piece of legislation. They resist seeing the totality of an issue, with all its implications, and with the issue of violence against women, more so perhaps because the offenses take place not only in the streets but also within the family. It is no less important than it ever was to secure the protection of the law for abused women. But it is time to reconsider the problem of violence against women in its wholeness. It is a crime, to be sure, but it is more than a crime. The human rights concept is helpful because it retains the legal framework while adding a broader vision.

Interdisciplinary Coordination

The multidisciplinary implications of violence against women must be considered in the development of both local action and in the broader arena of human rights advocacy. Violence against women differs from other kinds of interpersonal violence since much of it occurs within the family, or by a perpetrator known to the victim. In many cases custom and law are at odds: when women are abused for violating custom, legal institutions are mandated to bring the behavior under the rubric of law.

When society does intervene, programs and services to prevent violence, to protect the victim, or to prosecute and treat the abuser, cut across various disciplines, agencies, and institutions. A woman who has been battered may seek help from a shelter, the police, legal counsel, the prosecutor, child welfare services, public assistance programs, the court, and others.

Local agencies have begun to develop coordinated approaches to respond to the multidisciplinary aspects of violence against women. Police departments now undergo "awareness" training by battered women shelters or rape crisis centers. Multidisciplinary teams of representatives from the police, the District Attorney's office, and local services are set up to coordinate particular cases of family violence or child abuse. For example, police and child welfare personnel jointly conduct their interviews with child victims to reduce the trauma of repeated interviewing. A Canadian Interdisciplinary Project on Domestic Violence has united 10 national associations representing service providers, consumers of these services, and their advocates in the fields of criminal justice, social services, health care, education, and religion in order to explore new ways to promote interdisciplinary approaches to domestic violence issues.

This initial movement toward interdisciplinary solutions is carried into the international setting in several

"Violence against women is widespread and global."

ways. It reinforces a more holistic and universal view of the problem. As is beginning to happen, a fully developed dialogue on human rights for women can better develop when practitioners in a variety of disciplines examine issues of female abuse in international meetings. The relationship between violence and women's role in development are more apparent through interdisciplinary presentations of the issues. Mirer Busto (1990), a Chilean psychologist and president of Mujeres por la Vida, has asked for a global vision of the problem of violence against women, and urged that "women and men must work together and form interdisciplinary teams."

The movement to combat violence against women has its roots in local action. It is the power of locally based projects and coalitions from around the world—such as GABRIELA in the Philippines, Women under Muslim Laws in Bangladesh, and Mujeres por la Vida in Chile—that has begun to drive the international machinery. These coalitions bring to bear the moral authority of female victims of violence on U.N. human rights legislation, particularly on the ratification and implementation of the Convention on Elimination of All Forms of Discrimination against Women.

Although the anti-violence movement is not the only social action movement which is strong at the grass roots, it is distinctive in that it puts forth a clear, consistent call for the empowerment of the victim of abuse. Empowerment strategies emphasize putting the victim of violence in charge of assessing her situation,

> *"Violence against women must be considered a special category of human maltreatment."*

making her own decisions, and implementing them (contrasting with a medical model in which a professional diagnoses the problem, then provides the therapy or "cure"). A substantial activist literature has developed to facilitate the empowerment concept, providing training curricula, manuals for organizing volunteer programs, materials on special populations (including Indochinese, Latina, and Black women), as well as analyses of the empowerment concept itself. The Overseas Education Fund (OEF), a Washington-based nonprofit organization, has linked the concepts of law and empowerment in its Regional Law projects which include networks of practitioners around the world.

Including Women

Now that there are conceptual frameworks and a process for including women on the international human rights agenda, activist organizations and their networks are moving increasingly into the international arena.

Local projects have increased their potential impact by organizing national and regional coalitions. Filipinas, for example, have founded GABRIELA, an umbrella organization consisting of over 100 women's organizations, to combat battering, rape, prostitution, and sexual harassment (including forced boxing). A Network on Violence against Women (BUKLOD) has also been formed in the Philippines.

Activist projects gathered in Nairobi in 1985 at the Nongovernmental Tribunal of the United Nations Conference, following the United Nations Decade for Women. On the final day of the conference they convened informally to form the International Network against Violence against Women (INAVAW), a communication network for activists. INAVAW seeks to address the problem of violence by providing a greater understanding of its cross-cultural nature.

In January 1990, many grass-roots groups sent representatives to the Fifth Annual Conference of the International Women's Rights Action Watch (IWRAW), a network of over 2,000 individuals and organizations which focus on the ratification and implementation of the U.N. Convention on the Elimination of All Forms of Discrimination against Women. The U.N. Committee to End Discrimination against Women (CEDAW) has asked for increased reporting from nongovernmental groups on women and violence. Reports by local projects on violence against women can be channeled into the international network through IWRAW.

Grass-roots involvement in human rights work is not limited to the Women's Convention, however. The year 1994 has been designated the U.N. Year of the Family. Nongovernmental organizations are organizing to ensure that family violence will be put at the top of the agenda for programs associated with this U.N. Special Year (NiCarthy, 1989).

A Special Category of Human Maltreatment

Violence against women is widespread and global, and is tolerated as a social phenomenon, in institutions and custom and, to some degree, in law. The results are major human rights violations for women, which a number of U.N. human rights instruments have the potential to address.

Three remedial approaches to violence against women have been examined here with a view to assessing their usefulness in the conceptual framework of international human rights efforts. These three factors—legal reform, interdisciplinary approaches, and local activism—represent necessary coordinates for the international movement to eradicate violence. Violence against women must be considered a special category of human maltreatment because it is so complex, cuts across so many boundaries, and strikes at the root of so many primary human relationships.

By drawing on these three factors, which have developed at the local and national level, human rights for women can be brought before the international community in a manner commensurate with the universality and severity of the attack on women. The local record over the last two decades tells us that both law and custom can change, and that progress is possible even for a problem as entrenched as this one.

International Measures Can Reduce Violence Against Women

by Aruna Gnanadason

About the author: *Aruna Gnanadason of the Church of South India is director of the World Council of Churches' sub-unit on women in church and society headquartered in Geneva, Switzerland.*

Recent decades have brought into sharp focus the dimensions of the once well-kept secret of violence against women.

Around the world the women's movement has been calling attention to just how much violence women do experience, not only in the workplace and the public domain, but also in the apparent security of the home.

The Legitimacy of Domestic Violence

Women have recognized that they need not bear silently the scars of a dehumanized society which systematically condones and even legitimizes different expressions of violence.

The women's movement has created an environment for telling stories of physical and mental intimidation. Women can speak out their pain to a world that must become aware of the problem and seek ways to respond.

Women recognize that the violence they experience need not be seen as a personal or "unfortunate" incident for which they are responsible.

They see links between violence in the privacy of their lives and other systemic oppression, including the militaristic and violent patriarchal culture that has swamped the globe.

Women have demonstrated that violence affects every part of their lives and even the future of nations.

Aruna Gnanadason, "No Longer a Secret," *One World*, October 1991. Reprinted by permission of the World Council of Churches.

As *The Tribune*, newsletter of the International Women's Tribune Centre, wrote recently, "The well-being of women, their full participation in their country's plans, policies and programmes are essential if development is to take place that will really benefit the whole of the population.

"There will be no peace, no stable environment, no educational progress if women are afraid to take leadership positions and are suffering physical and emotional abuse."

A Global Problem

In no region or country are women exempt from different forms of violence. *The Tribune* article collates some staggering statistics:

• In Costa Rica, one of two women can expect to be a victim of violence at some point of her life.

• Sixty per cent of the persons murdered in Papua New Guinea in 1981 were women—the majority by their spouses during or after a domestic argument.

• One Canadian woman in four will be assaulted at some time, half of these before the age of 17.

• UN [United Nations] reports say India leads the world in "custodial rape"—committed by men in such positions of power as police officers, jail and hospital staff.

• In the US, a woman is beaten every 15 seconds. There is a rape every six minutes; and four women are killed by their batterers every day.

• The Mexican Federation of Women Trade Unions says 95 per cent of women workers there are victims of sexual harassment in the workplace.

• Three-quarters of the Sri Lankan women interviewed in an International Labour Office study of plantation workers reported beatings by their husbands or estate superintendents.

• In the Philippines, half of the women arrested by soldiers are forced to undress. According to a study on rape by the military, 14 per cent of them were slapped, boxed or severely mauled; an equal number were harassed and threatened with rape or death.

> *"In no region or country are women exempt from different forms of violence."*

• One of every four girls in Peru will be sexually abused before her sixteenth birthday.

• In France, 95 per cent of the victims of violence are women, 51 per cent at the hands of their husbands.

But women have begun to organize themselves to challenge the situation these statistics reflect. They are claiming their right to live in a safe environment where they can offer their gifts and capabilities freely and without fear.

Women of all sectors, urban and rural, of all religious persuasions and races, in every region and nation are transcending the paralysis of being the victim of forces beyond their control. Unwilling to remain passive, they are acting creatively to bring change.

• Tanzanian women have organized a research project, made a film, and held a seminar on sexual discrimination and violence and a National Day of Action, with the goal of creating a pressure group on this issue.

• The Asian Women's Human Rights Commission has widened the scope of its work to include all forms of violence against women—prostitution tourism, dowry deaths and other domestic violence, pornography, violence against Dalit women in India, rape, sex-specific forms of torturing female political prisoners. Among their strategies to create public awareness are fact-finding missions to trouble areas.

> *"Women . . . are claiming their right to live in a safe environment where they can offer their gifts and capabilities freely and without fear."*

• *Viol-Secours*, a crisis centre in Geneva, provides a 24-hour telephone line and counselling and educational programmes in companies on sexual harassment. Their legal experts are working on a review of Swiss laws, and they are campaigning to raise public awareness of this issue.

• In certain *barrios* in Lima, women demonstrated directly in front of houses where domestic violence was known to occur, resulting in some decrease in wife-abuse.

• The Fiji Women's Rights Movement organized a "Walk Against Rape" to protest the rising incidence of violence against women.

• Women at one US university campaigned against date rapists by writing their names on bathroom walls. Students at another university organized a candlelight vigil to demand greater action on date rape.

The slogan "the personal is political" has given women the power to go beyond their suffering and pain to challenge the different expressions of violence they bear and to usher in a world of greater justice and peace.

Forms and Roots of Violence

The definition of what in fact constitutes violence against women always raises questions.

Clearly it includes all forms of physical and sexual violence perpetrated on women without their consent, by persons known or unknown to the victim, inside or outside marriage or family.

Blatant forms of violence—wife-battering, rape, assault, burning to death (as in dowry deaths in India)—may threaten a woman's very survival.

But violence also takes subtler forms, difficult to identify or challenge, yet having a similar effect, eating into a woman's psyche and demoralizing her.

The latter includes implicit undermining of the contributions of women, putting women down with sexist remarks, making unwanted sexual advances and all other abuses of power relations.

Whatever form violence takes, it must not be divorced from its systemic roots in societies built on unjust power equations, in which some have the economic, political and social power to dominate the many and the use of force and violence has become the norm.

In such a context, everyone on the fringes of society experiences violence. All subjugated peoples are exposed to various forms of institutional violence, but women are the primary victims.

Added to the oppression they experience due to poverty or race, they are vulnerable to physical and other abuse at the hands of the men in their own families and communities.

Dalit women in India have come to recognize that besides struggling against the violence of an unjust caste structure, they must expose the patriarchal violence they experience at the hands of Dalit men.

A common myth assumes that violence against women is a phenomenon of poor, illiterate contexts and "dysfunctional" families.

In fact, the culture of patriarchal domination and violent retribution against any expression of what the dominant group sees as rebellion or dissent is symptomatic of all societies.

Women Do Not Ask for Abuse

Thus women in all contexts are subject to physical and sexual abuse. In no context do women "ask" to be beaten or to be raped or abused.

Violence in the home and society is overwhelmingly by men against women. There are rare cases in which a woman batters a man; and women have been known to kill an attacker after prolonged years of battering. But in more than 95 per cent of domestic assaults, the man is the assailant.

A feminist group in Bangalore, India, describes rape as "not merely a physical assault and symbolic of the degradation of womankind, but a violation of the most sensitive part of the female psyche."

But, the group adds, "the shocking sentiment implicit even today in the law, besides the attitude of society, is that a woman 'asks for it,' or in a spirit of condonation states that a rapist is an individual giving in to his natural virility!"

> *"In America a rape occurs every minute. It is as common as drinking tea. One drinks tea and commits a rape."*

Such old assumptions and attitudes are hard to deal with. In a public meeting, the Chief Minister of one Indian state recently criticized media reporting of attacks on women tourists.

"What is rape after all?" he asked. "In America a rape occurs every minute. It is as common as drinking tea. One drinks tea and commits a rape."

At a boarding school in Kenya, 271 teenage girls were attacked by male classmates in July 1991. Nineteen girls were said to have died of suffocation as they tried to hide and 71 were raped.

> *"More and more governments are reviewing their laws to ensure legal redress for victims."*

The *Kenya Times* reported the response of the school's deputy principal: "The boys never meant any harm against the girls. They just wanted to rape."

Such reactions may be isolated and could be exaggerated, but they unfortunately reflect some old assumptions and attitudes. No real change can be achieved unless these are radically exposed and changed.

Courts in many countries condone perpetrators of crimes against women with the excuse of the woman's past history—as though there are some women who can never be raped!

The root of the problem lies in a failure to understand patriarchy and patriarchal violence and to acknowledge these as the framework necessary for analyzing the structural inequalities in society.

Shifting Power

Without a shift in traditional ways of defining unequal power relations and the concepts that legitimize them, there is no way to tackle the systemic roots of the violence against women or to respond adequately to individual incidents.

But it is important to recognize some positive actions as well. Because of the vigilant care women are taking to ensure justice, more and more governments are reviewing their laws to ensure legal redress for victims.

The struggle for comprehensive legal protection is far from over. The pain women experience when they seek help continues to be trivialized, both in police stations and in law courts. But many countries are on the way.

The United Nations Commission on the Status of Women, at its most recent meeting in March 1991 in Vienna, pressed for more action on this issue.

A Canadian resolution on "Violence Against Women in All its Forms" recommended developing a framework for an international instrument to address the issue, calling on the UN Division for the Advancement of Women (DAW) to convene a meeting of experts on this. . . .

Meanwhile, other groups are moving forward. Ministers of 16 Western European countries met in Brussels in March 1991 to deal with the question of physical and sexual violence against women.

They made 30 specific recommendations to participating governments. The ministers committed themselves "to stimulate all Members of Government concerned to pay particular attention to problems related to physical and sexual violence against women."

In future meetings they will deal with issues such as violence against children and young girls, prostitution, pornography, trafficking in women, physical and sexual violence among minority groups and sexual harassment in the workplace.

For the churches, the Ecumenical Decade of the Churches in Solidarity with Women provides an opportunity to seek ways to be truly responsive to this urgent and vital demand from women around the globe for action in solidarity.

The church should indeed lead the way, by demonstrating that a Christ-centred community must condemn such gross expressions of injustice and that our faith has a word of challenge and hope for the women of the world.

Can the church live out that challenge and point to that hope? That is the question the faith community must ask itself as it works out ways to be in solidarity with women during the remaining years of the decade.

Chapter 6

How Widespread Is the Problem of Rape?

The Incidence of Rape: An Overview

by Nancy Gibbs

About the author: *Nancy Gibbs is an associate editor of* Time, *a weekly news-magazine.*

Be careful of strangers and hurry home, says a mother to her daughter, knowing that the world is a frightful place but not wishing to swaddle a child in fear. Girls grow up scarred by caution and enter adulthood eager to shake free of their parents' worst nightmares. They still know to be wary of strangers. What they don't know is whether they have more to fear from their friends.

Most women who get raped are raped by people they already know—like the boy in biology class, or the guy in the office down the hall, or their friend's brother. The familiarity is enough to make them let down their guard, sometimes even enough to make them wonder afterward whether they were "really raped." What people think of as "real rape"—the assault by a monstrous stranger lurking in the shadows—accounts for only 1 out of 5 attacks.

So the phrase "acquaintance rape" was coined to describe the rest, all the cases of forced sex between people who already knew each other, however casually. But that was too clinical for headline writers, and so the popular term is the narrower "date rape," which suggests an ugly ending to a raucous night on the town.

These are not idle distinctions. Behind the search for labels is the central mythology about rape: that rapists are always strangers, and victims are women who ask for it. The mythology is hard to dispel because the crime is so rarely exposed. The experts guess—that's all they can do under the circumstances—that while 1 in 4 women will be raped in her lifetime, less than 10% will report the assault, and less than 5% of the rapists will go to jail. . . .

Women charge that date rape is the hidden crime; men complain it is hard to prevent a crime they can't define. Women say it isn't taken seriously; men say it is a concept invented by women who like to tease but not take the consequences. Women say the date-rape debate is the first time the nation has talked frankly about sex; men say it is women's unconscious reaction to the excesses of the sexual revolution. Meanwhile, men and women argue among themselves about the "gray area" that surrounds the whole murky arena of sexual relations, and there is no consensus in sight.

In court, on campus, in conversation, the issue turns on the elasticity of the word *rape*, one of the few words in the language with the power to summon a shared image of a horrible crime.

At one extreme are those who argue that for the word to retain its impact, it must be strictly defined as forced sexual intercourse: a gang of thugs jumping a jogger in Central Park, a psychopath preying on old women in a housing complex, a man with an ice pick in a side street. To stretch the definition of the word risks stripping away its power. In this view, if it happened on a date, it wasn't rape. A romantic encounter is a context in which sex *could* occur, and so what omniscient judge will decide whether there was genuine mutual consent?

Others are willing to concede that date rape sometimes occurs, that sometimes a man goes too far on a date without a woman's consent. But this infraction, they say, is not as ghastly a crime as street rape, and it should not be taken as seriously. The New York *Post*, alarmed by the Willy Smith case, wrote in a recent editorial, "If the sexual encounter, *forced or not*, has been preceded by a series of consensual activities—drinking, a trip to the man's home, a walk on a deserted beach at 3 in the morning—the charge that's leveled against the alleged offender should, it seems to us, be different than the one filed against, say, the youths who raped and beat the jogger."

This attitude sparks rage among women who carry scars received at the hands of men they knew. It makes no difference if the victim shared a drink or a moonlit walk or even a passionate kiss, they protest, if the encounter ended with her being thrown to the ground and forcibly violated. Date rape is not about a misunderstanding, they say. It is not a communications problem. It is not about a woman's having regrets in the morning for a decision she made the night before. It is not about a "decision" at all. Rape is rape, and any form of forced sex—even between neighbors, co-workers, classmates and casual friends—is a crime.

> *"While 1 in 4 women will be raped in her lifetime, less than 10% will report the assault, and less than 5% of the rapists will go to jail."*

A more extreme form of that view comes from activists who see rape as a metaphor, its definition swelling to cover any kind of oppression of women. Rape, seen in this light, can occur not only on a date but also in a marriage, not only by violent assault but also by psychological pressure. A Swarthmore College training pamphlet once explained that acquaintance rape "spans a spectrum of incidents and behaviors, ranging from crimes legally defined as rape to verbal harassment and inappropriate innuendo."

No wonder, then, that the battles become so heated. When innuendo qualifies as rape, the definitions have become so slippery that the entire subject sinks into a political swamp. The only way to capture the hard reality is to tell the story.

A 32-year-old woman was on business in Tampa last year for the Florida supreme court. Stranded at the courthouse, she accepted a lift from a lawyer involved in her project. As they chatted on the ride home, she recalls, "he was saying all the right things, so I started to trust him." She agreed to have dinner, and afterward, at her hotel door, he convinced her to let him come in to talk. "I went through the whole thing about being old-fashioned," she says. "I was a virgin until I was 21. So I told him talk was all we were going to do."

But as they sat on the couch, she found herself falling asleep. "By now, I'm comfortable with him, and I put my head on his shoulder. He's not tried anything all evening, after all." Which is when the rape came. "I woke up to find him on top of me, forcing himself on me. I didn't scream or run. All I could think about was my business contacts and what if they saw me run out of my room screaming rape.

"Rape is rape, and any form of forced sex—even between neighbors, co-workers, classmates and casual friends—is a crime."

"I thought it was my fault. I felt so filthy, I washed myself over and over in hot water. Did he rape me?, I kept asking myself. I didn't consent. But who's gonna believe me? I had a man in my hotel room after midnight." More than a year later, she still can't tell the story without a visible struggle to maintain her composure. Police referred the case to the state attorney's office in Tampa, but without more evidence it decided not to prosecute. Although her attacker has admitted that he heard her say no, maintains the woman, "he says he didn't know that I meant no. He didn't feel he'd raped me, and he even wanted to see me again."

Her story is typical in many ways. The victim herself may not be sure right away that she has been raped, that she had said no and been physically forced into having sex anyway. And the rapist commonly hears but does not heed the protest. "A date rapist will follow through no matter what the woman wants because his agenda is to get laid," says Claire Walsh, a Florida-based consultant on sexual assaults. "First comes the dinner, then a dance, then a drink, then the coercion begins." Gentle persuasion gives way to physical intimidation, with alcohol as the ubiquitous lubricant. "When that fails, force is used," she says. "Real men don't take no for an answer."

The Palm Beach case serves to remind women that if they go ahead and press charges, they can expect to go on trial along with their attacker, if not in a courtroom then in the court of public opinion. The *New York Times* caused an uproar on its own staff not only for publishing the victim's name but also for laying out in detail her background, her high school grades, her driving record, along with an unattributed quote from a school official about her "little wild streak." A freshman at Carleton College in Minnesota, who says she was repeatedly raped for four hours by a fellow student, claims that she was asked at an administrative hearing if she performed oral sex on dates. In 1989 a man charged with raping at knife point a woman he knew was acquitted in Florida because his victim had been wearing lace shorts and no underwear.

> *"A date rapist will follow through no matter what the woman wants because his agenda is to get laid."*

From a purely legal point of view, if she wants to put her attacker in jail, the survivor had better be beaten as well as raped, since bruises become a badge of credibility. She had better have reported the crime right away, before taking the hours-long shower that she craves, before burning her clothes, before curling up with the blinds down. And she would do well to be a woman of shining character. Otherwise the strict constructionist definitions of rape will prevail in court. "Juries don't have a great deal of sympathy for the victim if she's a willing participant up to the nonconsensual sexual intercourse," says Norman Kinne, a prosecutor in Dallas. "They feel that many times the victim has placed herself in the situation." Absent eyewitnesses or broken bones, a case comes down to her word against his, and the mythology of rape rarely lends her the benefit of the doubt.

She should also hope for an all-male jury, preferably composed of fathers with daughters. Prosecutors have found that women tend to be harsh judges of one another—perhaps because to find a defendant guilty is to entertain two grim realities: that anyone might be a rapist, and that every woman could find herself a victim. It may be easier to believe, the experts muse, that at some level the victim asked for it. "But just because a woman makes a bad judgment, does that give the guy a moral right to rape her?" asks Dean Kilpatrick, director of the Crime Victim Research and Treatment Center at the Medical University of South Carolina. "The bottom line is, Why does a woman's having a drink give a man the right to rape her?"

Last week the Supreme Court waded into the debate with a 7-to-2 ruling that protects victims from being harassed on the witness stand with questions about their sexual history. The justices, in their first decision on "rape shield laws," said an accused rapist could not present evidence about a previous sexual relationship with the victim unless he notified the court ahead of time. In her decision, Justice Sandra Day O'Connor wrote that "rape victims deserve heightened protection against surprise, harassment and unnecessary invasions of privacy."

That was welcome news to prosecutors who understand the reluctance of victims to come forward. But there are other impediments to justice as well. An internal investigation of the Oakland police department found that officers ignored a quarter of all reports of sexual assaults or attempts, though 90% actually warranted investigation. Departments are getting better at educating officers in handling rape cases, but the courts remain behind. A New York City task force on women in the courts charged that judges and lawyers were routinely less inclined to believe a woman's testimony than a man's.

The present debate over degrees of rape is nothing new: all through history, rapes have been divided between those that mattered and those that did not. For the first few thousand years, the only rape that was punished was the defiling of a virgin, and that was viewed as a property crime. A girl's virtue was a marketable asset, and so a rapist was often ordered to pay the victim's father the equivalent of her price on the marriage market. In early Babylonian and Hebrew societies, a married woman who was raped suffered the same fate as an adulteress—death by stoning or drowning. Under William the Conqueror, the penalty for raping a virgin was castration and loss of both eyes—unless the violated woman agreed to marry her attacker, as she was often pressured to do. "Stealing an heiress" became a perfectly conventional means of taking—literally—a wife.

It may be easier to prove a rape case now, but not much. Until the 1960s it was virtually impossible without an eyewitness; judges were often required to instruct jurors that "rape is a charge easily made and hard to defend against; so examine the testimony of this witness with caution." But sometimes a rape was taken very seriously, particularly if it involved a black man attacking a white woman—a crime for which black men were often executed or lynched.

Susan Estrich, author of *Real Rape*, considers herself a lucky victim. This is not just because she survived an attack 17 years ago by a stranger with an ice pick, one day before her graduation from Wellesley. It's because police, and her friends, believed her. "The first thing the Boston police asked was whether it was a black guy," recalls Estrich, now a University of Southern California law professor. When she said yes and gave the details of the attack, their reaction was, "So, you were really raped." It was an instructive lesson, she says, in understanding how racism and sexism are factored into perceptions of the crime.

> *"A case comes down to her word against his, and the mythology of rape rarely lends her the benefit of the doubt."*

A new twist in society's perception came in 1975, when Susan Brownmiller published her book *Against Our Will: Men, Women and Rape*. In it she attacked the concept that rape was a sex crime, arguing instead that it was a crime of violence and power over women. Throughout history, she wrote, rape has played a critical function. "It is nothing more or less than a conscious process of intimidation, by which *all men* keep *all women* in a state of fear."

Out of this contention was born a set of arguments that have become politically correct wisdom on campus and in academic circles. This view holds that rape is a symbol of women's vulnerability to male institutions and attitudes. "It's sociopolitical," insists Gina Rayfield, a New Jersey psychologist. "In our culture men hold the power, politically, economically. They're socialized not to see women as equals."

This line of reasoning has led some women, especially radicalized victims, to justify flinging around the term rape as a political weapon, referring to everything from violent sexual assaults to inappropriate innuendos. Ginny, a college senior who was really raped when she was 16, suggests that false accusations of rape can serve a useful purpose. "Penetration is not the only form of violation," she explains. In her view, rape is a subjective term, one that women must use to draw attention to other, nonviolent, even nonsexual forms of oppression. "If a woman did falsely accuse a man of rape, she may have had reasons to," Ginny says. "Maybe she wasn't raped, but he clearly violated her in some way."

Catherine Comins, assistant dean of student life at Vassar, also sees some value in this loose use of "rape." She says angry victims of various forms of sexual intimidation cry rape to regain their sense of power. "To use the word carefully would be to be careful

> **"It may be easier to prove a rape case now, but not much."**

for the sake of the violator, and the survivors don't care a hoot about him." Comins argues that men who are unjustly accused can sometimes gain from the experience. "They have a lot of pain, but it is not a pain that I would necessarily have spared them. I think it ideally initiates a process of self-exploration. 'How do I see women?' 'If I didn't violate her, could I have?' 'Do I have the potential to do to her what they say I did?' Those are good questions."

Taken to extremes, there is an ugly element of vengeance at work here. Rape is an abuse of power. But so are false accusations of rape, and to suggest that men whose reputations are destroyed might benefit because it will make them more sensitive is an attitude that is sure to backfire on women who are seeking justice for all victims.

Rape Is Widespread

by Mary P. Koss and Mary R. Harvey

About the authors: *Mary P. Koss is a professor of psychiatry at the University of Arizona College of Medicine. She is the author of several books, including* I Never Called It Rape: The Ms. Report on Recognizing, Fighting, and Surviving Date and Acquaintance Rape *and* The Rape Victim, *from which this viewpoint was taken. Mary R. Harvey is a clinical and community psychologist and the cofounder and director of the Victims of Violence Program at Cambridge Hospital in Cambridge, Massachusetts.*

Experiencing sexual violence transforms people into victims and changes their lives forever. Once victimized, one can never again feel quite as invulnerable. Rape represents the most serious of all major crimes against the person, short of homicide. The focus of this viewpoint is on the crime of rape including its legal definitions [and] frequency. . . . It may help victims to know that their experience was not a rare event. Knowledge of the processes by which incidence and prevalence numbers are generated also facilitates appropriate rebuttal in instances where statistics are (mis)used to maintain the illusion that rape is an infrequent crime. . . .

Legal Definitions of Rape

The traditional common-law offense of rape is defined as "carnal knowledge of a female forcibly and against her will." Carnal knowledge means penile-vaginal penetration only; other sexual offenses are excluded.

FBI Definition. This definition of rape is adopted by the Federal Bureau of Investigation (FBI) for purposes of compiling the *Uniform Crime Reports*. The *Uniform Crime Reports* (UCR) compile the numbers of rape complaints that have been filed with local police authorities that the police considered to be legitimate incidents. The UCR definition of rape also is adopted by the National Crime Survey (NCS), which is the federal data-collection effort that aims at describing the extent of unreported crime. The one exception is that the FBI definition is extended to include "homosexual rape" in the NCS. This statement contains two problematic elements. First, carnal knowledge refers to penile-vaginal intercourse. The compilers of the NCS have not considered that the carnal knowledge definition cannot be extended to male victims; to do so would require a change in the quali-fying forms of penetration. Such

> *"Rape accounted for 6% of the total violent crime volume."*

changes would have implications for female as well as male victims. Second, it is inaccurate to refer to the rape of men as homosexual rape. Men who rape other men are not always homosexuals.

Reform Rape Definitions. In spite of the existence of an FBI definition of the offense, rape is not a federal crime (except in those instances where the crime occurs on federal property or on Indian reservations). Rather, rape statutes are

---

Types of Rape

Stranger rape	Rose, age 25, was accosted at knife point in a shop-ping mall parking lot and forced by a stranger into his car. He drove her to a rural area, raped her, stabbed her five times, set the car on fire, and left her. Although severely injured, she survived.
Acquaintance rape	Susan, age 23, went to the door of her house to find a man she recognized from one of her college classes. She opened the door to let him in the house, whereupon he threw her on the sofa and raped her.
Date rape	Diana, age 50, is vacationing in the Caribbean. She spends some of her time learning sailing and walk-ing along the beach with a fellow guest. At a hotel dance, she dances with this man, and he asks to walk outside. Once on the beach, this 6'4" man asks to have sex and forces her to cooperate by holding her down. Diana is too afraid to resist.
Multiple rape	Ann, age 21, was at a friend's home with a group of her peers. There were three men, one other woman, and herself present. When the other woman left, the three men raped her.
Marital rape	Unidentified caller, in her thirties, telephones a radio talk show on which marital rape is discussed. She describes her husband's sexual assaults and asks where to go for help.

written at the state level. Recent years have seen extensive reform of these laws. One of the reforms was to substitute other terms for rape including sexual assault, sexual battery, criminal sexual penetration, criminal sexual conduct, gross sexual imposition, and sexual intercourse without consent. The intent of these reforms was to place emphasis on the perpetrator's acts rather than the victim's experiences and to draw attention toward rape's violent as opposed to sexual aspects. We have retained the use of the term "rape" to refer to the most highly sanctioned form of sexual penetration offense.

In reform statutes, *rape* is defined as nonconsensual sexual penetration of an adolescent or adult obtained by physical force, by threat of bodily harm, or when the victim is incapable of giving consent by virtue of mental illness, mental retardation, or intoxication. Included are attempts to commit rape by force or threat of bodily harm. . . .

Incidence of Rape

The concept of *incidence* is borrowed from the field of epidemiology. This term has a precise meaning in relation to disease but now is routinely applied to mental health and crime phenomena. Incidence refers to the number of new cases that appear within a specified time frame. When applied to crime data, incidence refers to the number of separate criminal incidents that occurred during a fixed period of time—often a one-year period. Incidence often is expressed as a *victimization rate*, which is obtained by dividing the number of incidents that occurred in the time period by the number of persons in the population. The rate is then set to a standard population base, often 1,000 people.

> *"[Several] studies documented rates of rape that are far higher than federal estimates."*

The Uniform Crime Reports. Statistics on crime reported to local authorities have been compiled by the FBI for the past five decades. The UCR summarizes several violent index offenses that include criminal homicide, forcible rape, aggravated assault, and robbery. Included in the rape rate are attempts to rape where no penetration took place. In 1988, a total of 92,486 reported crimes qualified as rape according to the FBI definition. This figure translated into a victimization rate of 73 per 100,000 female Americans. By definition, 100% of the victims of rape in the UCR were female. Approximately 82% of the rapes reported in 1988 were completed by force; the remainder were attempts. Rape accounted by 6% of the total violent crime volume. The UCR presently does not provide any further information on the indexed crimes such as the relationship of victim and offender; however, a conversion to incident-based crime reporting is in progress among the states that will significantly increase the range of data that are available in the future. . . .

214

Independent Research. Rape incidence also has been estimated in a small number of specialized studies carried out under federal contracts including research that has focused on adolescents; college women; and adult women. All of these studies documented rates of rape that are far higher than federal estimates. Diana Russell conducted a pioneering study in 1978 that involved interviews with a random sample of 930 women residents of San Francisco. Detailed interviews were administered in respondents' homes by a trained female interviewer. Whenever possible, race and ethnicity were matched. There were 38 questions about sexual assault, only one of which used the word rape. Rape was defined according to California statutes as, "forced intercourse (i.e., penile-vaginal penetration, or intercourse obtained by threat of force, or intercourse completed when the woman was drugged, unconscious, asleep, or otherwise totally helpless and hence unable to consent)." In the 12 months prior to the survey, 25 rapes and rape attempts occurred among respondents that met the UCR definition, which resulted in an estimated incidence rate of 2,688 per 100,000 women. This figure is 7 times higher than the NCS estimate for San Francisco during the same year. In contrast to the picture painted by NCS data of that era, when two thirds of rapists were strangers, in Russell's data only 11% of the rapes and attempted rapes were perpetrated by strangers, whereas 62% were perpetrated by current or former husbands, boyfriends, lovers, and other male relatives (the remainder were perpetrated by nonromantic acquaintances).

A National Survey of Young People

S.S. Ageton inserted questions about sexual assault into the National Youth Study. Boys were questioned about their perpetration of assault, and girls were questioned about victimization. The nationwide sample of 1,725 adolescents age 11 to 17 were interviewed yearly for five years. Sexual assault was defined in this study "to include all forced sexual behavior involving contact with the sexual parts of the body. Attempted sexual assaults were counted." Two questions were used to operationalize this definition of sexual assault. They included the following: "How many times in the last year have you been sexually attacked or raped or an attempt made to do so?" and "How many times in the last year have you been pressured or pushed by someone such as a date or friend to do more sexually than you wanted to?" The latter item was intended to reflect date rape. It is unfortunate, but the responses to this item were later discounted when it was found that 75% of the girls responded yes to it. In hindsight, Ageton herself identified several problems with her approach including the vagueness of the date-rape item, and the assumption inherent in the first screening item that

> *"In a 12-month period, 76 per 1,000 college women experienced one or more attempted or completed rapes."*

girls who have had an experience that would legally qualify as rape will conceptualize their experience as a "sexual attack or rape." Nevertheless, Ageton developed estimated rape victimization rates for adolescent girls by extracting incidents involving violent force and/or the use of a weapon. The resultant estimates were 9.2 per 1,000 for 1978, 6.8 per 1,000 for 1979, and 12.7 per 1,000 for 1980. These are much higher than the rates reported in the NCS for girls age 13 to 19 for the years 1978 and 1979, which were 3.5 and 4.2 respectively. On a nationwide basis, Ageton's incidence rate for 1977 would translate into 540,000 sexual assaults of female teenagers. This rate alone is 7 times greater than the total number of rapes officially recorded for *all* women in that year by the *Uniform Crime Reports*.

> *"College-educated respondents recall more crimes than others, particularly in the category of assaultive violence."*

College Surveys

Mary P. Koss and colleagues administered 10 sexual victimization screening questions to a nationwide sample of 3,187 women college students at 32 colleges and universities selected to represent the higher education enrollment in the United States. There were six questions pertaining to rape that described various behaviorally specific scenarios but did not use the word rape. Typical items included the following: "Have you had sexual intercourse with a man when you did not want to because he used some degree of force such as twisting your arm or holding you down to make you cooperate?" or "Have you had other sexual acts with a man such as oral or anal intercourse or penetration with objects when you did not want to because he used some degree of force . . . or threatened to harm you to make you cooperate?" In a 12-month period, 76 per 1,000 college women experienced one or more attempted or completed rapes defined according to the UCR definition. (The use of state reform definition of rape doubled the incidence figure to 166 per 1,000 women.)

It can be instructive to compare these incidence rates to NCS figures for the year in which that data were collected (1985). A direct comparison with the NCS must be viewed with caution, however, because there are several inherent limitations of the validity of this undertaking. The first limitation involves differences in the populations from which the data were obtained. Whereas the NCS involves a representative sample of all U.S. households, the present sample was restricted to college students who have a higher than average education level. Although common sense might suggest that less educated persons would be subject to more victimizations, in reality the reverse is often found on crime surveys and is explained by a phenomenon known as "differential productivity." College-educated respondents recall more crimes than others, particularly in the category of assaultive violence. This tendency of educated respondents to evidence greater productivity is suspected of masking the negative association between social position and victimization.

There also is an important methodological difference between the survey of college students and the NCS that could affect the validity of the comparisons. The recall period in the NCS is limited to a six-month period, and the respondents' previous contact with the interviewer serves as a reference point for where to begin remembering. The college students were contacted only once and were asked subsequently to specify the number of victimizations that occurred in the previous year. A phenomenon known as "telescoping" may occur under these circumstances. Experiences may be recalled as having happened closer to the present than they actually did (forward telescoping), or further away from the present than they actually did (backward telescoping). Studies with NCS data have revealed that single, retrospective reports of victimization produce rates that are about one third higher than bounded recall. As the incidence data on college students were obtained from unbounded recall, they were reduced by one third to adjust for forward telescoping. The adjustment lowered the estimate of rape incidence among college women from 76 per 1,000 using the UCR definition to 50 per 1,000. Even after discounting the rate by one third, 1 in 20 college women experienced rape or attempted rape in a year as defined by the FBI (1 in 9 using a reform definition). This rate is still between 10 and 15 times larger than the 1985 NCS estimates for women age 16 to 19 (4.3 per 1,000) and age 20 to 24 (3.4 per 1,000).

Sexual Assault Widespread

Many people have trouble believing that this level of assault could exist without coming to the attention of police or institutional authorities. However, fewer than 5% of college student rape victims stated that they had reported their assault to the police; almost half told no one at all. Responses to follow-up questions revealed that 95% of the rapes involved one offender, and 84% of the incidents involved an offender known to the victim. In 57% of the rapes, the perpetrator was a date.

To generalize these results to a broader population base, a second study focused on more than 2,291 adult women in Cleveland, Ohio. A mailed survey was sent to over 5,000 women and a 45% response rate was

> *"Fewer than 5% of college student rape victims stated that they had reported their assault to the police."*

obtained. Whereas the college women averaged 21 years of age, these women averaged 36 years of age. A total of five questions were used to screen for rape and attempted rape, which were defined according to Ohio rape statutes. A typical item is the following: "Has a man made you have sex by using force or threatening to harm you? When we use the word sex we mean a man putting his penis in your vagina even if he did not ejaculate (come)." The incidence of rape in a 12-month period was 28 per 1,000 women based on the FBI definition (the rate was 62 per 1,000 using a reform definition). Even after reducing this rate to allow for telescoping, it is still 15 times larger than

> *"Sexual assaults constituted half of the crimes recalled by participants."*

NCS estimates for the year 1986, which were 1.2 per 1,000 for women collapsed across all ages. These data mean that 1 adult woman in 55 experienced a rape as defined by the FBI during a one-year period (1 in 24 using a reform definition). Many of these assaults occurred in highly intimate contexts. Specifically, 39% of the rapes were perpetrated by husbands, partners, or relatives of the victim. Only 17% of the rapes were perpetrated by total strangers. . . .

Prevalence Studies of Rape

Prevalence figures attempt to estimate the number of women who have been victimized by rape ever in their lives. Thus these figures may be more broadly meaningful to clinicians. It is unfortunate, however, that the prevalence literature is difficult to integrate because of major differences in the methods used by various investigators. The most troublesome variability is in the definition of the construct that was measured. A number of studies measure "sexual assault." In legal usage this term is synonymous with rape. In the prevalence literature, however, the term sexual assault often is treated as a generic term that subsumes rape as well as lesser degrees of unwanted and pressured sexual contacts not involving penetration, and even subsumes child abuse and incest. Therefore one has to be very careful in reading this literature to examine not only the reported prevalence percentages but also the definition that was used to select incidents that were included.

Our review has been limited to those studies of rape prevalence that used probability sampling methods (as opposed to studying anyone who happened to be conveniently available) and involved U.S. samples. The literature includes studies that have focused on *adolescents; college students; adult women; adult men;* and *special populations* including the elderly, nursing home residents, psychiatric patients, and prisoners; and *ethnic groups* including Hispanics and African-Americans. In the following sections, we will briefly review what the prevalence of rape and/or sexual assault is among these groups.

Adolescent Girls. The work by Ageton was discussed earlier. Her question to elicit sexual experiences was, "How many times in the last year have you been sexually attacked or raped or an attempt made to do so?" Between 5% and 11% of female adolescents reported affirmatively to this question across the several years of the study. E.R. Hall and R.B. Flannery used the telephone survey to ask 508 Milwaukee adolescents, "Has a guy ever used physical force or threat-ened you, to make you have sex when you didn't want to?" Among their re-spondents, 12% reported a sexual assault in their lifetime.

College Students. In their national sample of college students, Koss and col-leagues found that 15% of the women respondents had had an experience which met the Ohio legal definition of rape. An additional 12% had experienced at-tempted rape. A total of 10 screening items were used to obtain the data (a typi-cal screening item was presented previously). These findings mean that 1 in 3.6 college women has been a victim of rape or attempted rape in her lifetime. More than half (54%) of the women surveyed had been sexually victimized to some degree. Women reported that their rapes occurred on average 1 to 2 years previ-ously. The typical victim was 18.5 years old. One offender was involved in 95% of the rapes. Just 16% of the rapes involved a perpetrator who was a complete stranger; 57% of the rapes involved a date. The rapes happened primarily off campus (86%), equally as often in the man's house or car as in the woman's house or car. Victims were using intoxicants in 55% of the episodes. Prior mu-tual intimacy had occurred with the offender to the level of petting above the waist. The victims believed, how-ever, that they had made their non-consent to have sexual intercourse quite clear. Typically, the victim per-ceived that the offender used quite a bit of force, often involving twisting her arm or holding her down. Only 9% of the rapes involved hitting or beating. Forms of resistance used by the victims in their attempts to escape were reason-ing with the offender (84%) and physically struggling (70%). Many women were virgins prior to the rape. Almost half of the victims told no one about their rape; just 5% reported to the police, and only 5% visited a rape crisis center.

> *"One in 3.6 college women has been a victim of rape or attempted rape in her lifetime."*

Rape and the Media

These findings differ greatly from the view of date rape that has sometimes been promulgated by the popular media. For example, note this case history presented in *Newsweek* magazine.

> Colleen, 27, a San Francisco office manager, had been involved with her boyfriend for about a year when it happened. After a cozy dinner at her apart-ment, he suggested that she go to bed while he did the dishes. But a few mo-ments later he stalked into Colleen's bedroom with a peculiar look on his face, brandishing a butcher knife and strips of cloth. After tying her, spread-eagled to the bed, the formerly tender lover raped her brutally for three hours using his fist, the knife, a shampoo bottle, and other household objects.

Adult Women. A number of prevalence estimates for rape are available for adult women. The earliest was Russell's work. As indicated earlier, she defined rape according to California law, and 38 items were used to elicit information. Interviewers were matched for gender and ethnicity whenever possible. Russell found that 24% of her San Francisco sample had experienced completed rape, and 31% had experienced attempted rape. These categories were not mutually exclusive; when each respondent is counted only once, a total of 44% of the sample experienced a rape or attempted rape. Among the 644 women who had ever been married, 14% reported being physically forced by their husband to engage in penile-vaginal, oral, or anal intercourse.

> *"Among . . . 644 women who had ever been married, 14% reported being physically forced by their husband to engage in . . . intercourse."*

S.B. Sorenson and colleagues administered the following question to 3,172 participants from the Los Angeles site of the Epidemiological Catchment Area Studies (ECA): "In your lifetime, has anyone ever tried to pressure or force you to have sexual contact? By sexual contact I mean their touching your sexual parts, your touching their sexual parts, or sexual intercourse." The interviewers were not gender- or ethnicity-matched and other family members were present for half of the interviews. The results indicated that 14% of the women respondents had experienced one or more sexual assaults since age 16. The rates of sexual assault were found to vary with ethnic status and with education. Thus the rate of assault was 7% for Hispanic women and 16% among non-Hispanic white women. The rate of sexual assault among white women age 18 to 39 with college educations was 28%.

Varying Rates

I. Winfield et al. interviewed 1,157 participants in the Durham, North Carolina, site of the Epidemiological Catchment Area Studies (ECA) and asked the following question: "Have you ever been in a situation in which you were pressured into doing more sexually than you wanted to do, that is, a situation in which someone pressured you against your will into forced contact with the sexual parts of your body or their body?" Interviewers were not gender-matched. The remainder of the ECA interview focused on symptoms of mental illness. No definition of sexual assault is found in their report, but examination of the screening question presented above suggests that a broad spectrum of incidents were included without the ability to break out a separate rate for rape and attempted rape. The prevalence percentage reported by Winfield and colleagues is 6% for adult women in their lifetime.

D.G. Kilpatrick et al. used random-digit dialing techniques to telephonically contact a sample of 2,004 women residents of Charleston County, South Carolina. In the context of other questions about crime, two items about rape were included, of which the following is representative: "Has anyone ever tried to make you have sexual relations with them against your will?" A total of 9% of the respondents reported experiences of rape or attempted rape. In a later study, a subsample of 391 women in this sample agreed to report for a personal interview. The actual text of screening items is not given in the report, but the definition of rape required nonconsent, threat or use of force, and one or more types of completed sexual penetration. Although questions about other crimes were included, the sexual assault items were administered separately from the other crime items with an introduction designed to dispel the notion that the incident had to be a crime and to counteract the tendency to conceptualize rape in narrow, stereotypic terms. The results indicated that 53% of the women had been a victim of at least one sexual assault including 23% who had experienced completed rape and 13% who had experienced attempted rape. Sexual assaults constituted half of the crimes recalled by participants; completed rapes alone accounted for 19% of the crime volume.

Special Populations

The focus of research by Gail Wyatt has been comparisons of African-American and white women. The data were collected by an extensive standardized interview using gender- and ethnicity-matched interviewers. Participants were a stratified random sample of 126 African-American and 122 white women residents of Los Angeles County. The questioning about rape came after a lengthy period of the interview had passed to allow rapport to be established. Then respondents were read the following definition of rape: "I will be asking you about sexual experiences which may have occurred without your consent. These experiences may have involved a friend, relative, or stranger. . . . Rape is involuntary penetration of the vagina or anus by the penis or another object. Since the age of 18 have you ever been raped?" The results indicated that 1 in 4 African-American women and 1 in 5 white women reported at least one incident of an attempted or completed rape since the age of 18.

Prevalence data for men are available from the two ECA sites that included questioning about sexual assault. The prevalence rates reported for adult men vary from 0.6% to 7%. Prevalence rates in special populations are 49% among female psychiatric inpatients and 0% among male patients, 100% among female prisoners and 8% among male prisoners. . . .

Thus rape prevalence of approximately 20% for adult women has been reported by separate groups of investigators working in different regions of the United States, who have all modeled their definition of rape on legal standards. These cumulative findings suggest that 1 in 5 adult women has experienced a completed rape up to that point in her life (i.e., the time of the survey). If more extensive data existed it would be possible to project the lifetime chances of being raped, and they would present an even more devastating picture. These findings transform rape from a heinous but rare event into a common experience in women's lives.

The Incidence of Rape Is High

by Hilary Shelton

About the author: *Hilary Shelton is an associate program director in the Ministry of God's Human Community Unit of the General Board of Church and Society for The United Methodist Church.*

The awful scourge of violence in our society continues to grow; however, in no area does it increase faster than against women. Police, rape crisis centers, hospital emergency rooms, and battered women's shelters have recorded an increasing incidence of rape, sexual assault, and domestic violence against women in the United States.

This violence has no boundaries; it cuts across race, class, age, and religious beliefs. Its victims share one common trait: *they are all women.* According to a national crime survey, assaults against women have risen 50 percent, while assaults against young men have actually dropped 12 percent since 1974. Furthermore, the Senate Judiciary Committee reported in 1990 that three out of four women will be victims of violent crime during their lifetimes.

A Devastating Fact of Life

The high incidence of rape makes it a devastating fact of life for literally millions of American women. Even those women who are not direct victims of rape are affected. When a rape takes place, women live with the fear of an attack and the restriction of freedom such fear brings. Their anxiety is further justified by the hard statistical evidence of the widespread and growing prevalence of violent sexual crimes.

According to statistics compiled by the D.C. Rape Crisis Center, one in three women will be a victim of rape during her lifetime. Both the 1989 "Uniform Crime Report" and the "National Crime Survey" included statistics showing

From Hilary Shelton, "To Ensure Women's Safety," *Christian Social Action*, July/August 1991. Reprinted with permission.

that, in this country, every hour 16 women confront rapists and every six minutes a woman is raped. These same reports showed that over the past decade the rape rate has risen four times as fast as the total crime rate. Furthermore, a comparison of this sexual violence in US society to other countries shows that a woman is 20-times more likely to be raped in the United States than in Japan, 13-times more likely than in Great Britain, and 4-times more likely than in Germany.

In the past, rape was regarded merely as an act of sexuality with punishment being more consistent with other crimes against a man's property. Later, experts refuted the arguments and maintained that rape was truly an act of aggression, where the perpetrator is motivated by a desire to dominate, control, and degrade the victim. Today, most experts who work in the field of violent sexual crime assert that it is a combination of the two. One commonly used definition of rape is the "sexual expression of aggression."

Rape and the Judicial System

The criminal justice system in the United States has not been very efficient in addressing rape in this country. Despite the high incidence of rape, few perpetrators are ever arrested, and even fewer are convicted. According to statistics compiled by the US Senate Judiciary Committee, less than 40 percent of reported rapes result in arrest. The 1989 "National Crime Survey" indicated that while rape rates increased 5.3 percent from 1983 to 1988, arrest rates increased only 3 percent. Furthermore, the conviction rate is even lower than the arrest rate. The US Bureau of Justice reported the conviction rate for rape is only 3 percent, while the conviction rate for robbery is 18 percent.

Traditional perceptions of women and sexuality mean that many survivors of rape are victimized twice: (1) during the rape and (2) in the courts. Even the burden of proof placed on rape victims is exceptional. Survivors of rape are subjected to demeaning examination of their personal life, attire, and previous sexual history in order to establish that they did not consent to the act. Rape victims often report feeling humiliated, accused by, and alienated from the system that is supposed to help them.

> *"The high incidence of rape makes it a devastating fact of life for literally millions of American women."*

Police, judges, juries, and defense and prosecuting attorneys are all susceptible to traditional views of sexual activity and gender which obstruct justice for rape victims. The National Organization for Women's Legal Defense and Education Fund cites instances where judges dismissed rape cases because they found the defendant handsome or thought the victim "ended up enjoying (herself)."

Although not all victims of rape sustain serious physical injuries, for most, the experience of rape carries with it long-term psychological wounds. Dr.

Dean Kilpatrick recently testified before the House Select Committee on Children, Youth and Families that his studies found that victims of rape were 8.7 times more likely than non-victims to have attempted suicide and twice as likely to experience major depression. The claim was substantiated by a National Institute of Drug Abuse survey indicating one-third of all rape victims developed post-traumatic stress disorder. This same survey indicated that more than 40 percent of college women who have been raped carry the devastating psychological expectation of being raped again.

Acquaintance Rape

There is a myth about rape in our society, one in which a woman is pulled into the bushes by a complete stranger and brutally attacked. Although this is tragically true for too many rape victims, the overwhelming majority of rapes are committed by persons the victim knew before the crime took place. According to the House Select Committee on Children, Youth and Families, 60 percent to 80 percent of rapes are committed by men the victims knew. The study went on to show that of college rape victims, 10.6 percent were raped by strangers, 24.9 percent by non-romantic acquaintances, 21 percent by casual dates, 30 percent by steady dates, and 8.9 percent by family members. (It is estimated that one out of every seven married women will be raped by their husbands.)

"One commonly used definition of rape is the 'sexual expression of aggression.'"

Victims of acquaintance rape have a unique set of difficulties following their attack. One study found that these victims blame themselves more and rate themselves as less-recovered than victims of stranger rape for up to three years after the rape. This self-blame, along with peer pressure, threats by the perpetrator, disbelief and shock, and, in cases of rape by a family member, feelings of family loyalty contribute to a low reporting of the crime. In fact, some women don't report the crimes at all.

Underreporting of Rape

According to a 1990 study, reporting of rape is very low. Only 34 percent of stranger rapes and 13 percent of acquaintance rapes are reported to authorities, compared to the reporting rates of 53 percent for robberies, 45 percent for assaults, and 52 percent for burglaries. In addition to posing a problem for statisticians attempting to assess the need for rape services, underreporting means that many rape victims are going without help or treatment and rapists are going free, without punishment or treatment, to rape again.

Many women do not report a rape because they do not know that what has happened is considered a crime. Another major factor in the non-reporting of rape is distrust of the efficacy of the legal system—either the victim will not be believed or that nothing will be done in the courts. Other reasons for not reporting a rape include feelings of shame and embarrassment, fear of one's safety, and concern over the reaction of others.

Those women who do report rapes often take a long time to do so. One rape crisis center reported that only 28 percent of adult victims who reported the crime to the center did so within one week, while 68 percent of those who reported the crime to the center waited up to three years to make the report. Other women experience further emotional trauma when they report the crime of rape only to find out the statute of limitations has run out and victim compensation programs require reporting soon after the crime is committed.

To Dominate, Control

The US Department of Health and Human Services defines "domestic violence" as serious or repeated injury caused by a person who has family ties or a sexual relationship with the victim. Perpetrators use, or threaten the use of, physical or sexual assault to dominate, hurt, degrade, and/or gain control over the victim.

Public awareness of domestic violence has increased as studies prove violent behavior can be passed on from parents to children, and with the recognition that legal, psychological, and emotional assistance for victims is minimal. More recently, national attention has focused on the plight of victims who fight back against perpetrators of domestic violence. Despite the increased public awareness, however, widespread domestic violence continues.

An estimated three to four million American women are battered each year by their husbands or partners. Violence occurs once in two-thirds of all marriages. In fact, statistics show that, in the United States, a woman is more likely to be assaulted, injured, raped, or killed by a male partner than any other assailant. According to the 1983 Bureau of Justice Statistics, 95 percent of the victims of domestic violence are women. When males are victims of domestic violence, it is often the result of women attempting to detach themselves from male-initiated abuse. . . .

Because of fear and the perception of violence being a personal issue, violence against women often goes unreported. According to the Bureau of Justice Statistics 1986 report, "Preventing Domestic Violence Against Women," 49 percent of the victims of domestic violence didn't report the incident because they felt it was a private and personal issue, while 12 percent didn't report it because they feared a reprisal or repeated attack by the assailant.

> *"The overwhelming majority of rapes are committed by persons the victim knew before the crime took place."*

Research indicates that current laws concerning domestic violence are too lenient, in many cases creating the illusion that domestic violence is not a serious offense. According to testimony presented before the Senate Labor and Human Resources Committee in 1990, only 110 US cities had domestic violence intervention programs requiring mandatory arrest. . . .

Even when arrests are made, the rate of conviction in domestic violence cases remains low. This low rate can be tied, in part, to the actions, or in-actions, of prosecutors who frequently discourage victims from going forward with cases, place a low priority on domestic violence cases, fail to consider the safety of the victim when releasing offenders, and/or go as far as dismissing domestic violence cases.

The criminal justice system is not the only source that fails domestic violence victims. Many women in violent relationships unsuccessfully try to stop the violence by seeking assistance from sources including lawyers, health care personnel, family members, and clergy. According to "Understanding Domestic Violence," a 1988 study of more than 6,000 battered women in Texas, women had contacted, on the average, five different sources for help prior to leaving the home and actually becoming the residents of battered women's shelters.

Federal Programs

Federal programs to address violent crimes against women have been extremely limited, both in scope and funding. As with most crimes, rape and domestic violence fall primarily under the purview of state and local authorities. The federal government, however, has only a few small programs to assist states helping female victims of violence.

Rape Is Widespread on College Campuses

by Le Anne Schreiber

About the author: *Le Anne Schreiber, a former senior editor of the* New York Times, *is the author of* Midstream: The Story of a Mother's Death and a Daughter's Renewal.

At schools large and small, urban and rural, Midwestern and Ivy League, one out of seven female students is a victim of rape. By their own admission, one out of twelve male students commits or attempts rape, usually more than once. The problem of sexual assault on college campuses is national, widespread and unabated, and yet, despite the evidence, it is largely unaddressed by students, their parents or college administrators. Because the vast majority of these rapes go unreported except on the blanks of anonymous questionnaires, it is all too easy for college administrators to believe that it isn't happening in *their* quads, in *their* dorms, on *their* fraternity row.

Rape on Campus

In the rare case of a reported rape on campus, the temptation is to treat it as an isolated event, shocking, frightening and aberrant. That was the response of both students and officials at Syracuse University, a large private school located in central New York State, when an eighteen-year-old student reported that she had been raped near the chancellor's home during the first week of classes.

The following week, when another eighteen-year-old student reported that she had been raped in her dorm room by two young men who had escorted her home from a nearby bar, the temper of the campus began to change. Two hundred placard-carrying students marched to the administration building to demand that something be done. Seeing a public relations disaster in the making, Chancellor Melvin Eggers responded later that afternoon by appointing a task force to study

Le Anne Schreiber, "Campus Rape." This article originally appeared in the September 1990 issue of *Glamour* and is reprinted with permission.

the issue and report back to him within thirty days. During the month it took the university task force to do its work, four more rapes were reported.

The impact of six reported rapes in five weeks was shattering. Female students were afraid to go to the library after dark. The dean of student relations spent hours on the phone with concerned parents who wanted to know why the hefty tuition they were paying ($11,000 and climbing) couldn't ensure their daughters' safety. The student newspaper, *The Daily Orange*, began to read like a big-city tabloid. Student activists, with the support of concerned faculty and community members, staged rallies, marches and a candlelight vigil that brought five hundred scared students out of their rooms at midnight on a chilly October weekday. Rape became the issue that wouldn't go away, and the administration realized the only choice was to address it. To their credit, administrators resisted the temptation to take the easy way out.

Acquaintance Rapes

Yes, there was an easy way out. According to Edward J. Golden, the dean who fielded those angry calls, most parents were reassured as soon as they learned that five of the six incidents were date or acquaintance rapes. Two of the victims had met their assailants at Sutter's Mill, an off-campus bar on nearby Marshall Street, and accepted their offer of an escort back to their dorm rooms. Two other attacks had taken place in students' apartments after the victims and assailants had met at fraternity parties. The victim of the sixth reported rape said she had been assaulted by three male "friends." The circumstances implied that the women had been drinking; perhaps they led the men on. At the very least, they must have acted imprudently. As long as parents could find a way to blame the victim, they didn't have to worry about their own "blameless" daughters. Parents were all too ready to believe the problem was manageable, a simple matter of securing the campus against that lone psychopathic stranger who lurked at its edges.

Even students, who were much better informed than their parents about the circumstances of the six rapes, focused upon the threat posed by strangers and the solutions promised by heightened security. "Don't walk home alone" became the campus battle cry, even though students knew perfectly well that at least four of the six reported rapes might *not* have happened if the victims had returned home alone. At the very bar where two of the victims met their assailants, the owner posted a large new sign outside the ladies' room: "MAKE SAFETY YOUR FIRST CONCERN: SUTTER'S MILL REMINDS YOU DON'T WALK HOME ALONE." The uninten-

"At schools large and small, urban and rural, Midwestern and Ivy League, one out of seven female students is a victim of rape."

tional irony of that sign seemed lost on the hundreds of students who still gathered to drink and mingle in Sutter's Mill every weekend night. For most students, it was—and is—much more comfortable to fear an outsider than to look at the enemy within, to believe that rapists are men who jump out of bushes rather than men voluntarily ushered into dorm rooms.

> *"Parents were all too ready to believe the problem was manageable, a simple matter of securing the campus against that lone psychopathic stranger."*

The misguided notion that strangers were the problem and security the answer might have gone unchallenged if it had not been for the persistence of a few strong voices on campus. Dolores Card, program director of the community Rape Crisis Center of Syracuse and a member of the university task force, kept reminding everyone that "75 percent of adult rapes that come to my center are acquaintance rapes, usually committed in the victim's home; on college campuses the percentage is even higher." The reluctance to acknowledge this fact and the readiness to blame the victim is not unique to Syracuse. "Date rape comes too close," says Card. "Women need to distance themselves from the victim to feel safe. If you can find a reason why somebody else did something wrong, then you're safe. That's why female jurors are harder on victims than male jurors. I see it over and over, particularly in college-age women. Friends turn against friends, because they want to find something the victim did wrong so they can say, 'I wouldn't do that.' They just won't let the danger register.". . .

Coming Forward

One of the most powerful voices came from a completely unexpected source—a sophomore metal smithing major who had been the victim of the only rape reported at the university the previous year. Through a long, hard freshman year, Kristin Eaton-Pollard had remained anonymous, the unnamed victim of front page news stories and campus rumors. But one day in September 1989 she walked out of her psychology class at noon and saw yellow posters announcing that a protest rally was under way that very moment in front of the administration building. She joined the crowd listening to Card and others speak into a megaphone, and without having wished or planned for this opportunity, she worked her way to the front of the crowd and took the megaphone.

"I don't know how I mustered the courage," says Kristin, then a sophomore, "but I just looked at the crowd and told them that I was the rape victim they had read about in the *Daily Orange*. I was shaking. I said I knew some of the things the student who had been raped that weekend must be going through, how it felt to be judged and blamed, to be slandered by my peers and the media. I told them that if they were really serious about preventing rape, they should turn to people they hear making slanderous remarks about the victim and tell them they are wrong and tell them how much pain their remarks cause the victim."

By the time she finished speaking to the hushed audience, Kristin had altered her life forever—and regained a measure of the control she felt had been seized from her by the stranger who attacked her a year earlier. Edward Golden, the dean of student relations, who was in the crowd the day she spoke, asked her to be a member of the rape task force. Lynne Woehrle, one of the rally organizers, and two other women, themselves victims of rape, thanked Kristin for her bravery in coming forward. Together, they began making plans to form a support group on the campus for victims of rape. Within a month of founding Women for Women, they had received sixty calls for help and were able to provide counseling for over forty students, many of whom had never before admitted being raped.

"You can know the statistics," says graduate student Lynne Woehrle, "and as an administrator you can be worried about what that means for people in your community, but until you connect those statistics to a human being, I don't think you're motivated to make a real commitment to change." As a member of the task force, Kristin forced the Syracuse administration to make that connection. Recalling her own solitary struggle with the consequences of rape, she made repeated, impassioned pleas for a university rape-crisis center, which the administration

> *"75 percent of adult rapes . . . are acquaintance rapes, usually committed in the victim's home; on college campuses the percentage is even higher."*

agreed to open for students. She testified before a House of Representatives committee in support of a federal bill that would require colleges to make their annual crime statistics known to all prospective students. Above all, she is committed to creating a climate on campus that will make students feel more free to report sexual assault and seek help.

Lying to Friends

Kristin remembers how it felt to lie to her friends, to explain her visible cuts and bruises with a story about falling down steps. She remembers how it felt when a campus security guard came to her residence hall to give a lecture on crime prevention and belittled her case. "He had this smirk on his face and said, 'Let me give you an example. Three weeks ago, this girl was at a frat party drinking and decides to go alone near the park at three in the morning and she gets raped. What a shock!' And I'm sitting right there. I want to get up and run, but I can't run, because then everybody will know it's me.

"Society paints such a terrible picture of the rape victim. I didn't want to admit that I—who was thought of as an intelligent and strong-minded person, this fun-loving freshman nicknamed 'Kip'—I didn't want to admit that I was a victim of rape. It was my first year of college and I was trying to fit in. But as long as a rape victim feels she has to hide what happened to her, deep inside she is going to feel guilty. I began to think, 'Well, maybe it was my fault, to an extent. I wasn't drunk and I was only going two hundred yards to a friend's house, but I was walking along a street at night by myself. I was a pretty, small, powerless-looking female.' But it wasn't my fault. The rapist should be paying for this, not me."

> *"As long as a rape victim feels she has to hide what happened to her, deep inside she is going to feel guilty."*

If victims of stranger rape like Kristin feel blamed and guilty, victims of date and acquaintance rape are even more isolated. In fact, the crucible of judgment a victim of date rape must endure is so daunting that most assaults go unreported even to friends and family, much less to university and police authorities. In four of the five acquaintance rapes reported by students in 1990, the victims either would not identify their assailants or chose not to pursue prosecution. In the only case to be heard by the University Judicial Board, the three male students accused of raping a sophomore "friend" were acquitted of sexual misconduct; the victim, who reportedly received several threatening phone calls after filing a police report, accepted the help of the local district attorney's witness-protection project to transfer to another university.

The very term "date rape" seems to work against its victims. "When I first heard the term, I was elated," says Dolores Card. "I thought, 'Finally we can make people understand that rape primarily happens with people you know.' But as time goes by, a term meant to be descriptive has become a qualifier, as if date rape is somehow a lesser kind of rape." On many campuses the term has become another opportunity for blaming the victim, for making her feel partially responsible for the crime and guilty for reporting what is, in some minds, "just a date rape." If a victim has been drinking, which is often the case, she is regarded as an accessory to the crime against her, as if insobriety were as great an offense as rape. In fact, a widely accepted double standard on campus seems to hold that alcohol makes a woman more responsible for her behavior and a man less so.

The Issue of Rape

A group of ATO fraternity members who agreed to discuss the issue of rape on campus acknowledged that blame fixing was the main concern whenever a reported rape was discussed among students. "I can see why you'd keep it to yourself," said sophomore Geoff Bent. "Why would you want people to know you have been humiliated? If you say anything, you'd walk around feeling like everybody had their eyes on you, judging you. I wouldn't want to admit it. I'd want to keep it in."

To a man, all eight of the ATO's in this gathering insisted that they would not be sexually persistent in the face of a woman's "no." When pressed they remained convincingly firm. "No is no, it's a moral given," said junior Tristan Welling. "It's always been no is no," added Geoffrey Hunt, a redheaded sophomore from Boston. "That's life. There's always another night, another time."

Then how do they account for surveys indicating that one out of seven college women has been raped? "I think those statistics are possible," said sophomore Scott Delea. "For instance, maybe the first time you have sex with a girl, she said yes, so the next time you just presume it's okay, and it could be rape. Or you hear guys say, 'Oh, I was so wasted. I don't know what I did last night. Man, I could have done anything!' And you hear that a lot. *A lot!* Maybe in one out of six of those situations, the guy raped the girl."

Sophomore Sean Reed agreed that what is known as "blackout sex" could be a contributing factor in rape. "I think when you introduce alcohol, nos turn into maybes. You don't want to hear no when you're drunk, so your judgment somehow hears maybe. Or a lot of times it will be a maybe situation, and no one will say no, and no one will say yes, and it will just happen. That's the scariest situation."

A Judgment Call

"I know for a fact," said Tristan, "that when you first go to college, those first few weeks, the whole first semester sometimes, you just go wild. And women do it, too. I'm a junior now, and I can look back three years and say, 'Geez, that might have been a date rape.' There's a certain judgment call in that."

Tristan's comment prompted Sean to observe that the most dangerous time for female students is "the honeymoon period." When asked to explain the term, all eight of the fraternity brothers spoke virtually in unison, finishing each other's sentences, never contradicting.

"The honeymoon period," they explained, is the first few weeks of the school year, "when freshmen girls arrive on campus. They are so naive, especially the ones from small towns, or girls who have never been away from home, who returned every night to Mom and Dad. And the upperclassmen are there waiting for them. They know how to manipulate the girls, know what they can get away with, what they should say, what moves to make. Like that freshman girl who got raped by two guys she met on Marshall Street who said they were Syracuse football players. They probably weren't football players here or anywhere else."

> *"You don't want to hear no when you're drunk, so your judgment somehow hears maybe."*

"Instead of a one-day seminar," Tristan summed up, "the freshmen girls get a month-long lesson, physically and mentally grueling, and then they learn. But for that first month, they're not used to handling so many strangers, going out and seeing new faces every night. The school gets pretty small pretty quickly, but at first you're on a campus with fifteen thousand strangers and it is overwhelming."

In the minds of the ATO's, it was probably not a coincidence that all six of the year's reported rapes happened in the first five weeks of the school year, and that four of the six victims were freshmen. Dolores Card of the Rape Crisis Center of Syracuse confirms that an inordinate number of date rapes happen between the end of senior high school and the first few months of college. "I can't prove it," she says, "but I bet if a survey were taken of women who leave college in their freshman year, rape would be the most common reason they left." Card herself has counseled twenty-five freshmen women during a three-and-a-half-year period; all but five left their schools.

> *"An inordinate number of date rapes happen between the end of senior high school and the first few months of college."*

Addressing the Problem

Everyone involved in rape prevention agrees that a strong freshman orientation program on rape is crucial, and legislation has just been passed in New York State that makes such orientation mandatory for colleges receiving state funds. Yet few colleges, including Syracuse, have such a program in place. What Syracuse has instead is a new, very explicit policy statement on rape and sexual assault that makes any form of nonconsensual sexual behavior a violation of the student code punishable by possible suspension or expulsion. The code strikes fear into the hearts of young men who know that consent is not always explicit. "Do we have to get a written or videotaped 'yes'?" one male student asked.

Since most violations are never reported, the men in all likelihood have little to fear, and yet their confusion is sincere. The desire for an honest exchange on the subject was so great that the eight ATO's, who initially had to be pried away from a televised Syracuse basketball game, talked nonstop for over two hours, without making even quick exits for an update on the score. . . .

Dean Edward Golden admits that "institutions have to think about what impact a limited amount of publicity on this subject will have. Of course there is an impulse in all of us to hope it will just go away, but that impulse is not leading us. I believe the long-term impact of the publicity will be positive in that the more forthrightly we address the issue, the more we will increase the confidence of students and their parents."

In response to student and parent demands, the university has tightened security in its residence halls and begun to install a system of "blue lights" on campus—outdoor telephones that sound an alarm in security headquarters as soon as the receiver is lifted. The director of the new rape-crisis center will be responsible for instituting both an education program and support services for victims. And 3,600 new students will arrive on campus with a handbook that clearly states the university will not tolerate rape, sexual assault or "any actual or attempted nonconsensual sexual activity, including, but not limited to, attempted intercourse, sexual touching, exhibitionism, or sexual language of a threatening nature."

It is a beginning, made in good faith, and should there be any temptation to backslide, that chorus of voices will make itself heard.

The Incidence of Rape
Is Exaggerated

by Neil Gilbert

About the author: *Neil Gilbert is Chernin Professor of Social Welfare at the University of California, Berkeley. His most recent book is* The Enabling State: Modern Welfare Capitalism.

Newspapers and television broadcasts have recently reported that a plague of sexual assaults is sweeping the country. Detailed accounts of this problem appear not only on Oprah and Geraldo and in the *National Enquirer*, but also in steadier sources such as *Time*, the *New York Times*, and network newscasts, all of which claim that we are in the midst of a "silent epidemic." The epidemic is said to be silent, in part, because it involves a wide range of behavior that is not yet understood to be abusive. The feminist movement seeks to eradicate it by advancing programs that teach and enforce radical prescriptions to alter intimate relations between adults and children, and between men and women. . . .

Sexual Assault

Mary Koss's survey of 6,159 college students, sponsored by *Ms.* magazine, is the most widely cited study of sexual assault on campus. Her findings (reported in the *New York Times*, *Newsweek*, the *Boston Globe*, and *Time*, among other publications) reveal that at some time in their lives, 15 percent of the female students had been raped and another 11 percent had experienced an attempted rape, usually by an acquaintance. Forty-one percent of the women raped were virgins at the time of the attack. Less frequently cited is the finding that in just one year on college campuses, the 3,187 female respondents in this survey reported suffering 862 incidents of rape or attempted rape. While many of these women experienced more than one episode, this annual count represents a level of sexual assault that would claim victim to the vast majority of women at some

From Neil Gilbert, "The Phantom Epidemic of Sexual Assault." Reprinted from: *The Public Interest*, No. 103 (Spring 1991), pp. 54-65, © 1991 by National Affairs, Inc. Used with permission.

point in their college careers.

These results are bolstered by several smaller studies and impressionistic accounts. For example, interviews of 930 women in San Francisco led Diana Russell to estimate that at least 46 percent of American women will be victims of rape or attempted rape at some time in their lives. A survey of 2,400 students at Stanford University reveals that one-third of the women have suffered incidents of date rape. Offering a more intuitive view, the coordinator of the Rape Prevention Education Program at the University of California's Berkeley campus reports that from her observations of campus life, female students stand a one-in-four chance of being raped by an acquaintance. Another expert in the field, Andrea Parrot, reckons that more than 20 percent of late adolescents outside of college are victims of rape. Drawing on Koss's findings, Parrot came to this conclusion by assuming that college women experience a lower rate of acquaintance rape than women of their age cohort in the general population.

> *"The problem . . . is still orders of magnitude smaller than the epidemic highlighted in the media accounts."*

Taken together, the most frequently cited estimates of acquaintance rape and the sexual molestation of children indicate that close to half of the women in the United States are sexually assaulted before age twenty-one. Other figures, however, tell a different story, which is seldom reported by the media.

Under the Uniform Crime Reporting Program, the FBI routinely gathers statistics on almost all major offenses reported to local law-enforcement agencies throughout the country. According to these data, the number of attempted and completed rapes disclosed between 1979 and 1988 rose from 76,390 to 92,490. It is true, of course, that many incidents of rape are not officially reported, and no one knows exactly how many have occurred. Estimates of unreported crime can, however, be gleaned from the National Crime Survey of the Bureau of Justice Statistics (BJS), which draws on a probability sample of 59,000 households. Findings from these household interviews generally disclose rates of rape 50 percent to 140 percent higher than those reported to the local authorities. Disturbing as these figures are, the problem that they reveal is still orders of magnitude smaller than the epidemic highlighted in the media accounts.

Incidence of Rape

The figure below provides the FBI and BJS data; for purposes of comparability, the raw BJS data have been converted to the format of the FBI data, which show the number of rapes per 100,000 women. Measured by either survey, the incidence of rape climbed significantly between 1970 and 1980. Since 1980, however, officially reported rates have leveled off, and the rates derived from household surveys have declined substantially. As the data show, between 1980 and 1987 the rate confirmed by household respondents fell from 150 reported and unreported cases for every 100,000 women to 113.

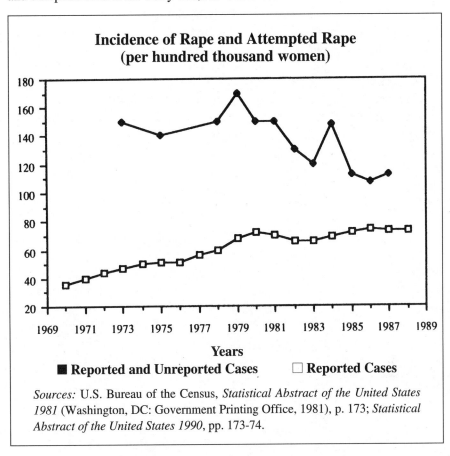

Incidence of Rape and Attempted Rape
(per hundred thousand women)

Years

■ **Reported and Unreported Cases**   □ **Reported Cases**

Sources: U.S. Bureau of the Census, *Statistical Abstract of the United States 1981* (Washington, DC: Government Printing Office, 1981), p. 173; *Statistical Abstract of the United States 1990*, pp. 173-74.

The situation conveyed by the figure is still, of course, deeply disturbing. Rape is a heinous offense, and the 141,000 cases reported and unreported in 1987 represent an enormous amount of human suffering. However, there is a staggering difference between a problem in which one of every thousand women is victimized and an "epidemic" of sexual assaults that harms one of ever two before they reach their mid-twenties. What accounts for this discrepancy?

A Matter of Definition

The obvious answer is that it is just a matter of definition. And to some extent this is true. Part of the variance among these findings can be attributed to the distinction between incidence rates (the number of cases per year) and prevalence rates (the proportion of women who, at some point in their lives, will be victimized); different sampling procedures; and assorted methods of gathering data. But the most telling factor is the investigators' different working definitions of sexual molestation.

For example, Diana Russell claims that 54 percent of her respondents were victims of incestuous or extrafamilial sexual abuse before age eighteen. This prevalence rate is based on a broad definition of sexual abuse: children who merely receive "unwanted kisses and hugs" are classed as victims, as are others who have not been touched at all (e.g., children who encounter exhibitionists). A lower rate of 38 percent was registered with a narrower definition that involved "unwanted sexual experiences ranging from attempted petting to rape" by nonrelatives and "any kind of exploitive sexual contact or attempted contact" by relatives. The information used to determine whether sexual abuse occurred was based on responses to fourteen screening questions such as these:

• Did anyone ever try to or succeed in touching your breasts or genitals against your wishes before you turned fourteen?

• Did anyone ever feel you, grab you, or kiss you in a way that you felt was threatening?

• At any time in your life has an uncle, brother, father, grandfather, or female relative ever had any kind of sexual contact with you?

In addition to finding a 38- to 54-percent rate of sexual abuse during their childhood, Russell discovered that more than a third of those included in her sample had been victims of rape or attempted rape after reaching age sixteen.

"Circumstances matter; it makes a difference what the man's intention was."

In the *Ms.* survey on campus sexual assault, Mary Koss was guided by what she calls a strict legal definition of rape: acts that involve the penetration of a woman "against consent through the use of force or threat of bodily harm, or intentional incapacitation of the victim." To identify victims of rape by this definition, survey respondents were asked ten questions about their sexual experiences, a few of which follow:

Have you had sexual intercourse when you didn't want to, because you were overwhelmed by a man's continual arguments and pressure? Because a man gave you alcohol or drugs? Because a man threatened or used some degree of physical force to compel you?

Date Rape

The report that one out of three female Stanford students has experienced date rape derives from a survey in which respondents revealed that they had "full sexual activity when they did not want to."

The results of these surveys, however, are misleading; in their efforts to capture the full extent of sexual molestation, the studies cast a large, tightly-woven net that snares the minnows with the sharks. If unwanted hugs and kisses are equated with the sexual abuse of children, we have all been victims. Russell's more restrictive definition may come closer to what people think of as sexual abuse, but it is hard to judge when she includes conduct that ranges from attempted petting to any kind of exploitive sexual contact.

Unlike Russell's perception of sexual abuse, which encompasses all sorts of physical contact, Mary Koss's view of rape is limited to sexual behavior that involves penetration. Koss, however, takes a strict legal definition and gives it a loose empirical interpretation. For example, if a woman said that she had had sexual intercourse when she did not want to, because a man gave her alcohol or drugs, Koss would label her a victim of rape. Presumably this is a case of "intentional incapacitation of the victim." Still, circumstances matter; it makes a difference what the man's intention was, how much alcohol the woman had ingested, and whether and how she expressed her lack of consent. Fifty-five percent of the women identified by Koss as rape victims had been drinking or taking drugs just before the episode. Did the man order a beer or a bottle of wine during dinner? Did she select the brand and split the bill? Was she too intoxicated to reason with the man? Did she physically resist his advances or run away? . . .

Sexual Coercion

According to Koss, respondents were identified as victims of "sexual coercion" if they had engaged in sexual intercourse because they were "overwhelmed by a man's continual arguments and pressure." The conventional script of nagging and pleading—"Everyone does it," "If you really loved me, you'd do it," "We did it last night," "You will like it,"—is transformed into a version of sexual assault.

Under these definitions of rape and sexual coercion, the kaleidoscope of intimate discourse—passion, emotional turmoil, entreaties, flirtation, provocation, demureness—must give way to cool-headed contractual sex: "Will you do it, yes or no? Please sign on the line below."

How do reasonable women view this matter? Most of the female students surveyed disagreed with the operational definition of rape in the *Ms.* study. Seventy-three percent of those whom the researcher defined as having been raped did not perceive of themselves as victims. Indeed, 42 percent of the women who were defined as having been raped had sex again with the men who had supposedly raped them. Among the college men surveyed, 84 percent of those identified as having committed rape disagreed with the

> *"Seventy-three percent of those whom the researcher defined as having been raped did not perceive of themselves as victims."*

researcher's interpretation of the incidents. Evidently, so did the women with whom they were involved, as 55 percent of these men had sex again with their putative victims.

There are several ways to interpret these reactions. Some would concur with Robin Warshaw's explanation that women who return to have sex with their attackers do so because they are confused and "fall back on typically self-blaming female explanations: I must have misunderstood him, I didn't make myself clear, I am wrong for feeling bad about this. He must really like me, because he asked me out again." Others would say that if reasonable people feel confusion rather than outrage, perhaps there is something to be confused about.

> *"The feminist prescription redefines conventional morality so as to give women complete control of physical intimacy between the sexes."*

It would be correct, then, to say that the vastly different estimates of the size of the problem are largely a matter of definition. But this explanation misses an essential point. What is at stake here is more than the semantic quibblings of social science.

A Feminist Prescription

A definition describes the essential character of a phenomenon and marks its boundaries. The definitions of sexual abuse and rape employed in the studies noted above extend the boundaries and transform the character of what is to be considered sexual assault. Most of the women in the *Ms.* survey did not regard their experience as rape—although according to Koss, they should have. Purporting to provide a strict definition of rape, her study actually issues a radical feminist prescription for the empowerment of women that is notably uneasy about physical intimacy between the sexes.

In her view, the slightest pressure constitutes use of force: all degrees of intoxication are the same; sweet talk and efforts at verbal persuasion are coercive; above all, the faintest demurral means no. The authorized script for male-female relationships precludes "Maybe," "I don't know," "If you would . . . ," "As long as. . . ." There is no place for qualification, uncertainty, and confusion, except perhaps when a woman says "yes." "Many feminists," according to Susan Estrich, "would argue that so long as women are powerless relative to men, viewing 'yes' as a sign of true consent is misguided." Estrich herself agrees that "yes" may often mean "no."

The feminist prescription redefines conventional morality so as to give women complete control of physical intimacy between the sexes. Advances by males, in almost any form, that do not receive clear and explicit consent are deemed coercive or assaultive. Passion, spontaneity, and the smile or nod that implies assent are all ruled out of intimate discourse, to be replaced by rational calculation and formal understanding. The awesome complexity of human interaction is reduced to "No means no" (even though "yes" may also mean "no").

But research that defines almost half of women under twenty-five as victims of sexual molestation is only part of the radical feminist effort to impose new norms governing intimacy between the sexes. . . .

The estimates of sexual assault calculated by feminist researchers are advocacy numbers, figures that embody less an effort at scientific understanding than an attempt to persuade the public that a problem is vastly larger than commonly recognized. Advocacy numbers are derived not through outright deceit but through a more subtle process of distortion. Under the veil of social science, rigorous research methods are employed to measure a problem defined so broadly that it forms a vessel into which almost any human difficulty can be poured. Some argue that efforts of this sort can serve a useful purpose, because social problems are sometimes larger than commonly recognized. And since the media gravitate toward alarming numbers, a bit of definitional stretching may be necessary to bring the problem into public view. Among those who practice social advocacy, this is known as "consciousness raising" and is deemed a respectable function of advocacy numbers.

One way of looking at the tremendous estimates of sexual assault, then, is to see them as part of the struggle to influence social policy for a good cause. From this perspective feminist advocates may claim a measure of success, when we consider the proliferation over the last decade of publicly subsidized rape crisis centers and training programs to prevent sexual abuse, along with the growing support industry of consultants, books, videos, and other educational paraphernalia. There is some indication, though, that public support for these efforts may be on the wane. In 1990 Governor Deukmejian eliminated all of the funding for California's extensive program of training to prevent sexual abuse. These funds were cut in the wake of a budget deficit and a report from the legislative analyst's office that found both the effects and appropriateness of the prevention program—particularly when directed at young children—highly questionable.

> *"One way of looking at the tremendous estimates of sexual assault, then, is to see them as part of the struggle to influence social policy."*

Consciousness Raising

In one respect the use of advocacy numbers to measure sexual assault is unique. Most consciousness raising requires that the public be exposed to the problems of other people. The people who have the problem—whether it is homelessness, mental illness, poverty, or AIDS—are well aware of it. According to the feminist researchers who promulgate advocacy numbers, sexual assault raises a different sort of issue: it not only afflicts a much higher proportion of people than other social problems (perhaps half of women under twenty-five and many more afterward), but most of the victims are also unaware of their affliction or unwilling and unable to acknowledge it. In this case the function of advocacy numbers is to alter consciousness more than raise it, to change social perceptions of what constitutes common experience in heterosexual relations. The difference between a sexual-assault rate of 25 or 50 percent and one of 0.1 percent is more than a matter of degree. It is the difference between the view that male-female relations are normally enjoyable for most people and the view that they are inherently antagonistic and dangerous. To argue for the higher rate is to try to shift our understanding of the battle of the sexes: the model suggested by Spencer Tracy and Katherine Hepburn is to be replaced by one in which Conan the Barbarian violently thrashes his cavemate.

> *"The burgeoning rates of sexual assault advanced by radical feminists have been almost immune to critical examination."*

While the problem of sexual assault may well be greater than is suggested by the National Crime Survey figures, it has certainly not reached the epidemic proportions indicated by the advocacy numbers. Radical feminists who promote advocacy numbers aim not so much to solve the problem of sexual assault as to change social perceptions of its basic nature. In pursuit of this objective, they find it necessary to instill belief in an epidemic that would justify the feminist-prescribed social inoculation of every woman and child in society.

Trivializing Abuse

To argue that the advocacy numbers are implausible is not to deny the terrible gravity of sexual assault; after all, deplorable things that seldom occur are still deplorable. And the case against the advocacy numbers should be made, because their promulgation trivializes ruthless cases of abuse and feeds off the suffering of real victims. Yet the burgeoning rates of sexual assault advanced by radical feminists have been almost immune to critical examination, especially by other women.

It is tempting to suggest that the silence of the majority explains the relative absence of public debate over the size of this problem: the few women who are disaffected monopolize the discussion, while the many others with no ax to grind go quietly about their business. This may account, in part, for the ready acceptance of the advocacy numbers. But I think that a more complete explanation must take into account women's experiences over the last few decades. During that time, an unprecedented number of women have become heads of single-parent families and have begun to receive the minimal pay of entry-level workers. Not surprisingly, many feel socially and economically oppressed. Advocacy numbers on sexual assault may resonate with their feelings of being, not literally raped, but figuratively "screwed over" by men. If this is the case, it will require more than objective analysis to dispel the phantom epidemic of sexual assault.

The Problem of Rape on College Campuses Is Exaggerated

by Murray N. Rothbard

About the author: *Murray N. Rothbard is editor of the* Rothbard-Rockwell Report, *a publication of the Center for Libertarian Studies in Burlingame, California.*

A lot of strange things are happening on college campuses these days, and one of them is a great deal of kvetching about the alleged epidemic of "date rape." William Celis 3rd's special report to the *New York Times* on the subject is best summed up by its subtitle: "Agony on Campus: What Is Rape?" To a libertarian, or indeed to any sensible person, there is no problem: if the sex was coercive, and took place against the will of one of the parties, then it was rape and if not, not. If it was, you call in the gendarmes, and if it wasn't, you don't. So what's the big problem?

Second-Guessing Sex

But to the current generation of college students, things are very different. One says, "it's such a fuzzy topic," and another adds, "it's easy to look at sex and second-guess." There follows a lot of guff about how the feminist movement has succeeded in alerting countless coeds about this terrible problem. But why should it take feminist theoreticians to inform a girl that she has been raped? Why is this topic "fuzzy," when to this reactionary it appears clear-cut? What's going on here?

Reading on, we find that many men are confused about these rising protests by college females. The guys charge that "women with whom they have had sex did not say 'no' and did not physically resist, yet later complained of date rape." Other "angrier" men claim that "in some cases women have encouraged

Murray N. Rothbard, "'Date Rape' on Campus," *Rothbard-Rockwell Report*, February 1991. Reprinted with permission.

their advances." But the feminists lash back that these are "after-the-fact excuses." Instead, "sexual intercourse," they argue, "should proceed from clear mutual consent."

Now we're getting somewhere. For whether or not "encouragement" took place, it strikes me as crystal-clear that if the girl did not say no and did not physically resist, then sex did indeed take place by "clear mutual consent." What do the feminists want? Will they only be satisfied if (a) the two parties sign an express consent form before the act, and then (b) sign another one immediately after? And have them both notarized on the spot, with forms sent in triplicate to their respective attorneys and to the county clerk? If so, the notary publics in college towns are in for a thriving business, plus some Peeping Tom (or Tomasina) opportunities on the side.

The point is that, as in so many other aspects of human "relationships," the feminists are setting out to destroy romance (if that word is not yet obsolete), which thrives on spontaneity, and on implicit, non-verbal mutual understanding. Which is also the problem with the current mania for condoms and other elaborate birth-control machinations.

Sex and Drinking

A clue to the peculiar fuzziness of the current analysis of rape can be found in the assumptions of the famed Koss study, headed by the shrink Mary Koss, now of the University of Arizona. In trying to find out the extent of rape on the college campuses, Koss *defined* sexual assault as the use of force *or* "intercourse as a result of intentionally getting the woman intoxicated." And we find various references to women being reluctant to report the "rape" because one or usually both parties were "drunk" at the time.

Well, now, drinking indeed! Are we now to include in rape any sex taking place after liquor is imbibed? Isn't everyone familiar with the old poem and the social reality it reported: "Candy is dandy, but liquor is quicker?" Everyone is responsible for whatever he or she imbibes, unless the guy spiked the girl's drink without her knowledge (not mentioned in any of these cases) and everyone is responsible for their own actions, liquor or not. Come off it, ladies; "date rape" my foot!

> *"If the sex was coercive, and took place against the will of one of the parties, then it was rape and if not, not."*

Ah, now we see what is going on here. For generations now, girls, while consenting implicitly to sex, have wanted to assuage their guilt by being able to tell themselves afterward that they had not planned the action, and that they were merely "swept off their feet" by the charm of the guy and/or the magic of the moment. Hence, as all implicitly consenting parties have been long aware, the use of liquor is a marvelous catalyst of this feet-sweeping. Now, along comes our baneful feminist theoreticians who have been able to use their besotted theories to (a) free girls, once and for all, from guilt for their actions, and (b) to load that guilt onto the poor, hapless male population.

Establishing Consent

The *New York Times* article details one of the cases. During a brainwashing reeducation dorm lecture on date rape at Lehigh University, a male student was asked by a dorm official if he had ever committed rape. First saying "hell, no," the student was later talked by the lecturer into "realizing" that he had, and that "not saying no" was not sufficient to establish consent. (There was no notarized agreement!) Later, the poor guy, admitting that he was "very confused," wrote a self-criticism article to the student paper confessing his sins: "I was uninformed and incorrect in my actions," he groveled. Yeah, and I bet he now loves Big Brother (oops sorry, Big Sister). Poor Orwell never knew the full depths of Political Correctness when he fashioned his dystopia.

There are several ways by which this terrible crisis on the campus can be solved. One, we can go back to the prohibition of alcohol, which our culture is almost ready for in any case. Two, we can go back to the good old days of campuses before the 1950s, especially in the South: not only the banning of coed dorms, and abolishing coeducation altogether, but insisting on official chaperons for girls on every date, on dance-cards filled out in advance and cleared with the chaperon, on boys being barred from the entire girls' campus except one official room, etc. And finally, why not go the whole hog toward Left Puritanism and define all sex as per se coercive? That would clear up all the fuzziness and sex, or at least hetero-sex, could be outlawed completely. Or is that the point, after all?

Feminists Exaggerate the Incidence of Acquaintance Rape

by Norman Podhoretz

About the author: *Norman Podhoretz is editor-in-chief of* Commentary, *a conservative monthly journal published by the American Jewish Committee.*

If prostitution is the world's oldest profession, rape may well be the second oldest crime. But this ancient crime received, so to speak, a new lease on life in the mid-1950s when (as we learn from a scholarly paper written jointly by the "sexuality educator" Laurie Bechhofer and Professor Andrea Parrot of Cornell) a sociologist at Purdue named Eugene Kanin "documented the existence of sexual aggression within courtship relationships. Of the women he sampled 30 percent had been victims of rape or attempted rape while on a date."

Acquaintance Rape: A New Problem?

To be sure, Bechhofer and Parrot do not believe that this was a brand-new phenomenon. As they see it, "Forced sex between acquaintances has probably occurred as long as people have been involved in relationships with each other." This would seem to take us all the way to Adam and Eve, but Bechhofer and Parrot more modestly trace it only as far back as the rape of Tamar by her half-brother Amnon, the story of which in the biblical book of Samuel shows that its "dynamics . . . have not changed significantly over the past 2,000 years":

> Amnon forced Tamar to have sex despite her wishes. He got her into his bed through manipulation and then rejected her after the rape. Tamar was emotionally distraught by the rape, yet others simply trivialized her feelings.

"Despite its long history," however, it was not until Professor Kanin's pioneering research that this particular form of rape was "reported in the scholarly literature." Even then, according to the chronology supplied by Bechhofer and Parrot, another twenty-five years passed before it acquired a name. In September 1982, Karen Barett, a journalist, wrote an article for the feminist magazine *Ms.* in which (apparently ignorant of the book of Samuel) she drew attention to a "new and unusual" form of sexual aggression and called it "date rape." The problem was that this name narrowed the field to couples actually going out together, and so a broader designation was needed to cover the many instances in which the aggressor was previously known to his victim but had not taken her to dinner or whatever. Out of this necessity the term "acquaintance rape" was born.

> *"We are in the presence here of . . . a brazen campaign . . . to identify practically all men as rapists."*

The "experts," as they are always described in newspaper stories on the subject, persist in referring to acquaintance or date rape as a "hidden crime." Well, hidden it may have been for several thousand years, but hidden it is no longer. In an amazingly short time, a vast literature has sprung up, much of it emanating from the women's studies departments now enshrined on almost every campus in the country, but more and more of it also appearing in popular magazines and daily newspapers. Inevitably Oprah and Geraldo have also chimed in, and by now there can hardly be anyone left in America who has not been alerted to the existence of a problem which, though supposedly coterminous with the human race itself, and though now said by the feminist journalist Robin Warshaw to be "more common than left-handedness or heart attacks, or alcoholism," was not even recognized as a problem until practically the day before yesterday. . . .

If everyone has always understood that it was rape when a man used a weapon and/or physical violence or the threat of it to force a woman into sex, whether she had met him previously or not—and let me state here for the record that I myself consider life imprisonment none too harsh a penalty for any such man—why introduce the new category of date or acquaintance rape? The answer is that this is a way of applying the word "rape" to a multitude of situations in which, as Bechhofer and Parrot (and all other "experts") freely admit, "Assailants are more likely to use verbal or psychological coercion to overpower their victims than guns or knives."

Seduction Redefined

Now, if we pause for a moment and remind ourselves that overcoming a woman's resistance by "verbal and psychological" means has in the past been universally known as seduction, it will immediately become clear that we are in the presence here of nothing less than a brazen campaign to redefine seduction as a form of rape, and more slyly to identify practically all men as rapists. "Acquaintance-rape educator" Py Bateman, who once edited the *Journal of Sexual*

Assault and Coercion, more or less lets the cat out of the bag when she declares:

> Rape is not some form of psychopathology that afflicts a very small number of men. In fact, rape is not that different from what we see as socially acceptable or socially laudable male behavior.

(Incidentally, the "we" who see rape as "socially laudable" are especially prevalent, it seems, in America: ". . . every man who grows up in America and learns American English learns all too much to think like a rapist . . ." [Timothy Beneke, quoted by Warshaw].)

It is no wonder that the "experts," armed with the new category of "nonviolent sexual coercion" [a phrase used by Professor Charlene L. Muehlenhard and one of her students, Jennifer L. Schrag], are able to estimate that at least one out of four, and as many as one out of three, young American women are victims of rape or attempted rape by a date or acquaintance. The only wonder is that they come up with so low an estimate. Why not 100 percent?

Sex as Rape

And indeed there are feminists who do not shrink even from that. Susan Brownmiller [Founding Mother of the antirape movement and author of *Against Our Will: Men, Women, and Rape*] is sometimes seen as one of these, but she is not quite of their company. True, she walks up to the edge in the most famous sentence of her book— "[Rape] is nothing more or less than a conscious process of intimidation by which *all men* keep *all women* in

> *"To read this stuff [antirape literature] . . . is to be presented with a picture of women as timorous, cowering, helpless creatures."*

a state of fear" (the italics are definitely her own). But she also denies believing that heterosexual coupling is itself a species of rape. And she even gives her endorsement (albeit, one might say, against her will) to this form of intercourse:

> Anatomically one might want to improve on the design of nature, but such speculation appears to my mind as unrealistic. The human sex act accomplishes its historic [*sic!*] purpose of generation of the species and it also affords some intimacy and pleasure. I have no basic quarrel with the procedure.

The radical feminist critic Andrea Dworkin, on the other hand, *does*, to put it mildly, have a basic quarrel with the procedure. In her book *Intercourse* (1987), she denounces the "simpleminded prosex chauvinism of Right and Left," and in effect extends Brownmiller's definition of rape to the sex act itself:

> Without being what the society recognizes as rape, [intercourse] is what the society—when pushed to admit it—recognizes as dominance.

One of Dworkin's favorite metaphors for sex is "wartime invasion and occupation," and she describes it as evil up against the skin—at the point of entry, just touching the slit; then it breaks in and at the same time it surrounds everything. . . .

In this nightmare inversion of D.H. Lawrence, even the element of coercion is irrelevant; the woman's consent only makes her a "collaborator" with her "rapist":

> Physically, the woman in intercourse is a space inhabited, a literal territory occupied literally: occupied even if there has been no resistance, no force; even if the occupied person said yes please, yes hurry, yes more.

But Dworkin, believe it or not, goes even further:

> . . . occupied women [are] more base in their collaboration than other collaborators have ever been: experiencing pleasure in their own inferiority, calling intercourse freedom. It is a tragedy beyond the power of language to convey when what has been imposed on women by force becomes a standard of freedom for women: and all the women say it is so.

At one point, Dworkin (in one of her gentler characterizations) describes intercourse as "the pure, sterile, formal expression of men's contempt for women." But however great men's contempt for women may be, it could hardly match the contempt for women exemplified in the above quotations and pervading the literature which has been spawned by the antirape subdivision of the contemporary feminist movement.

Women Reduced to Helpless Victims

To read this stuff—not just outspoken radicals like Dworkin herself but mainstream academics like Andrea Parrot, who teaches not only at Cornell but also at SUNY, and liberal journalists like Robin Warshaw—is to be presented with a picture of women as timorous, cowering, helpless creatures who are at the mercy of any male they may be unfortunate enough to run into. Those young women who still feel no fear upon meeting the boy next door are portrayed as naive and are sternly (but compassionately) lectured on their need to recognize that this clean-cut fellow, or any other "regular guy," is far more

"If . . . women are terrified of men, they give off not the slightest whiff of it."

likely to rape them than (in Warshaw's words) the stereotypical "stranger (usually a black, Hispanic, or other minority) jumping out of the bushes . . . brandishing a weapon. . . ."

The women we meet here often blithely accompany their dates or acquaintances into empty houses or apartments, proceed to engage in "certain behavior, like kissing or heavy petting," and are then shocked— shocked!—to discover "men assuming that [this] behavior . . . is an automatic precursor to intercourse."

So widespread among the male sex is this outlandish "behavioral assumption" that a girl cannot even sleep in the same bed with a man without being pressured to go all the way. Here—direct from the pages of Robin Warshaw's *I Never Called It Rape*—is Carol, age 18, who attends a fraternity party with "some nice boy from the next suburb," where she does a little drinking. The next thing she knows,

> We went back to the guys' apartment and my friend Terri went too. It never occurred to me that anything was going to be going on. We were just going to be sleeping there.

But as Warshaw, in reporting on this case, comments ominously,

> just sleeping together is not what Carol's date had in mind. After they got into bed, he started kissing her, then escalated his sexual attention. Despite her repeated "No, no, no" and her physically pushing him away, he used the advantage of his six-foot-three body to overpower her five-foot frame.

Carol, incorrigibly innocent to the end, did not realize she had been raped. But thanks to the antirape movement, she realizes it now.

Thanks to the movement, too, she also realizes that she bears no responsibility whatever for what happened to her. For from earliest childhood, writes Warshaw, Carol, like all girls, had been "taught directly and indirectly (by parents, teachers, playmates, and pop-culture role models) to be passive, weak, and opinionless." Even after she became a young adult, she was "expected to be fearful and inhibited" and was not "encouraged to develop independence and self-reliance." (This, in 1988!) Now, having had her consciousness raised by what is perhaps the most important precept of the movement, she understands that in no way and under no circumstances does any blame attach to the victim of a rape. According to an exquisitely delicate formulation of this precept, "It's his penis, and only he is responsible for where he puts it.". . .

> *"Any male who has intercourse with any female, . . . without first practically getting a . . . consent form . . . , will wind up in jail."*

Myth or Reality?

"Sexual intercourse began/ In nineteen sixty-three/ (Which was rather late for me)—/ Between the end of the Chatterley ban/ And the Beatles' first LP." For any man old enough to know at first hand what those famous lines by Philip Larkin mean (and, I suspect, even for many younger men who grew up under the auspices of the sexual revolution of the 60's), reading the literature on acquaintance and date rape is bound to be a bewildering experience.

There is, for one thing, that endless parade of helpless and stupid females who pass through this literature. Where, the male reader is likely to wonder, have such females been hiding all his life, and what has become of all the others—those swaggeringly self-assured women flaunting their sexual allure—he sees everywhere he goes? If these women are terrified of men, they give off not the slightest whiff of it. On the contrary, what they communicate, in their dress, in their bearing, in their carriage, is a serene confidence in the great power they have over men. And as almost any male reader can confirm, it is a confidence to which they are richly entitled. "Where do they all come from? What do they want from me?" cries a middle-aged character in a Paul Mazursky movie as he sits ogling *this* parade from the table of an outdoor café in Los Angeles.

> *"Almost the entire range of normal heterosexual intercourse must be stigmatized as criminal."*

Adolescent Males

But if middle-aged men still feel this way, it is at least not as bad for them as it is for the adolescent male. An adolescent male is typically a creature in a state of perpetual sexual anguish. The sight of just about any girl at any time in any place can plunge him into a fever of lust, and what makes his plight even more maddening is the unfairness of it all. *He* may be in a state of endless turmoil over sex, but girls, the same girls who do this to him just by being there, seem able to take or leave sex at will. Though their very existence is a provocation even when they are not (or are they?) deliberately taunting and teasing him, neither he nor any other boy seems to have a comparable power over them. For them it is evidently as easy to say no to sex as it is impossible for him. From which he learns very early on that his only hope of ever breaking through this incomprehensible indifference is by not taking their no for an answer at any stage in the process of courtship—which, as he also learns very early on, is precisely what some (and probably most) of them want him to do.

Realities like these are not entirely absent from the literature on acquaintance rape, but they are presented in terms that are again bound to bewilder any normal male reader. According to Robin Warshaw, expressing the movement's party line on this matter, the whole thing is a "myth," a "dogma of what . . . it means to be male" into which boys are "indoctrinated" by "fathers, uncles, grandfathers, coaches, youth group leaders, friends, fraternity brothers, even pop stars." This, it appears, and not their bitter experience with girls, is why they come to "view their relationships with women as adversarial challenges," and why they end up believing

> that they must initiate sexual activity, that they may meet with reluctance from girls, but if they just persist, cajole, and refuse to let up, that ultimately they will get what they want.

So far as the feminist movement is concerned, any man who acts on this "myth" is on the road to becoming a rapist, if indeed he is not already there. For in the movement's eyes a woman's no always means no, her maybe always means no, and even—I do not exaggerate—her yes often means no: "Many feminists," writes Susan Estrich, late of the Dukakis campaign and now a professor at the Harvard Law School, "would argue that so long as women are powerless relative to men, viewing 'yes' as a sign of true consent is misguided." Or, as Muehlenhard and Schrag explain it in "Non-Violent Sexual Coercion":

> There could be many reasons why a woman might not resist a man's advances so that unwanted intercourse could occur without force. The woman may fear that resisting will make the man violent. She may be confused. Her socialization may make it difficult for her to resist.

Not only, then, is there never any justification for pressing ahead when the woman protests or resists, even mildly; if the "experts" get their way, any male who has intercourse with any female, including his wife or a girlfriend with whom he has been sleeping all along, without first practically getting a signed and notarized consent form to cover that particular episode, will wind up in jail. . . .

Criminalizing Normal Intercourse

To further the establishment of the new sexual dispensation, it becomes necessary to delegitimize any instance of heterosexual coupling that starts with male initiative and involves even the slightest degree of female resistance at any stage along the way. Hence almost the entire range of normal heterosexual intercourse must be stigmatized as criminal, and both women and men must be educated to recognize it as such. But to make sure that normal people are not put off by so weird a project, the new conception has to be framed in language that does not betray the antinomian radicalism behind it.

Here, then, is how Robin Warshaw translates the lunatic prescriptions of an antinomian radical like Dworkin into relatively bland "guidelines for change" that men are exhorted to follow if they are to avoid becoming rapists. Among these 11 guidelines are the following:

1. *Never force a woman to have sex*—even if she has "led" you on, even if she has slept with your friends, even if she at first said "yes" and then changed her mind before having sex, even if she had sex with you before. This includes *all* unwanted sexual contact—from kissing to "copping a feel." . . . When partners' desires conflict, the one who wants more activity has to yield to the one who wants less. . . .

> *"To the extent that men are . . . persuaded into . . . the new sexual dispensation, the number of 'wimps'. . . will multiply apace."*

2. *Don't pressure a woman to have sex.* Men often see their verbal pressuring as being less forceful than women do. Even when the words you use are not threatening, the woman may feel that she is in danger. . . .

6. *Do not confuse "scoring" with having a successful social encounter.* . . . You can have intercourse with 100 women and still not know anything about good sex or what it means to be a "real" man. Ejaculating is no big deal; having a mutually agreed-upon and sustained relationship is. . . .

8. *"No" means "no."* . . . When a woman says "no" that means "no." Stop. . . . Do not try to cajole her or argue with her. . . . If you think she's saying "no" to protect her "reputation" (even though you know she *really* wants to have sex with you), so what? When (and if) she's ready to have sex with you, let it be her choice to make. If a woman says "no" and really means "yes, but you have to convince me," then you don't want to be with her anyway. . . . Just walk away. . . .

A Proliferation of "Wimps"

To the extent that men are bullied or persuaded into following, or at least trying to follow, the "guidelines" of the new sexual dispensation, the number of "wimps" about whom women have been complaining ever since women's lib was born (though without ever seeing any connection between the two phenomena) will multiply apace. So—to the great joy of Andrea Dworkin and those "experts" like Muehlenhard and Schrag who believe that "discrimination against lesbians continues as a form of indirect sexual coercion," and constitutes "one more source of pressure for women to be in sexual relationships with men"—will the incidence of male impotence. The search for husbands, already so difficult that hordes of young women have taken to advertising in the personals columns, will in consequence grow even more desperate, and the already familiar female refrain, "Why are all the men I meet either wimps or married or gay?" will swell into an even mightier chorus. And yet, nature still being stronger after all than its antinomian enemies, most young men and most young women will not be repelled or frightened off and will play their naturally ordained parts in the unending and inescapable war between the sexes, suffering the usual wounds, exulting in the usual victories, and even eventually arriving at that armistice known as marriage.

Even these lucky ones, however, will have a harder time of it because of the lethal new poison which has been sprayed by the anti-date-rape brigades onto the battlefield of the war between the sexes in general and the struggles of courtship in particular. As for the unlucky ones, those young men and young women who will be too impressionable or too frightened or too weak to hold out against the imperatives of the new sexual dispensation, they will have its feminist authors to thank for a life of loneliness, frustration, resentment, and sterility.

Broad Definitions of Rape Are Harmful

by Cathy Young

About the author: *Cathy Young is a freelance writer in New Jersey.*

The vast majority of Americans, women or men, undoubtedly take a positive view of changes the women's movement has brought about in attitudes toward rape. It is now widely accepted that a woman does not have to be a paragon of chastity to prove she has been raped; that her sexual history should not be put on trial; that even if she has been having drinks with a man or invited him in, he has no right to force sex on her. These advances, however, may be undermined by the efforts of some feminists to so enlarge the concept of rape as to demonize men, patronize women and offend the common sense of the majority of both sexes.

Every Man Is a Potential Rapist

A recent example of this extremism was provided by a panel discussion on an ABC News special, "Men, Sex and Rape." Men and women in the audience as well as the panel were seated separately, implicitly reinforcing the message that every man is a potential rapist

Five of the six women panelists, among them legal scholar Catherine MacKinnon and *Backlash* author Susan Faludi, backed the view that rape, far from being a pathology, reflects the norm in male-female relations in our society. As proof, MacKinnon asserted that 47 percent of all American women have been sexually assaulted and 25 percent raped. When a male panelist questioned these numbers, she retorted, "That means you don't believe women. It's not cooked, it's interviews with women by people who believed them when they said it."

But not all researchers on the topic do believe their female respondents. University of Arizona psychologist Mary Koss, whose studies in the field are among the most frequently cited, wrote in a 1988 article that of those women

Cathy Young, "What Rape Is and Isn't," *The Washington Post National Weekly Edition*, June 29-July 5, 1992. Reprinted with permission.

whom the researchers classified as victims of rape by nonromantic acquaintances, only 27 percent considered themselves rape victims. In situations involving dating partners, only 18 percent of the researcher-classified victims thought they had been raped. (In surveys that directly ask women about forced intercourse, fewer than 10 percent report such experiences.)

Do these feminists believe women, or do they believe that women need expert guidance to know when they've been raped?

The reason for this startling "credibility gap" becomes clear when one looks at how the concept of rape has been broadened by the radical feminists. In their redefinition, physical force or threat of injury is no longer required.

> *"Advances . . . may be undermined by the efforts of some feminists to so enlarge the concept of rape as to demonize men, patronize women."*

In a recent volume of the *Journal of Social Issues*, for example, University of Kansas Professor Charlene Muehlenhard and three co-authors cite the finding that "the most common method men used to have sexual intercourse with unwilling women was ignoring their refusals without using physical force. . . . The prevalence of rape found in these studies would have been much lower if the definition had required physical force."

A couple is necking, and at some point she says, "Please don't," and perhaps pulls back a little; he keeps trying and she eventually goes along rather than push him away or repeat her refusal more forcefully. Is this rape? Yes, say the hardliners: She does not resist because of fear. Even if the man does not threaten her, his size and muscle implicitly do.

Attacks by Dates

But many people, myself included, will find it hard to believe that most women are afraid their dates will beat them up if they resist. Indeed, many who are attacked by strangers and have far stronger reasons to fear injury still fight back or scream.

Women have sex after initial reluctance for a number of reasons, and fear of being beaten up by their dates is rarely reported as one of them. Some may be ambivalent or confused; they may believe that they shouldn't want sex, and feel less guilty if they are "overpowered."

Sometimes both the man and the woman are drunk, which adds to the confusion and miscommunication. Some women may change their mind, perhaps because they get sexually excited by the man's attentions. Others may be genuinely unwilling but concerned about displeasing the man or hurting his feelings. As one student, prodded by a campus presentation on date rape to conclude that she was a victim, explained to a journalist, "I thought, 'Well, he's my friend . . . whatever happens, it's not going to be that bad' . . . no big deal."

Is it unfortunate that many women are brought up to be so anxious not to offend, to be liked? Yes. But the answer should be to encourage assertiveness, not make excuses for doormat behavior.

Psychological Coercion

The redefinition of rape also includes "psychological coercion" such as "continual arguments." Muehlenhard and her co-authors suggest that if lack of resistance cannot be regarded as consent when a women is threatened with being shot, it might be no different if she is threatened with being dumped. The old "If you loved me, you'd do it" line becomes a felony.

To the cutting-edge anti-date-rape activists, even a "no" is no longer necessary for a finding of coercion; the absence of an explicit "yes" will suffice. In the January/February 1992 issue of *Ms.*, a scene of clearly consensual (but wordless) rough sex from "Basic Instinct" is described as one in which "a woman experiences date rape and then kisses the perp."

All these definitional shenanigans might be funny if they didn't have serious practical consequences. Young men on college campuses are now being told in rape prevention workshops (mandatory for male freshmen at some schools) that they may have raped some of their seemingly willing sexual partners; and young women are being encouraged to abdicate responsibility for their sexual behavior by labeling unsatisfactory experiences as coercive. Harvard's Date Rape Task Force issued a report recommending that university policy define rape as "any act of sexual intercourse that occurs without the expressed consent of the person," as well as sex with someone impaired by "intake of alcohol or drugs."

> *"Many people, myself included, will find it hard to believe that most women are afraid their dates will beat them up if they resist."*

Redefining Rape

Of course, in the enterprise of redefining rape, there is no reason to stop at requiring verbal agreement. If a woman's failure to object to unwanted sex can be attributed to intimidation, so can explicit consent. Inevitably, on the outer limits, this patronizing line of thinking reaches the conclusion that in our oppressive society, there can be no consensual sex. Even if a woman thinks she wants it, that's only because her desire has been "constructed" by the patriarchy.

People have a right to the wackiest of ideas, but it is disturbing that some proponents of this theory are being treated as mainstream feminists. MacKinnon, who has emerged as a leading spokeswoman on sexual harassment and rape, has written such things as: "The similarity between the patterns, rhythms, roles and emotions, not to mention acts, which make up rape on one hand and intercourse on the other . . . makes it difficult to sustain the customary distinctions between violence and sex. . . . The issue is less whether there was force and more whether consent is a meaningful concept." When she appears on television or is quoted in the press, this (one would think) very relevant aspect of her beliefs is tactfully omitted.

Crusading

So anxious are they to extend the concept of rape, these crusaders become almost annoyed when discussions focus too much on violent attacks by strangers or near-strangers. They want to hammer in the point that the greatest danger to women comes from male friends, lovers, husbands. (University of Washington professor Marilyn Friedman has compared Rhett Butler sweeping up Scarlett O'Hara and carrying her upstairs to mass murderer Richard Speck.) They insist that rape at knifepoint in a parking lot is not different from an ambiguous encounter in which a woman is pushed further sexually than she wanted to go, and further, that women have no responsibility whatsoever to avert situations of the latter sort.

On the ABC panel, Naomi Wolf (who is author of *The Beauty Myth*) complained that "in this culture we tend to trivialize the harm that rape does to women." But if anything, much of the effort to broaden the definition of rape trivializes the horror of real sexual violence (by strangers or acquaintances).

The same program included footage of a treatment program for jailed sexual offenders who were made to listen to a recording of a woman calling 911 just as a rapist breaks into her house. The terrified woman gasps "He's here! He's here!" before her voice dissolves into screams and whimpers. One would have to be utterly removed from the real world to insist this is comparable to the experience of a woman who yields because she's tired of pushing away her date's roving hands.

A friend of mine, although acknowledging that some feminist rhetoric is excessive, believes that expanding the definition of rape to include noncoercive experiences is useful because it sensitizes the society to the pain that sexual pressure and manipulation often cause. But pressure and manipulation are not a one-way street; women can apply them too. Besides, the law is not there to ensure we have trauma-free relationships.

Trying to relabel insensitive behavior as illegal can only backfire: When a cad is accused of being a rapist, the unfairness of the charges may make him an object of sympathy, leading people to overlook his moral flaws.

Although I, personally, do not think that "no-maybe-yes" games are the stuff of romance, or that the vanishing of feminine coyness would be a great loss, to replace those rituals with new ones based on suspiciousness, calculation and consent forms in triplicate would hardly be a gain.

Chapter 7

Is the "Battered Woman's Syndrome" a Legitimate Defense?

CURRENT CONTROVERSIES

Battered Women and the Courts: An Overview

by Nancy Gibbs

About the author: *Nancy Gibbs is an associate editor at* Time, *a weekly newsmagazine.*

The law has always made room for killers. Soldiers kill the nation's enemies, executioners kill its killers, police officers under fire may fire back. Even a murder is measured in degrees, depending on the mind of the criminal and the character of the crime. And sometime this spring, in a triumph of pity over punishment, the law may just find room for Rita Collins.

"They all cried, didn't they? But not me," she starts out, to distinguish herself from her fellow inmates in a Florida prison, who also have stories to tell. "No one will help me. No one will write about me. I don't have a dirty story. I wasn't abused as a child. I was a respectable government employee, employed by the Navy in a high position in Washington."

Her husband John was a military recruiter, a solid man who had a way with words. "He said I was old, fat, crazy and had no friends that were real friends. He said I needed him and he would take care of me." She says his care included threats with a knife, punches, a kick to the stomach that caused a hemorrhage. Navy doctors treated her for injuries to her neck and arm. "He'd slam me up against doors. He gave me black eyes, bruises. Winter and summer, I'd go to work like a Puritan, with long sleeves. Afterward he'd soothe me, and I'd think, He's a good man. What did I do wrong?"

The bravado dissolves, and she starts to cry.

"I was envied by other wives. I felt ashamed because I didn't appreciate him." After each beating came apologies and offerings, gifts, a trip. "It's like blackmail. You think it's going to stop, but it doesn't." Collins never told anyone—not her friends in the church choir, not even a son by her first marriage. "I should have, but it was the humiliation of it all. I'm a professional woman. I didn't want people to think I was crazy." But some of them knew anyway; they had seen the bruises, the black eye behind the dark glasses.

She tried to get out. She filed for divorce, got a restraining order, filed an assault-and-battery charge against him, forced him from the house they had bought with a large chunk of her money when they retired to Florida. But still, she says, he came, night after night, banging on windows and doors, trying to break the locks.

It wasn't her idea to buy a weapon. "The police did all they could, but they had no control. They felt sorry for me. They told me to get a gun." She still doesn't remember firing it. She says she remembers her husband's face, the glassy eyes, a knife in his hands. "To this day, I don't remember pulling the trigger."

The jury couldn't figure it out either. At Collins' first trial, for first-degree murder, her friends, a minister, her doctors and several experts testified about her character and the violence she had suffered. The prosecution played tapes of her threatening her husband over the phone and portrayed her as a bitter, unstable woman who had bought a gun, lured him to the house and murdered him out of jealousy and anger over the divorce. That trial ended with a hung jury. At her second, nine men and three women debated just two hours before finding her guilty of the lesser charge, second-degree murder. Collins' appeals were denied, and the parole board last year recommended against clemency. Orlando prosecutor Dorothy Sedgwick is certain that justice was done. "Rita Collins is a classic example of how a woman can decide to kill her husband and use the battered woman's syndrome as a fake defense," she says. "She lured him to his death. He was trying to escape her." Collins says her lawyers got everything: the $125,000 three-bedroom house with a pool, $98,000 in cash. "I've worked since I was 15, and I have nothing," she says. "The Bible says, 'Thou shalt not kill,' and everybody figures if you're in here, you're guilty. But I'm not a criminal. Nobody cares if I die in here, but if I live, I tell you one thing: I'm not going to keep quiet."

> *"More American women—rich and poor alike—are injured by the men in their life than by car accidents, muggings and rape combined."*

If in the next round of clemency hearings on March 10, Governor Lawton Chiles grants Collins or any other battered woman clemency, Florida will join 26 other states in a national movement to take another look at the cases of abuse victims who kill their abusers. Just before Christmas, Missouri's conservative Republican Governor John Ashcroft commuted the life sentences of two women who claimed they had killed their husbands in self-defense. After 20 years of trying, these women have made a Darwinian claim for mercy: Victims of perpetual violence should be forgiven if they turn violent themselves.

More American women—rich and poor alike—are injured by the men in their life than by car accidents, muggings and rape combined. Advocates and experts liken the effect over time to a slow-acting poison. "Most battered women aren't killing to protect themselves from being killed that very moment," observes Charles Ewing, a law professor at SUNY Buffalo. "What they're protecting themselves from is slow but certain destruction, psychologically and physically. There's no place in the law for that."

> *"As the clemency movement grows, it challenges a legal system that does not always distinguish between a crime and a tragedy."*

As the clemency movement grows, it challenges a legal system that does not always distinguish between a crime and a tragedy. What special claims should victims of fate, poverty, violence, addiction be able to make upon the sympathies of juries and the boundaries of the law? In cases of domestic assaults, some women who suffered terrible abuse resorted to terrible means to escape it. Now the juries, and ultimately the society they speak for, have to find some way to express outrage at the brutality that women and children face every day, without accepting murder as a reasonable response to it.

But until America finds a better way to keep people safe in their own homes or offers them some means of surviving if they flee, it will be hard to answer the defendants who ask their judges, "What choice did I really have?"

Home Is Where the Hurt Is

Last year the A.M.A., backed by the Surgeon General, declared that violent men constitute a major threat to women's health. The National League of Cities estimates that as many as half of all women will experience violence at some time in their marriage. Between 22% and 35% of all visits by females to emergency rooms are for injuries from domestic assaults. Though some studies have found that women are just as likely to start a fight as men, others indicate they are six times as likely to be seriously injured in one. Especially grotesque is the brutality reserved for pregnant women: the March of Dimes has concluded that the battering of women during pregnancy causes more birth defects than all the diseases put together for which children are usually immunized. Anywhere from one-third to as many as half of all female murder victims are killed by their spouses or lovers, compared with 4% of male victims.

"Male violence against women is at least as old an institution as marriage," says clinical psychologist Gus Kaufman Jr., co-founder of Men Stopping Violence, an Atlanta clinic established to help men face their battering problems. So long as a woman was considered her husband's legal property, police and the courts were unable to prevent—and unwilling to punish—domestic assaults.

Notes N.Y.U. law professor Holly Maguigan: "We talk about the notion of the rule of thumb, forgetting that it had to do with the restriction on a man's right to use a weapon against his wife: he couldn't use a rod that was larger than his thumb." In 1874 North Carolina became one of the first states to limit a man's right to beat his wife, but lawmakers noted that unless he beat her nearly to death "it is better to draw the curtain, shut out the public gaze and leave the parties to forget and forgive."

Out of that old reluctance grew the modern double standard. Until the first wave of legal reform in the 1970s, an aggravated assault against a stranger was a felony, but assaulting a spouse was considered a misdemeanor, which rarely landed the attacker in court, much less in jail. That distinction, which still exists in most states, does not reflect the danger involved: a study by the Boston Bar Association found that the domestic attacks were at least as dangerous as 90% of felony assaults. "Police seldom arrest, even when there are injuries serious enough to require hospitalization of the victim," declared the Florida Supreme Court in a 1990 gender-bias study, which also noted the tendency of prosecutors to drop domestic-violence cases.

Police have always hated answering complaints about domestic disputes. Experts acknowledge that such situations are often particularly dangerous, but suspect that there are

> *"Domestic violence is not seen as a crime. A man's home is still his castle."*

other reasons for holding back. "This issue pushes buttons, summons up personal emotions, that almost no other issue does for police and judges," says Linda Osmundson, who co-chairs a battered wives' task force for the National Coalition Against Domestic Violence. "Domestic violence is not seen as a crime. A man's home is still his castle. There is a system that really believes that women should be passive in every circumstance." And it persists despite a 20-year effort by advocates to transform attitudes toward domestic violence.

While most of the effort has been directed at helping women survive, and escape, abusive homes, much of the publicity has fallen on those rare cases when women resort to violence themselves. Researcher and author Angela Browne points out that a woman is much more likely to be killed by her partner than to kill him. In 1991, when some 4 million women were beaten and 1,320 murdered in domestic attacks, 622 women killed their husbands or boyfriends. Yet the women have become the lightning rods for debate, since their circumstances, and their response, were most extreme.

What Choice Did She Have?

"There is an appropriate means to deal with one's marital problems—legal recourse. Not a .357 Magnum," argues former Florida prosecutor Bill Catto. "If you choose to use a gun to end a problem, then you must suffer the consequences of your act." Defense lawyers call it legitimate self-protection when a victim of abuse fights back—even if she shoots her husband in his sleep. Prosecutors call it an act of vengeance, and in the past, juries have usually agreed and sent the killer to jail. Michael Dowd, director of the Pace University Battered Women's Justice Center, has found that the average sentence for a woman who kills her mate is 15 to 20 years; for a man, 2 to 6.

The punishment is not surprising, since many judges insist that evidence of past abuse, even if it went on for years, is not relevant in court unless it occurred around the time of the killing. It is not the dead husband who is on trial, they note, but the wife who pulled the trigger. "Frankly, I feel changing the law would be authorizing preventive murder," argued Los Angeles Superior Court Judge Lillian Stevens in the Los Angeles *Times*. "The only thing that really matters is, Was there an immediate danger? There can't be an old grievance." And even if a woman is allowed to testify about past violence, the jury may still condemn her response to it. If he was really so savage, the prosecutor typically asks, why didn't she leave, seek shelter, call the police, file a complaint?

"The question presumes she has good options," says Julie Blackman, a New Jersey-based social psychologist who has testified as an expert witness in abuse and murder cases. "Sometimes, they don't leave because they have young children and no other way to support them, or because they grow up in cultures that are so immersed in violence that they don't figure there's any place better to go, or because they can't get apartments." The shelter facilities around the country are uniformly inadequate: New York has about 1,300 beds for a state with 18 million people. In 1990 the Baltimore zoo spent twice as much money to care for animals as the state of Maryland spent on shelters for victims of domestic violence.

Last July, even as reports of violence continued to multiply, the National Domestic Violence Hotline was disconnected. The 800 number had received as many as 10,000 calls a month from across the country. Now, says Mary Ann Bohrer, founder of the New York City-based Council for Safe Families, "there is no number, no national resource, for people seeking information about domestic violence."

The other reason women don't flee is because, ironically, they are afraid for their life. Law-enforcement experts agree that running away greatly increases the danger a woman faces. Angered at the loss of power and control, violent men often try to track

> *"There is an appropriate means to deal with one's marital problems—legal recourse. Not a .357 Magnum."*

down their wives and threaten them, or their children, if they don't come home. James Cox III, an unemployed dishwasher in Jacksonville, Florida, was determined to find his ex-girlfriend, despite a court order to stay away from her. Two weeks ago, he forced her mother at gunpoint to tell him the location of the battered women's shelter where her daughter had fled, and stormed the building, firing a shotgun. Police shot him dead. "This case illustrates the extent to which men go to pursue their victims," said executive director Rita DeYoung. "It creates a catch-22 for all battered women. Some will choose to return to their abusers, thinking they can control their behavior."

> *"The average sentence for a woman who kills her mate is 15 to 20 years; for a man, 2 to 6."*

"After the law turns you away, society closes its doors on you, and you find yourself trapped in a life with someone capable of homicide. What choice in the end was I given?" asks Shalanda Burt, 21, who is serving 17 years for shooting her boyfriend James Fairley two years ago in Bradenton, Florida. She was three months pregnant at the time. A week after she delivered their first baby, James raped her and ripped her stitches. Several times she tried to leave or get help. "I would have a bloody mouth and a swollen face. All the police would do is give me a card with a deputy's name on it and tell me it was a 'lovers' quarrel.' The battered women's shelter was full. All they could offer was a counselor on the phone."

Two weeks before the shooting, the police arrested them both: him for aggravated assault because she was pregnant, her for assault with a deadly missile and violently resisting arrest. She had thrown a bottle at his truck. Her bail was $10,000; his was $3,000. He was back home before she was, so she sent the baby to stay with relatives while she tried to raise bail. The end came on a Christmas weekend. After a particularly vicious beating, he followed her to her aunt's house. When he came at her again, she shot him. "They say I'm a violent person, but I'm not. I didn't want revenge. I just wanted out." Facing 25 years, she was told by a female public defender to take a plea bargain and 17 years. "I wanted to fight. But she said I'd get life or the electric chair. I was in a no-win situation."

It is hard for juries to understand why women like Burt do not turn to the courts for orders of protection. But these are a makeshift shield at best, often violated and hard to enforce. Olympic skier Patricia Kastle had a restraining order when her former husband shot her. Lisa Bianco in Indiana remained terrified of her husband even after he was sent to jail for eight years. When prison officials granted Alan Matheney an eight-hour pass in March 1989, he drove directly to Bianco's home, broke in and beat her to death with the butt of a shotgun. Last March, Shirley Lowery, a grandmother of 11, was stabbed 19 times with a butcher knife by her former boyfriend in the hallway of the courthouse where she had gone to get an order of protection.

Defense lawyers have a hard time explaining to juries the shame, isolation and emotional dependency that bind victims to their abusers. Many women are too proud to admit to their family or friends that their marriage is not working and blame themselves for its failure even as they cling to the faith that their violent lover will change. "People confuse the woman's love for the man with love of abuse," says Pace's Dowd. "It's not the same thing. Which of us hasn't been involved in a romantic relationship where people say this is no good for you?"

It was Denver psychologist Lenore Walker, writing in 1984, who coined the term battered-woman syndrome to explain the behavior of abuse victims. Her study discussed the cycle of violence in battering households: first a period of growing tension; then a violent explosion, often unleashed by drugs or alcohol; and finally a stage of remorse and kindness. A violent man, she argues, typically acts out of a powerful need for control—physical, emotional, even financial. He may keep his wife under close surveillance, isolating her from family and friends, forbidding her to work or calling constantly to check on her whereabouts. Woven into the scrutiny are insults and threats that in the end can destroy a woman's confidence and leave her feeling trapped between her fear of staying in a violent home—and her fear of fleeing it.

Many lawyers say it is virtually impossible to defend a battered woman without some expert testimony about the effect of that syndrome over time. Such testimony allows attorneys to stretch the rules governing self-defense, which were designed to deal with two men caught in a bar fight, not a woman caught in a violent relationship with a stronger man.

"A violent man . . . typically acts out of a powerful need for control—physical, emotional, even financial."

In a traditional case of self-defense, a jury is presented a "snapshot" of a crime: the mugger threatens a subway rider with a knife; the rider pulls a gun and shoots his attacker. It is up to the jurors to decide whether the danger was real and immediate and whether the response was reasonable. A woman who shoots her husband while he lunges at her with a knife should have little trouble claiming that she acted in self-defense. Yet lawyers still find jurors to be very uncomfortable with female violence under any circumstances, especially violence directed at a man she may have lived with for years.

Given that bias, it is even harder for a lawyer to call it self-defense when a woman shoots a sleeping husband. The danger was hardly immediate, prosecutors argue, nor was the lethal response reasonable. Evidence about battered-woman syndrome may be the only way to persuade a jury to identify with a killer. "Battered women are extraordinarily sensitive to cues of danger, and that's how they survive," says Walker. "That is why many battered women kill, not during what looks like the middle of a fight, but when the man is more vulnerable or the violence is just beginning."

A classic self-defense plea also demands a fair fight. A person who is punched can punch back, but if he shoots, he runs the risk of being charged with murder or manslaughter. This leaves women and children, who are almost always smaller and weaker than their attackers, in a bind. They often see no way to escape an assault without using a weapon and the element of surprise—arguing, in essence, that their best hope of self-defense was a pre-emptive strike. "Morally and legally a woman should not be expected to wait until his hands are around her neck," argues Los Angeles defense attorney Leslie Abramson. "Say a husband says, 'When I get up tomorrow morning, I'm going to beat the living daylights out of you,'" says Joshua Dressler, a law professor at Wayne State University who specializes in criminal procedures. "If you use the word imminent, the woman would have to wait until the next morning and, just as he's about to kill her, then use self-defense."

That argument, prosecutors retort, is an invitation to anarchy. If a woman has survived past beatings, what persuaded her that this time was different, that she had no choice but to kill or be killed? The real catalyst, they suggest, was not her fear but her fury. Prosecutors often turn a woman's history of abuse into a motive for murder. "What some clemency advocates are really saying is that that s.o.b. deserved to die and why should she be punished for what she did," argues Dressler. Unless the killing came in the midst of a violent attack, it amounts to a personal death-penalty sentence. "I find it very hard to say that killing the most rotten human being in the world when he's not currently threatening the individual is the right thing to do."

Those who oppose changes in the laws point out that many domestic disputes are much more complicated than the clemency movement would suggest. "We've got to stop perpetuating the myth that men are all vicious and that women are all Snow White," says Sonny Burmeister, a divorced father of three children who, as president of the Georgia Council for Children's Rights in Marietta, lobbies for equal treatment of men involved in custody battles. He recently sheltered a husband whose wife had pulled a gun on him. When police were called, their response was "So?" Says Burmeister: "We perpetuate this macho, chauvinistic, paternalistic attitude for men. We are taught to be protective of the weaker sex. We encourage women to report domestic violence. We believe men are guilty. But women are just as guilty."

"I find it very hard to say that killing the most rotten human being in the world when he's not currently threatening the individual is the right thing to do."

He charges that feminists are trying to write a customized set of laws. "If Mom gets mad and shoots Dad, we call it PMS and point out that he hit her six months ago," he complains. "If Dad gets mad and shoots Mom, we call it domestic violence and charge him with murder. We paint men as violent and we paint women as victims, removing them from the social and legal consequences of their actions. I don't care how oppressed a woman is; should we condone premeditated murder?"

Only nine states have passed laws permitting expert testimony on battered-woman syndrome and spousal violence. In most cases it remains a matter of judicial discretion. One Pennsylvania judge ruled that testimony presented by a prosecutor showed that the defendant had not been beaten badly enough to qualify as a battered woman and therefore could not have that standard applied to her case. President Bush signed legislation in October urging states to accept expert testimony in criminal cases involving battered women. The law calls for development of training materials to assist defendants and their attorneys in using such testimony in appropriate cases.

> "We paint men as violent and we paint women as victims, removing them from the social and legal consequences of their actions."

Judge Lillian Stevens instructed the jury on the rules governing self-defense at the 1983 trial of Brenda Clubine, who claimed that she killed her police-informant husband because he was going to kill her. Clubine says that during an 11-year relationship, she was kicked, punched, stabbed, had the skin on one side of her face torn off, a lung pierced, ribs broken. She had a judge's order protecting her and had pressed charges to have her husband arrested for felony battery. But six weeks later, she agreed to meet him in a motel, where Clubine alleges that she felt her life was in danger and hit him over the head with a wine bottle, causing a fatal brain hemorrhage. "I didn't mean to kill him," she says. "He had hit me several times. Something inside me snapped; I grabbed the bottle and swung." The jury found Clubine guilty of second-degree manslaughter, and Judge Stevens sentenced her to 15 years to life. She says Clubine drugged her husband into lethargy before fatally hitting him. "It seemed to me [the beatings] were some time ago," Stevens told the Los Angeles *Times*. Furthermore, she added, "there was evidence that a lot of it was mutual."

It is interesting that within the legal community there are eloquent opponents of battered-woman syndrome—on feminist grounds—who dislike the label's implication that all battered women are helpless victims of some shared mental disability that prevents them from acting rationally. Social liberals, says N.Y.U.'s Maguigan, typically explain male violence in terms of social or economic pressures. Female violence, on the other hand, is examined in psychological terms. "They look to what's wrong with her and reinforce a notion that women who use violence are, per se, unreasonable, that something must be wrong with her because she's not acting like a good woman, in the way that women are socialized to behave."

Researcher Charles Ewing compared a group of 100 battered women who had killed their partners with 100 battered women who hadn't taken that fatal step.

Women who resorted to violence were usually those who were most isolated, socially and economically; they had been the most badly beaten, their children had been abused, and their husbands were drug or alcohol abusers. That is, the common bond was circumstantial, not psychological. "They're not pathological," says social psychologist Blackman. "They don't have personality disorders. They're just beat up worse."

Women who have endured years of beatings without fighting back may reach the breaking point once the abuse spreads to others they love. Arlene Caris is serving a 25-year sentence in New York for killing her husband. He had tormented her for years, both physically and psychologically. Then she reportedly learned that he was sexually abusing her granddaughter. On the night she finally decided to leave him, he came at her in a rage. She took a rifle, shot him, wrapped him in bedsheets and then hid the body in the attic for five months.

Offering such women clemency, the advocates note, is not precisely the same as amnesty; the punishment is reduced, though the act is not excused. Clemency may be most appropriate in cases where all the circumstances of the crime were not heard in court. The higher courts have certainly sent the message that justice is not uniform in domestic-violence cases. One study found that 40% of women who appeal their murder convictions get the sentence thrown out, compared with an 8.5% reversal rate for homicides as a whole. "I've worked on cases involving battered women who have talked only briefly to their lawyers in the courtroom for 15 or 20 minutes and then they take a plea and do 15 to life," recalls Blackman. "I see women who are Hispanic and don't speak English well, or women who are very quickly moved through the system, who take pleas and do substantial chunks of time, often without getting any real attention paid to the circumstances of their case."

> *"Women who have endured years of beatings without fighting back may reach the breaking point once the abuse spreads to others they love."*

The first mass release in the U.S. came at Christmas in 1990, when Ohio Governor Richard Celeste commuted the sentences of 27 battered women serving time for killing or assaulting male companions. His initiative was born of long-held convictions. As a legislator in the early '70s, he and his wife helped open a women's center in Cleveland and held hearings on domestic violence. When he became lieutenant governor in 1974 and moved to Columbus, he and his wife rented out their home in Cleveland as emergency shelter for battered women. He and the parole board reviewed 107 cases, looking at evidence of past abuse, criminal record, adjustment to prison life and participation in post-release programs before granting the clemencies. "The system of justice had not really worked in their cases," he says. "They had not had the opportunity for a fair trial because vitally important evidence affecting their circumstances and the terrible things done to them was not presented to the jury."

The impending reviews in other states have caused some prosecutors and judges to sound an alarm. They are worried that governors' second-guessing the courts undermines the judicial system and invites manipulation by prisoners. "Anybody in the penitentiary, if they see a possible out, will be claiming, 'Oh, I was a battered woman,'" says Dallas assistant district attorney Norman Kinne. "They can't take every female who says she's a battered woman and say, 'Oh, we're sorry, we'll let you out.' If they're going to do it right, it's an exhaustive study."

Clemency critics point to one woman released in Maryland who soon afterward boasted about having committed the crime. Especially controversial are women who have been granted clemency for crimes that were undeniably premeditated. Delia Alaniz hired a contract killer to pretend to rob her home and murder her husband in the process. He had beaten her and their children for years, sexually abusing their 14-year-old daughter. The prosecutor from Skagit County, Washington, was sufficiently impressed by the evidence of abuse that he reduced the charge from first-degree murder and life imprisonment to second-degree manslaughter with a sentence of 10 to 14 years. In October 1989, Governor Booth Gardner granted her clemency. "Delia was driven to extremes. The situation was desperate, and she viewed it that way," says Skagit County public defender Robert Jones. "The harm to those kids having a mom in prison was too much considering the suffering they went through. As a state, we don't condone what she did, but we understand and have compassion."

The Alternatives to Murder

There is always a risk that the debate over clemency will continue to obscure the missing debate over violence. "I grew up in a society that really tolerated a lot of injustice when it came to women," says Pace University's Dowd. "It was ingrained as a part of society. This isn't a woman's issue. It's a human-rights issue. Men should have as much to offer fighting sexism as they do racism because the reality is that it's our hands that strike the blows." The best way to keep battered women out of jail is to keep them from being battered in the first place.

In a sense, a society's priorities can be measured by whom it punishes. A survey of the population of a typical prison suggests that violent husbands and fathers are still not viewed as criminals. In New York State about half the inmates are drug offenders,

> *"The best way to keep battered women out of jail is to keep them from being battered in the first place."*

the result of a decade-long War on Drugs that demanded mandatory sentences. A War on Violence would send the same message, that society genuinely abhors parents who beat children and spouses who batter each other, and is will-

269

ing to punish the behavior rather than dismiss it.

Minnesota serves as a model for other states. In 1981 Duluth was the first U.S. city to institute mandatory arrests in domestic disputes. Since then about half the states have done the same, which means that even if a victim does not wish to press charges, the police are obliged to make an arrest if they see evidence of abuse. Advocates in some Minnesota jurisdictions track cases from the first call to police through prosecution and sentencing, to try to spot where the system is failing. Prosecutors are increasingly reluctant to plea-bargain assault down to disorderly conduct. They have also found it helpful to use the arresting officer as complainant, so that their case does not depend on a frightened victim's testifying.

> *"Once the cycle of violence winds down in this generation, it is less likely to poison the next."*

Better training of police officers, judges, emergency-room personnel and other professionals is having an impact in many cities. "We used to train police to be counselors in domestic-abuse cases," says Osmundson. "No longer. We teach them to go make arrests." In Jacksonville, Florida, new procedures helped raise the arrest rate from 25% to 40%. "Arrests send a message to the woman that help is available and to men that abuse is not accepted," says shelter executive director DeYoung, who also serves as president of the Florida Coalition Against Domestic Violence. "Children too see that it's not accepted and are more likely to grow up not accepting abuse in the home."

Since 1990 at least 28 states have passed "stalking laws" that make it a crime to threaten, follow or harass someone. Congress this month may take up the Violence Against Women bill, which would increase penalties for federal sex crimes; provide $300 million to police, prosecutors and courts to combat violent crimes against women; and reinforce state domestic-violence laws. Most women, of course, are not looking to put their partners in jail; they just want the violence to stop.

A Minneapolis project was founded in 1979 at the prompting of women in shelters who said they wanted to go back to their partners if they would stop battering. Counselors have found that men resort to violence because they want to control their partners, and they know they can get away with it—unlike in other relationships. "A lot of people experience low impulse control, fear of abandonment, alcohol and drug addiction, all the characteristics of a batterer," says Ellen Pence, training coordinator for the Domestic Abuse Intervention Project in Duluth. "However, the same guy is not beating up his boss."

Most men come to the program either by order of the courts or as a condition set by their partners. The counselors start with the assumption that battering is learned behavior. Eighty percent of the participants grew up in a home where they saw or were victims of physical, sexual or other abuse. Once imprinted with that model, they must be taught to recognize warning signs and redirect their anger. "We don't say, 'Never get angry,'" says Carol Arthur, the Minneapolis project's executive director. "Anger is a normal, healthy emotion. What we work with is a way to express it." Men describe to the group their most violent incident. One man told about throwing food in his wife's face at dinner and then beating her to the floor—only to turn and see his two small children huddled terrified under the table. Arthur remembers his self-assessment at that moment: "My God, what must they be thinking about me? I didn't want to be like that."

If the police and the courts crack down on abusers, and programs exist to help change violent behavior, victims will be less likely to take—and less justified in taking—the law into their own hands. And once the cycle of violence winds down in this generation, it is less likely to poison the next. That would be a family value worth fighting for.

The "Battered Woman's Syndrome" Is a Legitimate Defense

by Alene Kristal

About the author: *Alene Kristal is a contributor to the* New York Law School Journal of Human Rights, *a publication that advocates using the legal system to improve human rights.*

Gladys, an impoverished black woman, had been battered by her husband throughout their marriage. The abuse began the day after they were married, and continued intermittently for the next seven years. Her husband Ernest's excessive drinking usually accompanied the violence, and the abuse occasionally occurred in public. One day, after a series of arguments during which an inebriated Ernest refused to give her money to shop for food for the family, he started to club and bite her while they were walking down the street. During the ensuing struggle, Gladys pulled a pair of scissors from her purse and stabbed her husband, killing him.

Pistol Whipped, Threatened, and Beaten

During a five-year marriage Sherry was frequently pistol whipped, threatened with knives, and once beaten so badly with a tire iron that she was hospitalized. Sherry filed for divorce and obtained restraining orders against her husband. Disregarding the restraining orders, he persistently stalked and harassed her, lurking in doorways and leaping out to assault her. She returned home one evening only to find him hiding in her darkened apartment. When he told her he was going to kill her and seemed to be groping in a kitchen drawer for a knife, she shot and killed him.

Brenda testified that her husband had twice tried to kill her, once by smother-

From Alene Kristal, "You've Come a Long Way, Baby: The Battered Woman's Syndrome Revisited," *New York Law School Journal of Human Rights* 9 (1991): 111-160. Reprinted with permission.

ing her with a pillow, and then by placing a radio in the bathtub while she was bathing. He had also threatened to kill her children if she pursued a domestic violence charge she had brought against him. In between these outbursts of acute violence, some of which had been witnessed by others, their marriage was superficially calm. One night, Brenda noticed a gun she had never seen before on a table by her husband's bedside. Convinced the

> *"Many battered women who kill their abusers start out intending to commit suicide."*

gun signaled an escalation in his intentions and that he would kill her with it, she picked up the gun and shot him after he had hit her.

Gladys, Sherry, and Brenda are representative of battered women who have asserted a defense of justifiable homicide. Usually, the woman has survived years of beatings, alternating with periods of relative domestic tranquility. Women who have raised evidence of Battered Woman's Syndrome in support of justifiable homicide have generally been the victims of at least two acute battering incidents. The cases tend to follow one of two scenarios: (1) at some point in the latest incident, the woman perceives a shift in her attacker, indicative of increased danger. As he is about to strike her, she repels the attack with deadly force, or (2), as in the case of Brenda above, after years of savage brutalization, the woman takes advantage of an opportunity to catch her abuser off-guard and kills him to defend herself from the brutality she knows will inevitably come when he awakens. . . .

The Violent Cycle

Who are these battered women? Experts in the field agree that they can be "everywoman"—they come from every nation, socioeconomic background and level of education; they are mothers and homemakers, and many are successful professionals. Lenore Walker, the preeminent expert on Battered Woman's Syndrome in the United States, defines the typical battered woman as one who is "subjected repeatedly to coercive behavior (physical, sexual, and/or psychological) by a man attempting to force her to do what he wants . . . and who, as a member of a couple, has experienced at least two acute battering incidents."

According to Walker, the dynamics of the abusive relationship occur in a cycle composed of three phases: tension-building, the acute battering incident, and the tranquil, loving or nonviolent phase. The first phase is characterized by minor battering incidents, such as slaps, controlled verbal abuse and psychological warfare. The woman allows the behavior to continue because the incidents seem comparatively minor, and because she desperately wants to prevent the violence from growing worse; she is also committed to preserving the relationship, and willing to make what seem like minor sacrifices to do so. This desire proves to be a double-edged sword, for her docile behavior legitimizes her partner's belief that he had a right to abuse her in the first place. During this phase the woman commonly goes to excessive lengths to rationalize her mate's behavior and conceal the abuse from others, isolating herself from potential sources of assistance. As the cycle progresses, "her [placatory] techniques become less effective, and violence and verbal abuse worsen." The spiralling effect of the loss of control adds exponentially to the pressure. At some point, the tension becomes so unbearable that the woman withdraws emotionally, triggering the next phase.

The acute phase is remarkable for its savagery and uncontrolled nature; the violence escalates to a point of a rampage, resulting in serious injury and sometimes death. At this point, the woman feels psychologically trapped. Her outwardly submissive demeanor functions as a defense mechanism, cloaking a sense of distance from the attacks and from their terrible pain. The knowledge that her attacker is so much physically stronger than she reinforces her need to maintain the appearance of calm.

The third phase is distinguished by forgiveness, relative tranquility and an illusory sense of resolution. The couple experiences profound relief that the violence has abated, and the batterer often exhibits warm, loving behavior towards his mate. He begs her forgiveness, and promises there will be no recurrences. This final phase is the one in which the woman sustains the greatest psychological harm. The two parties exhibit their mutual emotional dependence—her for his caring behavior, he for forgiveness. Dr. Walker explains, "Underneath the grim cycle of tension, violence, and forgiveness that make their love truly terrifying, each partner may believe that death is preferable to separation. . . . In fact, many battered women who kill their abusers start out intending to commit suicide themselves.". . .

> *"Expert testimony on the Battered Woman's Syndrome has gained increasing acceptance."*

There are two major hurdles facing a battered woman asserting self-defense in a homicide case. First, she must convince the court to admit expert testimony on Battered Woman's Syndrome. Second, she must convince the court that the syndrome explains sufficiently why she experienced such an immediate fear of death that it justified her killing in self-defense. . . .

Admissibility of Expert Testimony

[Since the beginning of the 1980s], expert testimony on the Battered Woman's Syndrome has gained increasing acceptance in most jurisdictions in the United States. . . .

The watershed case in admitting expert testimony of Battered Woman's Syndrome is *State v. Kelly*. In 1984, the New Jersey Supreme Court ruled that the testimony met the standards for admissibility as an expert opinion, and was relevant to a determination of the self-defense standard under New Jersey law. The New Jersey criminal code limits deadly force used in self-defense to situations where the "actor reasonably believes that such force is necessary to protect [her]self against death or serious bodily harm." In the first such decision of its kind, the court held that expert testimony on Battered Woman's Syndrome could be heard to determine whether the defendant's belief that the regular pattern of serious physical abuse, combined with the prior threats to kill her, formed a reasonable basis upon which she could determine that her life was in danger.

> *"The 'behavior of battered women who kill their abusers needs to be understood as normal.'"*

Gladys Kelly was charged with reckless manslaughter. The court reasoned that expert testimony on Battered Woman's Syndrome would be of vital importance in buttressing Kelly's credibility by demonstrating that her experiences paralleled those of other women in abusive relationships. Further, the court held that the expert testimony would be central to assessing the honesty of the defendant's belief that she was in imminent danger of harm. The testimony would also be relevant in dispelling the myths and misconceptions the jury held about battered women and their ability to leave the abusive relationship. . . .

A 1990 Ohio case illustrates the encouraging degree of acceptance accorded to expert testimony in battered women's assertions of justifiable homicide. In *State v. Koss*, the Ohio Supreme Court specifically overruled prior precedent, and found that the trial court should have admitted expert testimony to demonstrate how Battered Woman's Syndrome could have led the defendant to perceive she was in immediate fear of death and thus entitled to the affirmative defense of justifiable homicide. The court based its holding on an interpretation of proposed changes in the penal code which were designed to inject subjectivity into the reasonableness standard in homicide cases. At trial, Mrs. Koss sought to admit evidence that she suffered from Battered Woman's Syndrome, but the court refused to allow her to admit expert testimony to support her claim of justifiable homicide. She was found guilty of voluntary manslaughter and sentenced to eight to twenty-five years in prison. On appeal, the court in *Koss* emphasized that it was crucial for the jury to understand the defendant's state of mind at the time of the shooting, and that expert testimony was thus vital to the jury's assessment of whether she honestly believed she was in imminent danger. . . .

Standards of Reasonableness

The issue of reasonableness is at the heart of any defendant's claim of self-defense to homicide. Standards of reasonableness have plagued battered women asserting claims of self-defense, and have been the source of many battered women's convictions for homicide. This has been especially apparent in those self-defense cases where the battered woman seized an opportunity to kill her attacker during a temporary cessation in the abuse. Two categories of proof have emerged, as courts have approached the reasonableness question both from the standpoint of case law and statutory requirements. The more conventional view is that the defendant's actions must appear objectively reasonable to the average juror (the "reasonable man" standard).

> *"The traditional notion of self-defense . . . is totally at odds with battered women's experiences."*

This objective standard for self-defense is defined as the defender's belief that she was in imminent peril of death or serious bodily harm and that her "beliefs must not only have been honestly entertained, but also objectively reasonable in light of the surrounding circumstances." By contrast, the subjective standard embodies the theory that the "justification of self-defense is to be evaluated in light of *all* the facts and circumstances known to the defendant, including those known substantially before the killing" [*State v. Wanrow*, 1977]. These standards do not always reflect a bright line in the case law; decisions often exhibit an amalgam of the two theories, thus rendering the self-defense claim more complex.

The Objective Standard

The objective standard poses particular difficulties for battered women. As the court in *State v. Wanrow* so forcefully argued:

> [W]omen suffer from a conspicuous lack of access to training in and the means of developing those skills necessary to effectively repel a male assailant without resorting to the use of deadly weapons. . . . Until such time as the effects of [this nation's history of sex discrimination] are eradicated, care must be taken to assure that our self-defense instructions afford women the right to have their conduct judged in light of the . . . handicaps which are the product of sex discrimination. To fail to do so is to deny the right of the individual woman involved to trial by the same rules which are applicable to male defendants.

Although the *Wanrow* case did not address the issue of battered women, it did open the door for courts to employ the subjective view of reasonableness to women in justifiable homicide cases. In *Wanrow*, the court ruled that the defendant was entitled to assert self-defense when she had reason to believe the homicide victim was a dangerous man and was startled to find him in the living room after he broke into the house. In this landmark case, the court eloquently underscored the need for a subjective standard by stating that:

> [t]he impression created—that a 5'4" woman with a cast on her leg and using a crutch must, under the law, somehow repel an assault by a 6'2" intoxicated man without employing weapons in her defense, unless the jury finds her determination of the degree of danger to be objectively reasonable—constitutes a

. . . distinct misstatement of the law. . . .

The decision in *State v. Kelly* discussed above exemplifies some of the difficulties inherent in applying standards of reasonableness in battered women's assertions of self-defense. While the opinion clearly set precedent by ruling that expert testimony on Battered Woman's Syndrome was relevant to the issue of self-defense, the court seemed particularly concerned with its applicability in explaining why the defendant had remained in the abusive relationship. . . .

Doctrine of Retreat

A number of . . . cases . . . make reference, either directly or indirectly, to the doctrine of retreat. This factor has complicated courts' assessment of reasonableness in battered women's self-defense cases. Retreat is one of the most difficult concepts for courts to comprehend because the common misconception is that the woman should have left the situation before resorting to deadly force, thus negating the imminent danger factor. There is no common law or judicial construct requiring a battered woman to retreat, except at the instant she confronts and kills her abusive mate; nor does she waive her legal right to act in self-defense because she has chosen, for whatever reason, to stay in her own home. The *Leidholm* court underscored this view of retreat by noting that the defendant was under no obligation to leave her home as she was not the original aggressor, and that her failure to retreat was nullified by her honest,

> *"Women are systematically discriminated against in the courts."*

reasonable belief that she could not withdraw safely. However, despite the legal irrelevance of this issue, courts often find the question difficult to separate from a determination of the reasonableness of the defendant's behavior.

The standard most often cited in determining when an opportunity to retreat defeats the right of self-defense is when the actor knows that she can retreat with complete safety. The question of whether a battered woman can safely retreat is one ideally suited for explanation as part of an expert's testimony. The answer may well be pivotal to the woman's defense. The expert can testify to the factors common to battered women and educate the jury regarding the inapplicability of retreat to battered women in self-defense situations. Such testimony can include explanation of one of the symptoms battered women experience, principally the "constant re-experiencing of [prior traumatic] events [and] the psychic numbing and emotional anesthesia that is characterized by a diminished responsiveness to events in the outside world" [Cynthia K. Gillespie]. The expert can also demonstrate an issue central to these justifiable homicide cases: that all battered women experience a heightened awareness of their abusive mate's behavior, often being capable of perceiving subtle distinctions others would not notice. This ability makes the battered women more apt than an outsider to accurately detect a time when the batterer is truly likely to pose an imminent threat. In fact, this hypervigilant response mechanism to such signals of "unusual" violence has been characterized as a crucial survival skill.

Additionally, expert testimony can be vital in rebutting the retreat issue by demonstrating that extreme fear is the single most frequently cited reason battered women remain in their violent relationships. The witness can cite the numerous studies which document a battered woman's utterly realistic perception that her only choice is between staying and being beaten, or leaving and being killed. Given this Scylla and Charybdis choice, it is not surprising that so many of them decide to stay. . . .

Several states have completely abolished the objective standard of reasonableness, either in their state criminal statutes or by court decisions. Others, such as North Dakota, have followed the reasoning of those commentators advocating the approach used in the Model Penal Code. This approach represents a partial subjectivization of the objective, reasonable person standard by requiring only that a defendant demonstrate an honest belief in the necessity for using deadly force; once this is established, the reasonableness of her actions is not questioned.

Legal Gender Bias

A persistent and vigorous debate exists in the feminist community regarding the issues raised by battered women asserting claims of justifiable homicide. Some experts, like Lenore Walker, Elizabeth Schneider, and Cynthia Gillespie believe that the social conditions causing women to defend themselves are poorly understood in the courtroom, and that expert testimony can contribute significantly in improving courts' and juries' understanding. In this regard, Walker argues that it is especially vital to emphasize that the "behavior of battered women who kill their abusers needs to be understood as *normal*, not abnormal. Defending oneself from reasonably perceived danger of bodily harm or death ought to be considered a psychologically healthy response." And, as noted above, the woman's response is indicative of an ability to discern that the situation had escalated beyond the point at which she could reasonably expect to survive.

"Past actions of the abuser should be considered relevant in all cases and admitted into evidence."

The concern expressed by these experts is underscored by the masculine origins of the law of self-defense. As Gillespie observes, our notions of self-defense hearken back to a situation in which a man "stands and faces his adversary, meeting fists with fists . . . [and] doesn't use a weapon unless one is being used against him." Gillespie also contends that, even if the court uses the "reasonable person" standard rather than the "reasonable man" standard, fighting will still be defined in our society along sex stereotypical lines; and the outlook for the battered woman claiming she killed in self-defense will suffer accordingly. Moreover, the traditional notion of self-defense, which tends to be defined as an actor responding to a single encounter, is totally at odds with battered women's experiences.

> *"Expert testimony on Battered Woman's Syndrome should be admissible in all cases."*

Authorities also agree that the gender bias issue pervades the judicial and law enforcement systems in an insidious fashion. . . .

Gillespie points to the recent studies of gender bias undertaken in New York and New Jersey, both of which concluded that women are systematically discriminated against in the courts. In summarizing the findings, she observed that

> myths, biases and stereotypes about women pervade the decision-making process and often affect the outcome of cases. Women are apt to be regarded as inherently less credible than men and, when they appear in court seeking justice as victims of violence, they are frequently the targets of the most callous sort of victim blaming.

Gillespie deplores the gender bias exemplified by a judge's ruling that a woman had not made a sufficient case for self-defense to send the question to the jury, despite having heard evidence that her partner pistol-whipped her, pointed a loaded gun at her, and threatened to kill her just before she shot him. As she so convincingly argues, judges with gender-biased attitudes are common throughout our judicial system, even at the lower court level, where the battered woman who has killed her abuser in self-defense will first appear.

Gillespie further contends that this gender bias extends to the preoccupation of juries with the question of why the woman did not leave the violent relationship. She asserts that the question subsumes two assumptions: that controlling male violence "is the woman victim's responsibility, not the man's"; and that the family home belongs to him, and "he has the right to drive her out of it." As she points out, it is the woman who is forced (if she does decide to leave) to abandon her home and her possessions and surrender her freedom to hide behind locked doors in an overcrowded shelter. Moreover, these sexist attitudes are reflected in the fact that a woman's reasonableness is so suspect that she requires an expert witness to explain why, after she has been repeatedly beaten and threatened with death, she has good reason to fear her tormentor. . . .

Suggested Changes

The concept of imminence of the harm should be relaxed somewhat, as it is more appropriately applicable to the traditional equal force scenario, and has minimal relevance in most battering situations. One remedy, suggested by the Model Penal Code, and by the *Leidholm* court [1983], would open up the time frame sufficiently for the battered woman to act *before* her abuser strikes her again. Alternatively, courts could define a statutory requirement of "imminence" as "impending," which would be perfectly consistent with a gap in time between the perception of the imminent event and its occurrence.

It has also been suggested that the subjective, rather than the objective, standard should be employed uniformly in determining whether the actor's behavior meets the test of reasonableness. As noted earlier, the subjective standard is not only more applicable to battered women's self-defense claims, it is more logically in line with the concept of *mens rea* [criminal intent] implicit in our criminal law system. Further, past actions of the abuser should be considered relevant in all cases and admitted into evidence to provide the jury with an understanding of the defendant's genuineness of belief. At a minimum, Gillespie proposes that the "reasonable man" standard be replaced by the "reasonable person" standard, rendering the standard gender neutral.

In addition, some commentators have proposed the abolition of the retreat doctrine in battered women's self-defense cases. The doctrine poses two major obstacles: it requires a battered woman to flee her home, and it is frequently confused with the question of why the woman stayed in the relationship. Failing a formal repeal of the retreat portion of a statute, appropriate jury instructions explaining that the woman had no affirmative obligation to terminate the relationship or to leave her home would sufficiently emasculate the doctrine and restore a more balanced approach to justifiable homicide cases.

The Use of Expert Testimony

Most advocates of reform agree that expert testimony on Battered Woman's Syndrome should be admissible in all cases. While some critics have argued that this is a recommendation of a separate law for battered women, this assertion lacks merit. Significantly, expert testimony on a wide variety of subjects is admissible in all jurisdictions, and testimony about Post Traumatic Stress Disorder in particular can be useful to defendants of *either* gender in a variety of contexts, including rape and child abuse.

Defense attorneys should emphasize, through the use of expert testimony, the notion that the battered woman was responding appropriately to her situation, and that her fear of death or serious harm was, indeed, reasonable. This testimony should underscore the battered woman's characteristically heightened sense of awareness to danger, as well as the view that battered women are more likely to be killed themselves if they attempt to escape their violent relationships. Further, testimony explaining the "flashback" sensations battered women experience would help serve to convince a jury of the woman's perception of imminent danger. While some explanation of why the

"Battered women are more likely to be killed themselves if they attempt to escape."

woman remained in the relationship is useful to allay confusion, attempts should be made to de-emphasize the concepts of learned helplessness and victimization. This will minimize the sexual stereotyping of the actor, which only serve to highlight the apparent contradiction of a helpless woman who took direct action to save her life.

The Battered Woman Defense

One recommendation not mentioned by any of the experts above is to take the legal solutions one step further by creating a new category of self-defense, tentatively entitled the Battered Woman Defense. This proposal would include a completely subjective standard of reasonableness, such as that used by the court in *Leidholm*, and would eliminate completely the requirement for imminence of the harm as it is currently employed. The standards of proof would include: (a) that a defendant offer, through expert testimony by a mental health professional experienced in diagnosing Battered Woman's Syndrome, evidence that she had been through a minimum of two acute battering cycles before the killing; (b) a requirement that a defendant demonstrate an honest belief that her abusive spouse's behavior had escalated to such a degree within the 48 hours preceding the homicide that she was in fear for her life or of grave bodily injury; and (c) a statutory rejection of the retreat doctrine, thus simplifying the jury's ability to reach a conclusion regarding the defendant's actions.

This suggested reform would address many of the significant difficulties currently associated with battered women's self-defense claims. It is believed, by many of the experts mentioned above, and by this author, that the current formulations of criminal codes are poorly equipped to address battered women's circumstances with sufficient fairness. The approaches used in even the more enlightened jurisdictions are, at best, efforts to fit a square peg into a round hole, as battered women who resort to killing their batterers often do not conform to the legal standards used to maintain a claim of self-defense. While it is certainly true that legislation codifying this proposal would likely encounter many obstacles to passage, it would go far in eliminating much of the gender bias inherent in the criminal codes and allow juries to assess more accurately the blameworthiness of a battered woman defendant.

The "Battered Spouse Syndrome" Is a Legitimate Defense

by Julia J. Chavez

About the author: *Julia J. Chavez is a contributor to the* Southwestern University Law Review, *a journal of the Southwestern University School of Law in Los Angeles, California.*

In the past several years, a movement has begun among social scientists and lawmakers alike to address the problem of wife battery. An increase in the number of women convicted for using deadly force resulting in the death of a spouse has brought this problem to the forefront of women's issues. Moreover, as the participation of women in social sciences, law, and the legislature has increased, the need for information concerning this trend has received greater recognition. Consequently, scientific studies charting what has become known as the battered woman syndrome and increased social awareness of the problem have resulted. However, some states have addressed the issue by statute, usually allowing admission of evidence of battery in spousal homicide cases. In states that have not passed legislation regulating courtroom treatment of spousal battery, there is broad judicial discretion concerning its treatment under laws governing the admission of evidence.

Equal Protection and Gender

However, a disturbing trend is emerging as increased focus is placed on the gender specific issue of battered women: the issue of battered men has been excluded from the social and legal agenda. Although statistics document a relatively small number of men battered by their wives, the issue is one that must be addressed in light of recent changes in state evidence laws allowing battered

From Julia J. Chavez, "Battered Men and the California Law," *Southwestern University Law Review* 22 (1992): 239-256. Reprinted with permission.

wife syndrome to be admitted into evidence in cases of spousal homicide. The issue raises the possibility that the socially accepted gender distinction between battered husbands and battered wives is unnecessary and inaccurate; that, in fact, wife battery and husband battery are two aspects of one condition— spousal battery. Given the possibility that battered spouses should not be

> *"Wife battery and husband battery are two aspects of one condition—spousal battery."*

segregated by gender, the issue raises constitutional equal protection questions.

The United States Constitution guarantees equal protection under the law to people who are similarly situated. In recent years, the United States Supreme Court has recognized that the Equal Protection Clause extends not only to racial classifications, but also to classifications based on gender. Most cases challenging a gender classification have addressed the exclusion of women. Conversely, laws challenged by men as being unfairly favorable to women arise less frequently. One must ask whether a law containing language that favors women and excludes men furthers or hampers the efforts to realize a society that provides equal protection regardless of gender. . . .

The California Law

On October 11, 1991, female defendants in California received the right to introduce evidence that allows the jury to hear how past experiences of spousal abuse have impacted their perception of imminent danger. Additionally, the law authorizes expert testimony to increase juror understanding of the lasting psychological effect of spousal abuse. The language of the law creates a class of defendants that are eligible to use the law. Specifically, the new law states: "In a criminal action, expert testimony is admissible by either the prosecution or the defense regarding *battered woman's syndrome*, including the physical, emotional, or mental effects upon the beliefs, perceptions, or behavior of victims of domestic violence. . . ."

The effect of permitting expert testimony concerning spousal abuse is that battered woman syndrome becomes a justification for self-defense. Traditionally, self-defense is available only when the defendant has a reasonable belief that he or she is in imminent danger of death or bodily injury. The California Supreme Court has set forth the following guidelines for determining self-defense:

> (1) the defendant's acts causing the victim's death were motivated by an actual (also referred to as "genuine" or "honest") belief or perception that (a) the defendant was in imminent danger of death or great bodily injury from an unlawful attack or threat by the victim and (b) the defendant's acts were necessary to prevent the injury; and (2) a reasonable person in the same circumstances would have had the same perception and done the same acts.

In California, juries are instructed to judge the defendant's actions by the actions of a reasonable person in the same circumstances, knowing what the defendant knew at the time. A juror is considered to be representative of a reasonable person and is asked to make a judgment based on his or her personal knowledge and experience without expert testimony as to the defendant's unique perspective. Therefore, the theory of self-defense appears gender neutral.

However, the 1991 addition to the California evidence code acknowledges that the circumstances of a woman who is repeatedly battered may be outside the knowledge of the average juror. Thus, experts are allowed to tell the jurors about the psychological impact of repeated battery and its effect on a woman's ability to perceive imminent danger. The language of the law makes it gender biased both on its face and in application because it specifically classifies women as the only group able to benefit. "Battered woman's syndrome" must, by definition, exclude men.

A battered male defendant may attempt to use the recent law by analogy. However, denial or acceptance of the attempt will depend on individual judges. Thus, the battered male defendant does not have the same protection afforded a battered female defendant.

It takes little imagination to postulate popular response to a law that allows a criminal defense for men that women may only attempt to use by analogy. Yet, the California legislature has, in effect, done just the opposite by passing a law with language that excludes men solely by reason of gender. Given the low ratio of battered men to battered women, it is not surprising that the situation of battered women has been closely studied while the problem of battered men has been largely ignored. Here, the legislature addressed the well-documented and scientifically accepted issue of battered women. However, through its failure to include battered men, the legislature has passed a fatally underinclusive law. The recent California law denies battered men the opportunity to have the jury consider their subjective perceptions, while at the same time, affords this opportunity to a group of similarly situated women.

> *"The Equal Protection Clause extends . . . to classifications based on gender."*

Battered Woman Syndrome

While the issue of battered men is a relatively recent phenomena, historically, battered women were not uncommon. At common law a woman was considered the property of her husband and under his complete control. Thus, she had no recourse at law for the abuse she suffered at home. Her options were drastically limited by her social position as her husband's chattel, her economic dependence on him, and pressure from her family, friends, and society.

With the advent of the women's movement, women now have more resources available to remove many of the restraints that, in the past, have kept them in abusive relationships. However, it is widely recognized that some women are unable to make use of available social resources because of a condition known as the battered woman syndrome.

Repeated wife battery usually consists of a specific pattern of behavior. The pattern begins with the "tension building" stage. During this time, the wife is accommodating and passive in an effort to avert the coming violence. At the same time, the batterer's behavior becomes increasingly erratic and unpredictable. The second stage, known as the "battering" stage, is characterized by severe violence, which can last up to twenty-four hours. Finally, in the "remorseful" stage, the relationship is loving, and the batterer is filled with remorse. He promises never to hurt the woman again and treats her well, until the tension building stage begins again.

Women who have been through more than two of the above cycles are considered battered women. As a result of the pattern of violence, they tend to have some of the following characteristics in common: low self-esteem; traditional views about the home, family, and sex role stereotypes; denial of terror and anger; passivity; severe stress reactions including psycho-physiological complaints; and isolation. These characteristics comprise the psychological symptoms common to battered women and define the battered woman syndrome.

Learned Helplessness

The psychological manifestations of battered woman syndrome have been characterized by many as learned helplessness. One commentator likens the condition to experiments conducted by behavioral scientists:

> Behavioral scientists have known for years how to make rats (and dogs and cats and other animals) just give up. Any first year psychology student has read about it or tried it. You apply electric shocks—or some other unpleasant stimulus—in a manner that is unpredictable to the animal and also uncontrollable. Do that long enough, whenever the animal wants to eat or sleep or move about, and the animal will eventually stop trying, even when the shocks are turned off.

Psychologists believe that this behavior, resulting from repeated battery, stops women from leaving an abusive relationship. The sense of learned helplessness, brought about by the pattern of abuse, changes a woman's sense of reality, and she becomes passive and submissive.

"The language of the [California] law makes it gender biased."

Inequality between men and women imposed by society increases the helpless response. Many women are financially dependent upon their mate. This dependence makes it more difficult to escape from an abusive relationship. Moreover, the added burden of caring for and supporting minor children may cause a woman to stay in an abusive relationship. Most women are reluctant to leave children with a man that has shown abusive tendencies. Thus, economic dependence and social attitude further the helpless response. If a woman has fewer alternatives, then it is more likely that she will suffer the abuse and, correspondingly, become unable to halt the sequence of violence.

Battered Husband Syndrome

As noted above, the subject of battered women has become a leading women's issue in recent years; at the same time, the issue of battered men has been "cloaked in secrecy." Admittedly, the number of battered women exceeds that of battered men. Yet, the similarities between the two abusive situations are striking. Necessarily, social and economic differences between men and women dictate that battered men and battered women will have different psychological reactions to the abuse. Different, however, does not necessarily mean less severe or less worthy of serious analysis and protection under the law.

The difference in reaction to spousal abuse between men and women is dictated in large part by society's stereotypes. Traditional attributes of men include physical strength, dominance, and aggressiveness, while for women they include weakness, submissiveness, and vulnerability. For a man to come forward and admit that his wife abused him is to admit that he possesses none of the traditional male attributes.

> *"The battered male defendant does not have the same protection afforded a battered female defendant."*

In the eyes of his peers, he is not a man. This stereotype imposed by society lessens the number of men that report this type of abuse and increases their feelings of doubt and confusion.

Given the criticism of police officers for their insensitivity in the handling of battered women cases, one can easily imagine police response to a man reporting a battery inflicted by his wife. Male police officers epitomize the traditional male attributes of physical strength, dominance, and aggressiveness, thereby increasing a man's reluctance to seek help and increasing his fear of ridicule and rejection from those able to provide him with assistance. Moreover, male family and friends seldom offer emotional support. Most feel uncomfortable with the situation because of social stereotypes. They feel that their masculinity requires a response that mirrors society's stereotype. Even female family and friends are unlikely to fully understand the emotional impact of the situation and so may react in conformity with the same societal stereotypes as men.

Because of this stereotype, men often find themselves isolated and alone with their problem. This attribute is indeed shared with battered women. Like a battered woman, the man ultimately "loses respect for himself, resulting in feel-

ings of guilt and self-loathing." It has been suggested that the feelings a man suffers may be more pronounced than those suffered by a woman because a battered man who chooses to stay in the relationship is further from society's norms and expectations than is a battered woman. An abused woman is still conforming to the traditional at-tributes of weakness, submissiveness, and passivity, while a battered man who does not fight back contradicts

> *"The [California] legislature has passed a fatally underinclusive law."*

society's expectations. Both battered men and women must deal with feelings of inadequacy, physical injury, guilt, shame, and embarrassment. Clearly, the similarities between battered women and battered men suggest that both are as-pects of the larger problem of domestic violence.

In addition, the theory of learned helplessness is not confined to women. Men may also be treated in such a way as to provoke a helpless response. The cycle of violence, unprovoked and unexpected, causes the same reaction in the abused, regardless of gender. Soon the victims lose the will to try to change their situation; they learn that there is no pattern to the violence and, thus, no way to deal rationally with the batterer.

Men, however, may not experience the economic pressure present in most women's decisions. Men usually have economic freedom from their wives. Consequently, they have an additional alternative that is unavailable to many women. While this lack of an additional alternative is an important element in the helplessness that women learn to feel, it should not be given too much weight. Women have access to social services, as well as family and friends, where help may be sought. Despite these resources, women often stay in an abusive relationship. Similarly, men may also choose to stay in an abusive rela-tionship despite their economic freedom, perhaps to keep an open relationship with their children. Thus, this economic difference should be taken into ac-count, but should not be determinative in a legislative decision to exclude men from the classification of persons able to benefit from expert testimony con-cerning the psychological effects of spousal abuse.

A Larger Syndrome

Battered husband syndrome was introduced as a scientific theory in the late 1970s. It began at a scholarly meeting, with Suzanne Steinmetz's presentation of a paper entitled "The Battered Husband Syndrome." Steinmetz has since published several papers on the same topic. Other researchers followed suit. At the same time, there is continuing criticism of the theory for its alleged cloud-ing of the wife battery issue. For example, Mildred Daley Pagelow, a prominent author on the subject of battered woman syndrome, suggests that the issue of battered husband syndrome tends to trivialize women's demands for civil rights. The issue has been hotly debated by social scientists.

The debate concerning battered husband syndrome revolves around the issue of whether there are enough men who are victims of this type of abuse to warrant calling their common psychological symptoms a syndrome. Most of the researchers agree that instances of men battered by their wives do exist. In her article about the myth of battered husband syndrome, Pagelow documents the number of males that made use of social resources for battered spouses. Although she concludes that battered husband syndrome does not exist, her charts do document men making use of social resources. From this documentation, one can then infer that the number of battered men must be higher than the represented number to account for those men who do not use the available services.

If the debate focuses exclusively on the number of men who are battered, then how does one decide how many men it takes to create a battered husband syndrome? Again, the social scientists and researchers are divided on the issue. The definition of a syndrome is "a group of symptoms or signs typical of a disease, disturbance [or] condition. . . ." Logically, one must have a large enough occurrence of the abnormality to be able to definitively characterize the symptoms and signs. This, however, may be done with a relatively small group. One researcher defines the group of battered men as "minuscule compared to female victims." Yet, nothing dictates that one group of people must be defined in relation to another group of people. Additionally, nothing dictates that men must have their own exclusive syndrome. Both battered men and battered women display common characteristics. This evidence strongly suggests that abused men are actually part of a larger syndrome, namely, battered spouse syndrome, that the legislature has mistakenly classified as applying to women only.

Deadly Force and the Victims of Abuse

The group of signs and symptoms that characterize both battered woman syndrome and battered husband syndrome tends to distort the victim's perception of reality. An abused person gauges and reacts to particular situations differently than a nonabused person. This difference in perception arises in a legal context when a battered spouse has killed the batterer. The favored defense for such an act is self-defense. Defendants must convince the jury that they perceived themselves to be in imminent danger of death or bodily injury and that the use of deadly force to defend themselves was reasonable under the circumstances. For a battered woman or a battered man, perception, as well as the term "reasonable," must be modified. Modification is the practical result of the recent California law, except the law allows modification for women only.

"A battered man who does not fight back contradicts society's expectations."

In a perfect case of self-defense, the perception of imminent harm is one that the jury agrees is reasonable. For example, the aggressor has a weapon and has threatened to use it to kill the victim. In cases like this, where a battered woman or man has defended him- or herself with deadly force, there is no need for introduction of the battery syndrome. The perception of the need for deadly force is not connected to the psychological results of battery and is viewed as reasonable by the jurors.

> *"Abused men are actually part of a larger syndrome, namely, battered spouse syndrome."*

Unfortunately, in most situations where a battered man or woman has killed a spouse, it is a case of imperfect self-defense. The spouse is rarely armed with a deadly weapon and is often asleep or has walked away. To a reasonable juror, the perception of the need for deadly force may seem unreasonable. California law addresses this situation by allowing the introduction of testimony that may permit jurors to find that an abused *woman's* perception was reasonable in light of past experience with the batterer. Abused men are at a disadvantage in that they are unable to use the recent California law, except by analogy. Thus, unless an individual judge allows testimony concerning past battery, abused men are at the mercy of a juror's perception of what is reasonable.

One may argue that the physical differences between men and women impact on the reasonableness of the use of deadly force. While both men and women suffer similar psychological impairments resulting from the abuse, men are not justified in using deadly force as often as women. Men usually have the option of subduing a woman without using deadly force, an option most women do not have. There are, however, situations where one can imagine that a man may have to use deadly force to subdue a woman who has threatened him. In some situations a woman may have a physical advantage over the man. Men that are elderly, sick, disabled, or simply physically smaller than their wives may find themselves in this situation. When a male defendant seeks to use the defense, he would find it more difficult to convince the jury that his actions were reasonable. However, difficulty in convincing a jury is not a legitimate reason for developing an exclusionary gender classification for the use of this type of expert testimony in spousal abuse cases. . . .

Missouri and Maryland

While some jurisdictions have addressed the battery problem by allowing only evidence of battered woman syndrome, some have passed gender-neutral laws allowing both men and women to use the law. These laws usually characterize the syndrome as "battered spouse syndrome." In these jurisdictions, it is recognized that no need exists for a separate syndrome for men and women; both genders are perceived as suffering from different aspects of the same psychological condition. The legislatures have chosen to address the problem with language that does not create gender classifications. Missouri and Maryland are two states that have done so.

Missouri recently passed a statute that uses the language "battered spouse syndrome" to characterize the type of evidence that will be admissible with expert testimony. Additionally, the language in the remainder of the statute is fairly nongender specific. The legislature uses words such as "defendant," "individual," "actor," "accused," and "spouse." In the two instances in which gender is specified, the male gender is used. In most instances female defendants will be using this statute, but the inclusion of the male gender identification acknowledges that men also may use this statute in their defense. Newspapers, touting this new law as a step forward in women's rights have, as an afterthought, mentioned the fact that men may also use the law. Use by men is considered a secondary effect of the law; yet, it is nevertheless a reality.

Similarly, the Maryland statute refers to "battered spouse syndrome" instead of battered wife syndrome. It also uses nongender specific language such as "spouse," "cohabitant," and "individual." While men are not explicitly noted in the statute, the fact that it is nongender specific makes their use of the statute a real possibility. Most psychological literature referring to spousal battery identifies the syndrome as battered woman syndrome.

> *"In some situations a woman may have a physical advantage over the man."*

Therefore, the use of a nongender specific label in both state statutes must have been a deliberate attempt to avoid the constitutional equal protection problem raised by excluding a group of defendants based on gender. . . .

A Simple Change in the Language

The Equal Protection Clause of the United States Constitution requires that states provide equal protection to people similarly situated. California's attempt to allow evidence of past spousal abuse ignores the male victims of spousal abuse. Based on cases interpreting the Equal Protection Clause of the United States Constitution, section 1107 of the California evidence code cannot exclude a group of defendants based on gender. The solution to the problem lies in a simple change in the language of the statute from "battered woman's syndrome" to "battered spouse syndrome." The new wording would give both battered women and battered men the protection guaranteed to them under the United States Constitution. However, as easy as this may seem, it also entails a change in perception and attitude by members of the legislature and the public.

It has taken many years for women to formulate and pass laws aimed at equalizing a legal system that has traditionally discriminated against them. However, to accomplish this goal by excluding a group of male defendants that may need the same protection as women is not progress. Nevertheless, women cannot take all the blame for a law that is discriminatory by gender. The vast majority of legislators are men. They too must attempt to see beyond the stereotypes that society imposes upon them. They must not only address the inequalities in the legal system that affect women, but must also allow for redress of nontraditional problems faced by men. California should follow the lead of states like Missouri and Maryland in passing laws narrow enough to address a specific problem and, at the same time, include all who may need the legal opportunity to present their entire case.

The "Battered Woman's Syndrome" Is Not a Legitimate Defense

by Coramae Richey Mann

About the author: *Coramae Richey Mann has received advanced degrees in clinical psychology and sociology from Roosevelt University and the University of Illinois, both in Chicago. Her research has centered on the criminal justice system's treatment of youths, racial minorities, and women.*

Although the rates of killing one's spouse or relatives have been remarkably stable over the years, domestic violence has "come out of the closet" recently. As result of such exposure, this form of violent behavior is viewed currently as a serious problem in American society. Typically, because seven out of every ten incidents of domestic violence reported in the National Crime Survey were committed by a woman's husband, ex-husband, boyfriend, or ex-boyfriend, little empirical attention has been directed to the woman who kills in intimate encounters. Yet in a replication of an earlier study of family violence, Murray A. Straus and Richard J. Gelles report that "women are about as violent within the family as men." These researchers found decreases in both overall violence and severe violence (wife beating) in husband-to-wife violence and a slight decrease in the rate of severe wife-to-husband violence, but an increase in the rate of overall wife-to-husband violence between 1975 and 1985.

To Obtain a Clearer Picture

As J.A. Fagan, D.K. Stewart, and K.V. Hansen point out, "Explanations of violence, both inside and outside the home, must incorporate situational or contextual factors as well as an assessment of the relationships of violent individuals to these environments." The exploratory, descriptive study of female homicide of-

From Coramae Richey Mann, "Getting Even? Women Who Kill in Domestic Encounters," *Justice Quarterly*, March 1988. Reprinted with permission of the Academy of Criminal Justice Sciences.

fenders on which this article is based was undertaken in order to obtain a clearer picture of such offenders and the "life pressures and the concomitant personal stress" that resulted in another person's death (B. Bunch, L.A. Foley, and S.P. Urbina). The data from field research in six of the largest cities in the United States concern arrested females who killed persons who were, or once had been, in intimate sexual relationships

> *"Women are about as violent within the family as men."*

with them: husbands, ex-husbands, common-law and ex-common-law husbands, both heterosexual and homosexual lovers, live-in lovers, and ex-lovers.

The Women Who Killed

The data for the larger study consist of 296 randomly selected, cleared homicide cases from Chicago, Houston, Atlanta, Los Angeles, New York, and Baltimore for the years 1979 and 1983 in which the offenders were females. These six cities were chosen because their homicide rates were equal to or higher than the national rates for both years and were proportionately representative of murder by region according to the F.B.I. Uniform Crime Reports for 1979 and 1983. The random sample represents 42.9 percent of all the women arrested for homicide in the six cities in 1979 and 42.3 percent of that total in 1983. The total of 164 cases in 1979 and 132 cases in 1983 reflects the decrease in female homicide arrests at the national level.

The subgroup of 145 women who killed someone in a domestic encounter constituted almost one-half (49.5%) the total sample of 293 cases (out of 296 cases) where the victim-offender relationship was known. In 1979 the domestic homicides (52.8%) exceeded the nondomestic homicides (47.2%), but by 1983 they lagged behind (45.5% versus 54.5%).

The complete homicide files of the sampled cases for 1979 and 1983, some of which included photographs and autopsy reports and any other police record sources such as arrest and fingerprint files and F.B.I. reports, were examined minutely. I recorded information from these documents on previously designed research schedules after I had assigned each case a code number to insure confidentiality. The seven-page schedule included demographic and social characteristics of the offender and victim, offense data, and criminal justice data.

Over a two-year period, I spent approximately one to two weeks in each city abstracting information from police department and criminal court files. After I left the field sites, several followup contacts were necessary to obtain missing or additional data, particularly court dispositions.

The following results of aggregate data collected on the 145 women who killed in domestic encounters include comparisons with nondomestic cases and with previous studies of such offenders regarding the homicide, the victim-offender relationship, and characteristics of the female homicide offender. The findings conclude with a profile of the female offender and the final disposition of her case.

Location. Not surprisingly, the women who committed domestic homicide were most likely to kill in either their residence or the victim's, a finding reported by almost every investigator who examined the location of the homicides studied; . . . 83.2 percent of the domestic homicides commonly take place in a residence (victim's residence, 2.8%; offender's, 18.9%; both, 57.7%; or someone else's, 4.2%). . . . Within the residence, the living room was the most frequent homicide location (30.4%) in the study described here, followed by the bedroom (23.2%), and the kitchen (17.6%).

Time, Day, Month. It is generally accepted that murders take place on weekend nights, peaking in the summer months and at the Christmas holiday season. M.E. Goetting, for example, found increases in the incidence of wives who committed homicide during June and July and again from December through February, usually on weekend evenings. In contrast, the present study showed no discernible monthly patterns; the homicides were spread almost evenly throughout the year, with slight increases in the warmer months (April through August).

Another contrary finding was that these domestic killings were slightly less likely to be committed on the weekend (49.0%) than during the week. . . .

> *"Women who committed domestic homicide were most likely to kill in either their residence or the victim's."*

As to time of day, typically the women in the six cities studied committed the homicide between 8:00 P.M. and 3:00 A.M. (52%). The mode time was 3:00 A.M., a finding that generally coincides with other studies defining domestic homicide committed by wives as a "night crime."

Firearms the Principal Weapons

Weapon. Times have changed since A. Wolfgang reported in 1958 that in Philadelphia "wives usually stabbed their mates." More recent studies reveal a "dramatic increase in firearms as principal weapons" used by women who kill. . . . Over half the female domestic homicide offenders used firearms (51.7%), while 44.1 percent used knives. This finding must be qualified, however, because an examination by year shows that in 1979 a firearm was the most likely weapon of choice (56%), but by 1983, knives were chosen more frequently (50%) than guns (45%). Further, the choice of weapon varied geographically; women in western and southern cities were more apt to employ a gun than were women in eastern cities.

A significant difference was found between the homicide methods adopted by the domestic homicide killers and by the nondomestic offenders. Although both groups used guns and knives most frequently, and domestic homicide offenders exceeded the nondomestic group in using both weapons, the nondomestic female killers were more likely to use other methods such as clubbing weapons, strangling, drowning, and hands and feet. This finding appears to be explained by the preponderance of infant and child killings within this subgroup.

The important variables regarding the circumstances of the homicide are the interpersonal relationship between the victim and the offender, a demographic description of the victim (gender, race, and age), and the contribution of alcohol and/or narcotics to the crime.

Victim-Offender Relationship. The most frequent affiliation between the domestic homicide offender and her victim was common-law marriage (31.9%), followed closely by a relationship as lovers (29.1%) and by legally married status (25.0%). In most cases, despite the lack of legal marital status, the victim and the offender shared or had once shared an intimate sexual and personal existence.

Homicide an Intraracial, Intersexual Event

The Victim. As in the case of the female offenders, 91 percent of whom were nonwhite, the majority of the victims were also nonwhite (91.7%). This finding reinforces the well-established notion that homicide is an intraracial event. Cross-tabulations of the domestic and nondomestic homicide offenders' subgroups reveal a significant racial difference: victims of women who killed in domestic encounters were more frequently nonwhites, while white victims were killed more frequently in nondomestic situations.

Not unexpectedly, because previous accounts define domestic homicides as intersexual, (although five female victims were either current or ex-homosexual lovers of the female homicide offenders), the majority of the victims were males (96.6%) who ranged in age from 19 to 71 years (mean=37.9). Most of the victims of both female homicide groups were over 25 years of age, but among the nondomestic homicide offenders a substantial proportion of the victims was also under 25. Again, this finding is believed to reflect the nondomestic offenders' tendency to kill children.

Substance Involvement. . . . Narcotics use generally was not as serious an intervening factor as alcohol for either the offender (8.7%) or the victim (12.2%). Even so, a substantial increase in the involvement of narcotics before the homicide was found in the victims between 1979 and 1983 (7.6 to 18.4%), while such use doubled for offenders over that period (6.1 to 12.2%).

> *"Over half the female domestic homicide offenders used firearms."*

In such homicide events, usually either the victim or offender had been under the influence of alcohol. This study was no exception; over one-third (36.2%) of the offenders and more than half (58.3%) of the victims had been drinking before the homicide. In fact, as determined by autopsies, 22 percent of the victims were drunk. . . .

A comparison of domestic and nondomestic homicide victims as to alcohol involvement revealed that those killed in a domestic encounter were more likely than victims in nondomestic situations to have been drinking at the time of the offense. Whereas victim involvement with alcohol before the homicide decreased from 60.9 percent in 1979 to 54 percent in 1983, the converse was true in the case of the female offenders. In 1979, 32.8 percent of the women had been drinking before the homicide, as compared to 40.8 percent in 1983.

A Profile of Women Who Kill in Domestic Encounters

Age and Race. As William Wilbanks notes accurately, "Women become murderers at a somewhat older age than men." In his Miami study, for example, Wilbanks reports that female homicide offenders had a peak age of 25 to 44 years, as compared to 15 to 24 years for male killers. Another South Florida study by B. Bunch et al. found female killers to be considerably older with a mean age of 29.34 years. . . .

An older offending group [was also found] among the domestic killers in the present six-city study, who ranged from 13 to 64 years (mean=33.6 years). . . . A significant difference [is found] between domestic and nondomestic homicide offenders when age is reclassified as "under 25 years" and "over 25 years"; domestic killers are revealed in the older bracket.

"Over one-third of the offenders and more than half of the victims had been drinking before the homicide."

Every study of female homicide has reported a preponderance of black female offenders. This finding also holds true here; 84.1 percent of the domestic homicide offenders were black, 9.0 percent were white, and the remaining 6.9 percent were Hispanic. . . . It is notable that in the total study there were no Native American or Asian-American female killers.

Socioeconomic Level. A few studies of female murderers examined education and employment as crude measures of the offenders' socioeconomic status. Previous information on education has been skimpy, and this was certainly the case in this report on domestic killers; this subgroup contained more missing cases than valid cases. Keeping this warning in mind, I found a tentative mean of 10.9 years of education (range=7 to 16 years) for women who killed in domestic encounters.

Employment offers a more reliable index of the female homicide offenders' possible socioeconomic level. Available sources indicate that such offenders either are on public assistance, are in menial employment or prostitution, or are unemployed. In P.D. McClain's study, 66.7 percent of black female homicide offenders were unemployed; in this study, among the domestic homicide offenders for whom information was available, the percentage was 63.2. The homicide files also revealed that the 35.9 percent who were employed were laborers or worked in semiskilled occupations. Within the employed group, domestic homicide offenders predominated (60.9%) over the nondomestic murderers (39.1%).

> *"Women who killed in domestic encounters . . . tended to premeditate the event."*

Marital and Maternal Status. Earlier I pointed out that the most frequent marital status was common-law. Combining common-law status with married, divorced, separated, and widowed status (not by crime) reveals, not unexpectedly, that the women who killed in domestic encounters were more likely than the nondomestic female killers to have ever-married or common-law status. Conversely, women who killed in nondomestic situations were predominantly single compared to the domestic killers.

If we can assume that the women in the common-law category are also single (at least not married legally to the victim), we note some rather intriguing differences. Such a regrouping reveals that the percentage of single women exceeds that of ever-married women in both domestic (56.5% versus 43.5%) and nondomestic (60.6% versus 39.4%) homicides. This difference appeared in 1983.

R. Weisheit introduces an interesting dimension of marital status and living arrangements through "indicators of independence and autonomy." An application of this perspective suggests dependency on the part of the domestic homicide group and more freedom, independence, and autonomy among the nondomestic, single homicide group. Associated closely with the independence-autonomy index is the responsibility for children, or maternal status. In the 97 cases where information was located, it was found that 80.4 percent of the female domestic killers were mothers who, on the average, had one or two children. This finding suggests that members of this offender subgroup are not only ever-married and dependent, but also may lack independence because of their status and responsibilities as mothers.

Premeditation, Motive, and Prior Records

Premeditation and Offender's Role. Most reports indicate that women who kill do not preplan the homicide and usually act alone in committing the offense. A notable exception is found by Bunch et al., who report that 70 percent of the incarcerated female killers in their study planned the crime but only 22.2 percent committed the offense alone. In the present study of women who killed in domestic encounters, a mixed finding tends to lend partial support to both positions: these women were lone offenders (97.2%) who tended to premeditate the event (58.3%).

Motive. The motive given most frequently for domestic homicide was self-defense (58.9%), a reactive form of violence resulting from an argument or fight with the victim reported commonly in other studies of female homicide offenders.

Yet one result in this study that appears to differ from other researchers' findings concerns the extent of responsibility for the homicide. Previous studies emphasize the self-defense aspect of female homicide cases and suggest that the "helpless little woman," in an altercation in which she is at a physical disadvantage, kills the "bullying big man," who has a history of battering her. Women who killed in domestic encounters provide no exception to this scenario and in fact, denied responsibility for the killing (51.8%) more frequently than nondomestic female killers (48.2%). Although they denied responsibility for the slaying, and attributed it to self-defense or some other cause, the women in this study quite often seemed responsible. One typical example is a 30-year-old Puerto Rican offender, who killed her 31-year-old spouse in a domestic argument in which the victim was drunk. He began to break up the household furniture, and at one point in the altercation, he threatened the offender with a chair. She shot him in the *back* of the head six times with his .38 pistol, and claimed self-defense. Apparently the court agreed; the case was dismissed.

As noted previously, drinking by the victim appeared to influence the incidence of his or her death. . . .

Previous research indicated that most women who kill do not have previous arrest records, although P.D. McClain provides a notable exception in her finding that 62.5 percent of the black female homicide offenders had prior records. The present study tends to corroborate those studies in showing that criminal histories are uncommon: 50.8 percent of the domestic killers had no prior arrest records. It is noteworthy, however, that in 36 out of 120 valid cases of women who killed in domestic encounters (30%), the women had records of previous arrests for violent crimes such as assault, battery, and weapons charges. . . .

Expected and Unexpected Findings

In summary, the picture of domestic killings by females reveals an offense that is most frequently intersexual and intraracial, committed by a woman who tends to be older than most male or other female murderers. She is typically an unemployed black mother who preplans the killing and then acts alone in committing it. The homicide usually involves a firearm, typically a pistol, as the weapon of choice, and takes place in a residence on a Tuesday, Thursday, or Saturday night. . . .

> *"She shot him in the* back *of the head six times with his .38 pistol, and claimed self-defense."*

I discovered many expected and some unexpected findings in this exploratory six-city study representing over 40 percent of women murderers in those metropolitan areas. Among the expected findings, I found verification for most of the research results on female homicide offenders, reported first over a quarter of a century ago by M.E. Wolfgang on Philadelphia women and as recently as 1987 by A. Goetting on Detroit women. Findings that homicides committed by women are intersexual, intraracial and intrafamilial corroborate earlier reports. Findings that women who kill are usually older, members of minority groups, and of lower socioeconomic status also supported previous research findings.

> *"These women were the victors in the domestic fight."*

On the other hand, in contrast to earlier studies, no discernible pattern could be found regarding the month or season of the domestic homicide; firearms have become more prevalent as the weapon of choice; there has been an increase in single female offenders who kill in domestic encounters; the homicides tend more to be preplanned now than in the past; and self-defense as a motive in such cases is questioned strongly. The last finding seems most problematic.

"Battered Woman's Syndrome" Not Relevant

When I presented these findings at the annual meeting of the American Society of Criminology, women in the audience challenged the analysis of motives and suggested that the female domestic homicide offenders might have been battered women responding to abuse in self-defense. In-depth readings of the case files, had however, indicated the contrary possibility that these women were the victors in the domestic fight.

The "battered woman syndrome," when used as a rationale for self-defense in a homicide case, suggests that the act was reasonable and necessary because the offender "reasonably believed she was in imminent danger of serious bodily harm or death and that the force she used was necessary to avoid that danger," according to A.E. Thar. Further, in comparison with male victims, researchers often refer to women's smaller size, their lack of expertise in hand-to-hand fighting, and the fact that "the fist or the body of the large male may itself be the deadly weapon," thus leaving a weapon as the woman's only resort. In other words, as L.P. Eber put it, "(T)hese women are only killing their husbands because they realize that there is no other way to end the abuse."

In addition to the individual case analyses, several other indicators suggest that the "battered woman syndrome," although not to be rejected, is not necessarily relevant in many of the domestic homicides studied. First, the majority of the offenders were single and (at least theoretically), could have left the abuser, particularly because they did not appear to reflect the "learned helplessness" typical of battered women. Second, premeditation of the homicide in more than half of the cases (56.3%) challenges the notion of "reasonableness," particularly the "objective immediacy standard" or the woman's belief that she is in immediate danger. Third, previous arrest histories suggest that some of these offenders were neither helpless nor afraid of their victims. Misdemeanor arrest data were available on 126 of the 145 domestic homicide offenders; felony arrest information was obtained on 123 cases. Forty-eight of the subjects (38.1%) had 1 to 30 previous misdemeanor arrests, while 36 women (29.3%) had 1 to 13 prior felony arrests. In separate examination, the domestic homicide offenders who claimed self-defense were found to have more prior arrests than the nondomestic offenders claiming self-defense. Even more revealing is the finding that 36 of the female domestic killers (30%) had violent offense histories and constituted 42.9 percent of all offenders with such backgrounds; yet half of them claimed self-defense.

Alcohol involvement by both the victims and offenders was significantly greater where self-defense was the excuse for the homicide. A conceivable interpretation of this finding, based on individual case analyses, is that both parties were drinking, a domestic fight ensued, and the female homicide offender won.

Courts Should Not Allow Testimony on "Battered Woman's Syndrome"

by Gerald Caplan

About the author: *Gerald Caplan is a professor of law at George Washington University in Washington, D.C.*

The rules of self-defense, so long a settled part of our law, may be changing for "battered" women who have killed their husbands. Some courts, relying on expert-witness testimony from feminist psychologists, have enlarged the defense to allow acquittals in cases which otherwise would have ended in manslaughter or murder convictions. In Ohio, Governor Richard Celeste commuted the sentences of 25 battered women who had finally attacked their husbands, and other governors are thinking of following suit.

Moments of Kindness and Violence

The prosecution of Janice Leidholm is illustrative. Janice was charged with murdering her husband, Chester, in the early morning hours of August 7, 1981, at their farmhouse near Washburn, North Dakota. The Leidholms had, in the words of the North Dakota Supreme Court, a volatile marriage, "filled with a mixture of alcohol abuse, moments of kindness toward one another, and moments of violence." The homicide itself followed a rather tepid alcoholic argument—"Chester was shouting and Janice was crying"—during which Chester prevented Janice from calling the police by "shoving her away and pushing her down." Eventually the quarrel subsided and they went to bed; once Chester was asleep, Janice arose, secured a butcher knife, and in a few minutes, "from shock and loss of blood," Chester was dead.

An inventive lawyer might have tried to jiggle these facts into a temporary-insanity defense, a suspect diagnosis often employed to camouflage ordinary rage in appealing forensic garb. (It was used successfully in the famous "burning bed" case, where the defendant poured gasoline around her husband's bed and set fire to him as he slept in alcoholic stupor.) Instead, defense counsel advanced a theory that should have been curtly dismissed by the court. He argued self-defense "in reaction to severe mistreatment" by Chester over the years. Under longstanding legal principles, this was no defense. For one thing, evidence of Chester's past brutality would be inadmissible—Chester was not on trial—unless it illuminated the events immediately preceding the killing. If Janice could show that as a result of past beatings, she had learned to see signs of impending attacks that would not be apparent to an untutored observer, only then could she detail her victimization for the jury. But since even the most imaginative attorney could not argue that Chester, asleep, was mounting an attack, Janice was not entitled to argue self-defense.

Inexplicably, the trial judge ruled otherwise. He both admitted the evidence of prior abuse and instructed the jury on self-defense. More surprising, on appeal the North Dakota Supreme Court not only agreed but, in reversing Janice Leidholm's manslaughter conviction, held that on retrial she was entitled to a far more favorable instruction on the law of self-defense. As the instruction had been given at her trial, the jury was to decide whether Janice had behaved reasonably, like a person of ordinary prudence and circumspection. That was wrong, the North Dakota Supreme Court held. The true test was whether she had acted reasonably according to *her* standards.

Reasonable Violence?

This is no minor distinction. Since Janice depicted herself as having little self-esteem, and being so dependent upon Chester that she was unable to leave him, the test—what might be called "the reasonable battered wife" standard—is a contradiction in terms. It makes no sense to define "the reasonable person" in terms that themselves evidence unreasonableness—e.g., "hot-blooded," "impulsive," "helpless." What is the reasonable violent person, or the reasonable helpless person? More important, defining the legal standard subjectively deprives it of its value for making moral judgments, for deciding whether Janice Leidholm is blameworthy.

> *"It makes no sense to define 'the reasonable person' in terms that themselves evidence unreasonableness— e.g., 'hot-blooded,' 'impulsive,' 'helpless.'"*

In any case, under any definition of reasonableness, the reasonable thing for Janice to have done was to leave Chester, not kill him.

Why Janice didn't do so is unclear. One possibility—perhaps the most obvious one—is that things were not as bad as she said. Another, offered by some feminist psychologists, is that Janice suffered from "battered-woman syndrome."

Dr. Lenore Walker, the inventor of this concept, claims that victims of battered-woman syndrome are unable to leave their abusers even when circumstances permit. According to Dr. Walker, over time a battered wife despairs of being able to control her husband's violence. "Repeated batterings, like electrical shocks, diminish . . . [her] motivation to respond." The victim gives up and settles into a languid state of "learned helplessness," a concept Dr. Walker borrowed from laboratory experiments which showed that dogs subjected to repeated shocks eventually become too dispirited to accept opportunities to escape.

> *"Most women have enough sense to leave a man before he lands the first blow—or, at least, immediately thereafter."*

Dr. Walker has written three books, including *Terrifying Love: Why Battered Women Kill and How Society Responds*. More troublingly, she has been a witness in over 150 criminal cases.

As a witness, Dr. Walker's approach is to depict the battered woman as "just like you and me" and to denounce as prejudice or ignorance any hint that battered wives are other than victims of circumstance. There is, she asserts, "nothing special about their personalities." Experience, of course, suggests the opposite: that most women have enough sense to leave a man before he lands the first blow—or, at least, immediately thereafter. Dr. Walker disagrees. "Any woman" who meets up with the wrong man "is in danger of becoming a battered woman."

Murder, Not Self-Defense

This is either poor social science or empathy caricatured; and may explain why Dr. Walker has been able to find self-defense in cases that the layman would recognize as first-degree murder. In one, a wife, though separated from her husband, hired a hit man, lured her husband back into the house, and, after the hired killer had fired two shots, yelled to him, "He's not dying fast enough—hit him again." Fortunately, in that case, the court excluded Dr. Walker's testimony as irrelevant.

But common sense is often left outside the courtroom door. In another case, involving a woman who shot her sleeping husband twice, following his threat to kill their baby, the expert witness, Julie Blackman, argued that the wife "exhibited characteristics of . . . [battered-woman] syndrome. . . . I emphasized . . . [her] unsuccessful attempts to leave the relationship . . . [and] although the [husband's] threat did not closely precede . . . [the killing] . . . she reported that she had relived her fear as she stood at the foot of the bed and fired the gun into her husband's sleeping body." It worked. The wife, incredibly, was acquitted on grounds of self-defense.

Although Dr. Walker acknowledges that battered women do exhibit "bizarre" behavior, she attributes this to their victimization. Once free of their husbands, "most . . . cease to manifest any so-called behavioral disturbances or personality disorders, [proving] that . . . their previously abnormal behavior was directly caused by their victimization." A homicide by a battered woman is "simply a terrified human being's *normal* response to an abnormal and dangerous situation."

All this sounds more like tract than treatise (and Dr. Walker, in her professional success, reminds one of the missionaries who went to Hawaii to do good and wound up doing well). Reduced to its essence, battered-woman syndrome is not a physician's diagnosis but an advocate's invention. It means: Blame the deceased.

Unfortunately, the term has received judicial recognition. The early decisions did exclude expert testimony on battered-woman syndrome as unscientific. The District of Columbia Court of Appeals, for example, cited Dr. Walker's remark—"I tend to place all men in an especially negative light"—as evidence of bias; and the Wyoming Supreme Court accused her of reaching her conclusions before "engag[ing] in research . . . to substantiate those theories." But as Dr. Walker and others continued to publish, judicial resistance wilted. Most courts now allow expert testimony on battered-woman syndrome (the Ohio Supreme Court reversed a decade-old precedent to admit it), and a few have swallowed Dr. Walker's "learned helplessness" adaptation in one gulp. The New Jersey Supreme Court, for example, mimicked Dr. Walker by finding that battered women "become so demoralized and degraded by the fact that they cannot predict or control the violence that they sink into a state of psychological paralysis and become unable to take any action at all to improve or alter the situation."

Not Helpless

Of course, such reasoning doesn't explain how women who are that helpless manage to stab their husbands repeatedly in the chest with butcher knives, shoot them at close range, or hire hit men to do the job. Nor does it explain why, if battered women are capable of such violent actions, they are incapable of non-homicidal responses such as leaving the house.

"Battered-woman syndrome is not a physician's diagnosis but an advocate's invention."

Far-fetched as Dr. Walker's theories are, however, one can't read many accounts of abused women without wanting to say something on their behalf. The small number of battered women who kill should not be grouped with the premeditated murderer or hired killer. Many acted only after years of cruelty. The killing was an outburst, the accumulation of years of rage. Even when the victim was, like Chester, asleep, his death may not have been the product of calculation. A woman just abused may be unable to calm herself (as the law requires) once the moment of danger has passed. Nor is flight always possible. Some women don't flee their homes because no safe port exists where an enraged husband can't find them or their children; they are cornered, and, so cornered, they are explosive.

But this is learned violence, not helplessness. Lenore Walker's insistence that killing "out of anger would be a male's response" is wrong; the impulse to retaliate is universal. "If one allows that the accumulated irritation of a working day can be . . . [discharged] by kicking the dog," writes psychiatrist Anthony Storr, there is no reason why more serious grievances "should not be stored for much longer, perhaps even a lifetime"; and, at times, produce outbursts like Janice Leidholm's, disproportionately savage to the immediate provocation, but revenging a history of victimization.

Under modern law, however, such acts are forbidden. The law holds a monopoly on punishment, requiring the victim to seek its protection. Janice was expected to give evidence to convict Chester. But if Janice was like most, she didn't want Chester put away, only better behaved, and refused to cooperate once an arrest rendered him contrite. And if the North Dakota police were like most, they quickly tired of responding to domestic-violence calls from the same household. Even if indefatigable, they had no legal way of preventing a determined man from attacking his wife.

Victims like Janice don't often appreciate this. Probably Janice thought the legal system incapable of effectively taking her side. Perhaps, like Bernhard Goetz, she had become unhinged by its failure to protect her in the past. Perhaps she believed that her status as one who has been repeatedly victimized accorded her greater rights to look after herself. But regardless of what Janice believed, she was not entitled to acquittal; death is not the penalty the law assigned for Chester's offenses.

Not Self-Defense

Judges who allow expert testimony on battered-woman syndrome don't fully understand this. They install, perhaps unwittingly, an escape route lacking a scientific predicate and appealing to popular prejudice. And judges who allow a jury to find self-defense where the victim was asleep, or eating or bathing, or otherwise unoffending when slain ignore long-settled, dearly won legal principles evincing respect for life.

If a jury needs to know why Janice or any other defendant thought she was in danger or why she didn't leave a life-endangering situation, she can speak for herself, without a hired translator. Then, if convicted, she will have established grounds for leniency, and the sentencing judge, in extending mercy, will be both honoring the law and showing due regard for the defendant. Not perfect justice, but perhaps it is as close as we can get.

Battered Women Who Kill Do Not Deserve Clemency

by Stanton Peele

About the author: *Stanton Peele is a contributing editor to* Reason *magazine and a psychologist and health care researcher.*

The governors of Ohio and Maryland both pardoned a number of women imprisoned for killing their mates. The reasoning underlying the actions of Ohio Gov. Richard Celeste and Maryland Gov. William Donald Schaefer was that the women had not been allowed to describe adequately in court how their lives and well-being had been threatened by their husbands. They could have argued self-defense, of course; under the law, a person may defend herself with force if she is physically threatened and has no alterative. But it was by no means clear that these women had no alternative.

A Moment of Opportunity

In recent years, we have come to a new understanding of the motives that drive women to murder their spouses. In many cases, these women are not threatened at the moment they kill. Rather, they have endured long-term abuse, while feeling unable to extricate themselves from the relationship. They then kill a husband or lover, with whom they usually live, at a moment of opportunity. In the seminal case depicted in the film *The Burning Bed*, Francine Hughes set her husband on fire as he slept.

Such women are said to suffer from "battered-woman syndrome." They are so psychologically debilitated by abuse that they lose their judgment and their ability to protect themselves. Eventually, they may come to feel that murdering a spouse is the logical way out of the situation. Professional organizations such as the American Psychological Association and the American Psychiatric Association have filed amicus-curiae briefs in support of the battered-woman defense.

One psychologist, Lenore Walker, has testified in more than 100 trials in which defendants claimed to have been incapacitated by battered-woman syndrome.

Courts now routinely accept battered-woman syndrome. New York University law professor Holly Maguigan told *Newsday:* "Given that the highest court of New York has endorsed battered-woman syndrome, a judge refusing to admit it [as a defense] would be subjected to intense scrutiny." Meanwhile, a New York assemblywoman introduced legislation to grant clemency to battered women who kill their mates, and a California assemblyman proposed a law that would codify the battered-woman defense. Following the lead of Celeste and Schaefer, the governors of New York, Texas, and several other states are considering pardons for battered women.

Undermining Responsibility

But the battered-woman defense, however well intentioned, does not serve the goal of reducing family violence. Indeed, by undermining personal responsibility, the acceptance of this concept may actually contribute to the problem.

The details of cases said to involve battered-woman syndrome rarely fit the generic definition. Quite often, the abuse victims and the men they kill seem to have been involved in consensual relationships, from which the women derived basic emotional gratification. The women refused to leave the relationships when given a real opportunity to do so because they welcomed the intensity of their spouses' feelings. Francine Hughes, for example, had separated several times from her husband Mickey, only to return to him voluntarily.

The relationships that culminate in the killing of a spouse are often marked by escalating violence in which both men and women participate. Men are more likely to physically assault a spouse, and they tend to inflict more damage when they do so. But the final assault may not be the first time the woman has tried to hurt the man, and in some cases the violence seems very much premeditated.

The *Baltimore Sun* investigated several of the women freed by Schaefer. Among other things, it discovered that one woman had hired a hit man to kill her husband and then collected on her husband's life insurance. An article in the *Columbus Dispatch* reported that 15 of the 25 women pardoned by Celeste had not been physically abused. Six had discussed killing their spouses before doing so, and two had tracked down and then killed husbands from whom they were separated.

> *"The women refused to leave the relationships when given a real opportunity to do so because they welcomed the intensity of the spouses' feelings."*

More troubling still are cases where battered-woman syndrome is used to excuse abuse and neglect of children. In their book *Intimate Violence*, researchers Richard Gelles and Murray Straus report that entire families are characterized by cultures of violence. In households where men abuse women and women retaliate against men, there is also much more violence against children.

In 1989, for example, the body of 3-year-old Andrew Mitchell was found in a shallow grave in Queens, New York. Andrew's mother, Geraldine Mitchell, admitted to burying the boy after her companion, George Chavis, had beaten him to death. Mitchell described how Chavis frequently beat her and her child. "He got jealous because I paid more attention to Andrew than to him," she testified. She also reported that, shortly before her son's death, Chavis scalded the boy with hot water and that she then beat her son for crying.

Mitchell pleaded guilty to manslaughter as part of an agreement for her testimony at Chavis's murder trial. But her attorney claimed the prosecution charged her with a crime only "because she's black and poor." The attorney argued that Manhattanite Hedda Nussbaum was not charged in a similar case in which she allowed her husband, Joel Steinberg, to beat to death their 6-year-old adopted daughter, Lisa. Nussbaum had let Lisa lie comatose on a bathroom floor for 12 hours before she called for help. During this time, she smoked cocaine with Steinberg.

A Textbook Example

During the Steinberg trial, Nussbaum was regarded as a textbook example of the battered woman, having given up all self-respect and personal independence in response to Steinberg's derision and assaults. The national media portrayed her sympathetically; a 1989 *People* cover story was titled, "Hedda's Story." At the same time, many people—feminists included—were appalled that a woman could participate in the abuse and death of a child, even if the woman was being assaulted herself.

In the 1990 book *What Lisa Knew*, Joyce Johnson describes Lisa's body as "a map of pain," covered with scratches, bruises, and dirt. Johnson, like the jury that tried Steinberg, felt Nussbaum was implicated in Lisa's death. For Johnson, Nussbaum was a wholly self-absorbed individual, incapable of looking beyond her own pain to understand—or care about—Lisa's. (A baby boy who also lived with Steinberg and Nussbaum was found tethered and urine-soaked by the police investigating Lisa's killing.)

In any case of abuse within a family, there are likely to be serious problems all around. In March 1991, Jane Scott was arrested in New York for leaving her 7-month-old boy in an unlocked apartment while she went on a six-day crack binge. She returned to find the baby had starved to death. Scott reportedly told a neighbor that she had left the apartment because her boyfriend had beaten her. The neighbor said that she replied to Scott, "If he beat you up, what makes you think he wouldn't beat the baby up?"

Bibliography

Books

Julie A. Allison and Lawrence S. Wrightsman — *Rape: The Misunderstood Crime*. Newbury Park, CA: Sage Publications, 1993.

Robert T. Ammerman and Michel Hersen, eds. — *Assessment of Family Violence: A Clinical and Legal Sourcebook*. New York: John Wiley & Sons, 1992.

Constance A. Bean — *Women Murdered by the Men They Loved*. Binghamton, NY: Haworth Press, 1992.

Douglas J. Besharov, ed. — *Family Violence Research and Public Policy Issues*. Washington, DC: AEI Press, 1990.

Carol Bohmer and Andrea Parrot — *Sexual Assault on Campus: The Problem and the Solution*. New York: Lexington Books, 1993.

Jerry Brinegar — *Breaking Free from Domestic Violence*. Minneapolis: CompCare Publishers, 1992.

Eve S. Buzawa and Carl G. Buzawa — *Domestic Violence: The Criminal Justice Response*. Newbury Park, CA: Sage Publications, 1990.

Dorothy Ayers Counts, Judith K. Brown, and Jacquelyn C. Campbell, eds. — *Sanctions and Sanctuary: Cultural Perspectives on the Beating of Wives*. Boulder, CO: Westview Press, 1992.

R. Emerson Dobash and Russell P. Dobash — *Women, Violence, and Social Change*. New York: Routledge, 1992.

Andrea Dworkin — *Letters from a War Zone: Writings, 1976-1989*. New York: Dutton, 1989.

Richard J. Gelles and D. Loseke — *Current Controversies on Family Violence*. Newbury Park, CA: Sage Publications, 1993.

Edward Gondolf — *Man Against Woman: What Every Woman Must Know About Violent Men*. Bradenton, FL: Human Services Institute, 1989.

Margaret Gordon and Stephanie Riger — *The Female Fear*. New York: Free Press, 1989.

Robert L. Hampton, ed. — *Black Family Violence: Current Research and Theory*. Lexington, MA: Lexington Books. 1991.

Marsali Hansen and Michele Harway, eds. — *Battering and Family Therapy: A Feminist Perspective*. Newbury Park, CA: Sage Publications, 1993.

Bibliography

Nat Hentoff — *Free Speech for Me—but Not for Thee: How the American Left and Right Relentlessly Censor Each Other.* New York: HarperCollins, 1992.

N. Zoe Hilton — *Legal Responses to Wife Assault: Current Trends and Evaluation.* Newbury Park, CA: Sage Publications, 1993.

Catherine Itzin, ed. — *Pornography: Women, Violence, and Civil Liberties: A Radical View.* New York: Oxford University Press, 1993.

Scott Johnson — *When "I Love You" Turns Violent.* Far Hills, NJ: New Horizons, 1993.

Barrie Levy, ed. — *Dating Violence: Young Women in Danger.* Seattle: Seal Press, 1991.

Mark Rosenberg and Mary Ann Fenley, eds. — *Violence in America: A Public Health Approach.* New York: Oxford University Press, 1991.

Diana E.H. Russell — *Rape in Marriage.* Bloomington: Indiana University Press, 1990.

Peggy Reeves Sanday — *Fraternity Gang Rape: Sex, Brotherhood, and Privilege on Campus.* New York: New York University Press, 1990.

Diana Scully — *Understanding Sexual Violence: A Study of Convicted Rapists.* Boston: Unwin-Hyman, 1990.

Elizabeth Stanko — *Everyday Violence: How Women and Men Experience Sexual and Physical Danger.* London: Pandora Press, 1990.

Michael Steinman, ed. — *Women Battering: Policy Responses.* Cincinnati: Anderson Publishing Co., 1992.

Periodicals

Robert James Bidinotto — "Freed to Rape Again," *Reader's Digest*, October 1991.

Jane Caputi and Diana E.H. Russell — "'Femicide': Speaking the Unspeakable," *Ms.*, September/October 1990.

CJ the Americas — "Arrests Can Increase Domestic Violence," June/July 1992. Available from 1333 S. Wabash, Chicago, IL 60605.

Jean Bethke Elshtain — "Battered Reason," *The New Republic*, October 5, 1992.

Jean Bethke Elshtain — "Women and the Ideology of Victimization," *The World & I*, April 1993.

Eric Felten — "A Redefinition of the Issue of Rape," *Insight*, January 28, 1991.

Suzanne Fields — "Rape as Sport: The Culture Is at the Root," *Insight*, May 3, 1993.

David Frum — "Women Who Kill," *Forbes*, January 18, 1993.

Marcia Gillespie — "Delusions of Safety: A Personal Story," *Ms.*, September/October 1990.

Linda Hall and Peter Rothberg — "She Asked For It," *Lies of Our Times*, September 1991.

Violence Against Women

Linda Hasselstrom — "A Peaceful Woman Explains Why She Carries a Gun," *Utne Reader*, May/June 1991.

Kathleen Hirsch — "Fraternities of Fear: Gang Rape, Male Bonding, and the Silencing of Women," *Ms.*, September/October 1990.

Michelle A. Holden — "Self-Defense or a License to Kill?" *Prison Life*, May 1993. Available from PO Box 267, Sussex, WI 53089.

J. Hollyday — "Ending the War Against Women," *Sojourners*, August 1990.

Michele Ingrassia et al. — "Life Means Nothing," *Newsweek*, July 19, 1993.

Wendy Kaminer — "Feminists Against the First Amendment," *The Atlantic*, November 1992.

David A. Kaplan et al. — "The Incorrigibles," *Newsweek*, January 18, 1993.

Rhonda L. Kohler — "The Battered Woman and Tort Law: A New Approach to Fighting Domestic Violence," *Loyola of Los Angeles Law Review*, April 1992.

Cindi Leive — "The Dangerous Truth About Acquaintance Rape," *Glamour*, June 1993.

Anne Matthews — "The Campus Crime Wave," *The New York Times Magazine*, March 7, 1993.

Gene Ruffini — "The Super Bowl's Real Score," *Ms.*, November/December 1991.

Ruth Schmidt — "After the Fact: To Speak of Rape," *The Christian Century*, January 6-13, 1993.

Diana Scully — "Who's to Blame for Sexual Violence?" *USA Today*, January 1992.

Todd Seavey — "A Better Class of Sleaze," *Reason*, November 1992.

Brenda Seery and Michelle Clossick — "Analysis" (Results of *Ms.* magazine's Violence Survey), *Ms.*, March/April 1991.

Ruth Shalit — "Radical Exhibitionists," *Reason*, July 1992.

H. Robert Showers — "Pornography and the Law," *The World & I*, December 1992.

Walter W. Steele Jr. and Christine W. Sigman — "Reexamining the Doctrine of Self-Defense to Accommodate Battered Women," *American Journal of Criminal Law*, Fall 1990.

Shawn Sullivan — "Wife-Beating N the Hood," *The Wall Street Journal*, July 6, 1993.

Organizations to Contact

The editors have compiled the following list of organizations that are concerned with the issues debated in this book. All have publications or information available for interested readers. For best results, allow as much time as possible for the organizations to respond. The descriptions below are derived from materials provided by the organizations. This list was compiled at the date of publication. Names, addresses, and phone numbers of organizations are subject to change.

Batterers Anonymous (BA)
8485 Tamarind, Suite D
Fontana, CA 92335
(714) 355-1100

Batterers Anonymous is designed to rehabilitate men who abuse women. It aims to completely eliminate physical and emotional abuse and seeks positive alternatives to abusive behavior. BA believes that through increased awareness of their problem, batterers are better able to cope with abuse issues and can develop skills for handling stress. It publishes a manual entitled *Self-Help Counseling for Men Who Batter Women*.

Center for Libertarian Studies (CLS)
875 Mahler Rd., Suite 105
Burlingame, CA 94011
(415) 348-3000

CLS promotes scholarly analysis of social, economic, political, and philosophical problems from a libertarian perspective. It opposes censorship, including the censorship of pornography. Its publications include the *Journal of Libertarian Studies* and the *Rothbard-Rockwell Report*.

Center for Women Policy Studies (CWPS)
2000 P St. NW, Suite 508
Washington, DC 20036
(202) 872-1770

CWPS was established in 1972 as a feminist policy research center. It believes that the economic, legal, and social status of women must be improved. To this end, it conducts research and provides information about family violence and sexual violence against women. The center publishes the quarterly journal *Response to the Victimization of Women and Children* as well as policy papers on a variety of issues.

Emerge: A Men's Counseling Service on Domestic Violence
18 Hurley St., Suite 23
Cambridge, MA 02141
(617) 422-1550

Emerge seeks to end male violence against women by helping batterers to explore the causes of their violence and to find alternatives to battering. It also offers community workshops and classes on the abuse of women from a male perspective. Emerge distributes articles on abusive men as well as the pamphlet "What You Should Know About Your Abusive Partner."

Family Research Laboratory (FRL)
126 Horton Social Science Center
University of New Hampshire
Durham, NH 03824-3586
(603) 862-1888

Since 1975, FRL has devoted itself primarily to understanding the causes and consequences of family violence. The laboratory has conducted numerous studies on the extent and nature of family violence and sexual abuse. It has published more than 150 articles and more than two dozen books on family violence, including *Physical Violence in American Families: Risk Factors and Adaptations to Violence in 8,145 Families* and *Stopping Family Violence*.

The Heritage Foundation
214 Massachusetts Ave. NE
Washington, DC 20002
(202) 546-4400

The foundation is a conservative public policy institute dedicated to the principles of free competitive enterprise, limited government, individual liberty, and a strong national defense. It believes that national security concerns justify limiting the media and that pornography should be censored. It publishes the monthly *Policy Review*, the periodic *Backgrounder*, and the *Heritage Lecture* series, all of which sometimes address issues of violence and pornography.

Men's Rights, Inc. (MR)
PO Box 163180
Sacramento, CA 95816
(916) 484-7333

Men's Rights is concerned with sexism and men's problems. MR believes that women are as likely as men to initiate violence within relationships and that "The Battered *Woman's* Defense" is a sexist term that should be replaced with "The Battered *Person's* Defense." MR publishes the newsletter *New Release* along with position papers and articles.

National Clearinghouse for the Defense of Battered Women
125 S. 9th St., Suite 302
Philadelphia, PA 19107
(215) 351-0010

Created in 1987, the clearinghouse provides assistance, resources, and support to battered women who have killed or assaulted their abusers while attempting to protect themselves from life-threatening violence or who are coerced into crime by their abusers. Its publications include a newsletter entitled *Double-Time*, as well as an annotated bibliography, a statistics packet, and a variety of articles and papers on abuse issues.

National Coalition Against Censorship (NCAC)
275 Seventh Ave.
New York, NY 10001
(212) 807-6222

NCAC is an alliance of organizations committed to defending freedom of thought, inquiry, and expression by engaging in public education and advocacy on national and local levels. It believes censorship of violent materials is dangerous because it represses intellectual and artistic freedom. NCAC maintains a library of information dealing with First Amendment issues and publishes the quarterly *Censorship News*.

National Victims Resource Center (NVRC)
Box 6000
Rockville, MD 20850
(800) 627-6872

Established in 1983 by the U.S. Department of Justice's Office for Victims of Crime, NVRC is crime victims' primary source of information. The center answers questions by using national and regional statistics, a comprehensive collection of research findings, and a well-established network of victim advocates and organizations. NVRC distributes all Office of Justice Programs (OJP) publications on victim-related issues, including *Female Victims of Violent Crime* and *Sexual Assault: An Overview*.

Violence Policy Center (VPC)
1300 N St. NW
Washington, DC 20005
(202) 783-4071

VPC conducts research and explores alternatives to commonly accepted views on violence. A primary goal of the center is the widespread dissemination of this information in an effort to educate the public, news media, and policy makers. The center functions as a clearinghouse for information on firearms violence and the firearms industry. Its publications include *More Gun Dealers Than Gas Stations* and *Putting Guns Back into Criminals' Hands*.

Women Against Pornography (WAP)
PO Box 845, Times Square Station
New York, NW 10036-0845

WAP is a feminist organization that seeks to change public opinion about pornography so that Americans no longer view it as socially acceptable or sexually liberating. It offers tours of New York's Times Square that are intended to show firsthand that "the essence of pornography is about the degradation, objectification, and brutalization of women." WAP offers slide shows, lectures, and a referral service to victims of sexual abuse and sexual exploitation. Its publications include *Women Against Pornography—Newsreport*.

Index

more dangerous to leave, 263-264
unable to, 263, 277, 278, 305
see also domestic violence
Bible
endorses child abuse, 34, 169
endorses subjugation of women, 20, 168
blame, of the victim
is fair, 67-70, 244
is unfair, 173-174, 230
makes people feel safer, 228, 229
boys, 203
learning to hate women, 77, 79
participation in sports, 41, 43

Canada, 99, 102, 142, 149-150, 190, 196, 203
Caplan, Gerald, 301
Cart, Julie, 59
Catholic church
ignores sexual violence, 167-169
pedophile priest scandals and, 175
reforms needed
allow men to be nurturing, 171-172
on handling sexual abuse, 173-175
recognize gays' rights, 175
recognize women's equality, 170-171
teach about sexuality positively, 172-173
should act against sexual violence, 167-175
censorship, 52
feminist-far right coalition for, 132-133, 136, 141-142
harms of, 132, 135-140
of pornography
feminist debate over, 131-134, 179
would hurt women, 131-134
would reduce rape, 124-126, 127-130
con, 141-151
Chapman, Jane Roberts, 189
Chavez, Julia J., 282
chemical dependency
among rapists, 48
in domestic violence cases, 157, 158, 160-161, 165
see also alcohol abuse
children
beating of, 34, 177, 307-308
learning violence, 139-140
sexual abuse of, 167, 169, 204
by homosexuals is exaggerated, 175
is exaggerated, 236, 238, 241
is underreported, 33-34
long-term effects of, 170
pornography causes, 121
rapists often were victims of, 47, 48-49, 50
torture of, 195
Christian right, 132-133, 136, 141-142
classes, economic
reporting of abuse and, 34
sports participation, 39-40, 44
violence more prevalent among lower, 296-297
myth of, 39, 173, 176, 183, 202

clemency, for battered women, 260-261, 266, 268-269
is wrong, 301, 306-308
colleges
freshmen at, 232-233
rape at, 224
administrators' response to
effective, 227-228, 233-234
ineffective, 63-66, 70, 209
alcohol use and, 76, 228, 230, 231, 232, 244, by athletes, 60, 63-66
due to women's carelessness, 67-70, 244
as unjust view of problem, 230-231
education about, 233-234, 245, 256
fraternities and, 61-62, 231-233
is exaggerated, 243-245, 249-250
is widespread, 227
Koss study on, 216-217, 219, 235-240, 244, 254-255
Syracuse University, 227-234
victims of are harassed, 229-231
women's fight against, 201
Crime Control Institute, 105
criminal justice system
does not discourage rape, 53-58, 210
domestic violence policy, 155-156, 225-226, 281
judges' beliefs about, 87-89, 90-91, 94, 100
prosecutors' reluctance, 86-87, 94, 98, 100
reforming can reduce wife abuse, 82-93
favors men over women, 264, 279
con, 266-267
used to discourage sexual violence, 194-196

date rape. *See* acquaintance rape
doctors
can act to reduce wife abuse, 164-166
underreport child abuse, 34
domestic violence
causes of
economic distress, 184
family privacy, 26-32
pornography, 122-123
sexism, 33-38, 202
as limited explanation, 176-181
traditional gender roles, 19-25, 34, 93, 140, 180, 184
committed by women, 202, 261, 282-291, 307-308
cycle of, 96, 156, 265, 273-274, 285
economic impact of, 186
extent of, 19, 30, 34, 82, 95, 164-165, 226, 261
internationally, 190-191, 200
feminist activism against, 22, 23-24, 29-30, 177, 188, 201
homelessness and, 184-185
laws regarding
defer to family privacy, 27, 92
favor male domination, 28-29
history of, 19-24, 83-84, 262

316

Index